CW01574822

THE DIVINITY LINK

Tantra, Shamanism, Gods & Self Healing

By Julian Wilde

Author of “The Real Rasa”

Julian Wilde © Copyright 2008

All rights reserved

No parts of this publication may be reproduced, stored in a retrieval system, or transmitted in any form or by any means, electronic, mechanical, photocopying, recording or otherwise without the prior permission of the copyright owner.

British Library Cataloguing In Publication Data
A Record of this Publication is available
from the British Library

ISBN 978-1-84778-002-7

First Published 2008 by
Exposure Publishing,
an imprint of
Diggory Press Ltd
Three Rivers, Minions, Liskeard, Cornwall, PL14 5LE, UK
WWW.DIGGORYPRESS.COM

INTRO – A TANTRICAL, MAGICAL, ECSTATICAL, SHAMANICAL COMPENDIUM!

Thanks for picking up this book. There are thousands and thousands of books out there on Tantra, Shamanism, Gods and Goddesses, Self Healing. Why would I want to add to that ever growing pile? It's not like I'm going to make a lot of money (if any!) from my efforts. If you're going to part with cash for this book you deserve some kind of pledge from me. So here it is – I solemnly promise that everything you read in this book is real, is from my direct experience. Nothing is made up, dredged up from dodgy sources. Nothing is fictionalised for dramatic effect. This is the true account of my spiritual unfolding and the things I've learned along the way. You may not like what I have to say, you may not like the way I express myself, but at least I'm being honest with you from the start.

And it's a big subject - the spiritual search. The quest for meaning in our lives. The searching for answers to those all important questions – why are we here? Why am I here? What should I be doing in this life? Is there more than this?

When the priests of our present culture can't satisfy us, when the teachings of the dominant religious tribe no longer resonate with us, no longer feed us, then it's natural to look elsewhere. It's permissible too. No one has the right to say you should be a Jew, a Muslim, a Christian, a Hindu, a Buddhist. You and only you are responsible for finding and maintaining your path, your worldview, your practice.

And it doesn't matter where you find it. Maybe from somewhere exotic, on the other side of the globe. Maybe from sometime else, in the land of your ancestors – or someone else's ancestors. Or maybe it's a synthesis you seek, the "best" from Daoism, Buddhism and Hinduism, or the "best" from the Celtic spiritual legacy mixed with the wisdom of the Native Americans. Maybe a synthesis of Tantra and Shamanism, or Tantra and Wicca, or Paganism and Christianity. It's entirely up to you, no one else.

To mix and match is your freedom. It has its problems too, there's a possibility that, in just following the path of easy options, you miss out on necessary challenges and explorations. That said, even those following a "straightforward" vehicle, a well documented route, such as Zen Buddhism or Sufism, often manage to do that self same thing - to follow where their attractions and aversions lead them, rather than follow their true heart, the needs of the soul.

And to follow our true heart, we need to know it, to be able to hear it when it speaks to us. That can be difficult, drowned as the heart's voice is in the clamour of the world and in the whinging and crowing of our egos. It takes courage and determination to even keep asking the question, "What should I be doing?"

For all of us somewhere, there's a work waiting, a set of tasks, a road to travel. This book is about that search and how, for me, the answer was waiting in a dark, mysterious cave 35,000 years ago. It took the shape of a Shaman God, a God of Animals, a God of mystery, of religious aspirations and worldly pleasures. The Hindus know Him as Shiva. I didn't know Him at all! It took me literally a decade to even notice that this deity had been floating around in my life, in dreams, in my poetry etc. I'm aware of how dumb I sound but it's the truth. I didn't take any notice. I didn't heed the call.

After a long, long time, I began to listen, to pay attention to my dreams, to pay more attention to the images and messages that kept surfacing in meditation. I re-read my own poetry!

Things are different, very different for me now. This Shamanic deity, the alleged inventor of Tantra and Tantric techniques (No! Not just the same old, tired, multi-orgasm, sexual trip that most people associate with Tantra!) is a constant presence in my life. He teaches, guides, supports and protects me. Gives me a good kicking occasionally too.

And life is different for those around me too. I have a few friends who elected to follow me into the wilderness, so to speak, to try and find their own God/dess, to seek reunion with lost parts of themselves, to search for what the Hindus call "darshan", a face to face intimacy, an encounter with God/dess, a mutual recognition and blessing. You can read two of these accounts deeper into the book.

So how do we achieve darshan? And how do we define Tantra, a convenient name for my personal path (though religious Shamanism would equally suffice)? Well, Tantra...the path of ecstasy. An ancient, ancient wisdom with modern, psychologically sound practices. Sounds fantastic, doesn't it! If you've read my first book "The Real Rasa", and you should, it's pretty cool, you may or may not be delighted to learn that this book is more of the same. I warble on and on merrily about cosmic energies, time and space, Gods and Goddess, Tantric sex, karma and all that religious stuff. Occasionally I throw in some bad jokes and bad language (though not too much – my teacher told me off after the first book!). Nothing much has changed! You don't even get a break from my poetry!

"The Real Rasa" had its critics. Interestingly, most of them focused on the style, my voice, rather than on the content. Some said I was too fierce, some said I was too irreverent. Some said I let myself down by too much bad language. All of that may be true. I make no excuses. When the spirit calls you have to respond. The book was a sincere response. I'm an ordinary, flawed human being, so all my creations may be slightly flawed too! I set out to write it as I talk it, to talk it as I walk it, and in that I succeeded. The message of the book, that one can have a direct and intimate relationship with the various Buddhas, Gods and Goddesses of Tantra, or deities of any path come to that, remains valid and important.

Anyway - you don't need to read The Real Rasa first to enjoy and understand this book. I cover some basic terms and principles again and explain stuff as I go – so no sweat! And it's all my interpretation of what I've been taught - in other words just my opinion. Take on board as much or as little as you like.

If you haven't read any of my stuff before and you're not used to my style, the flavour of my writing – then apologies in advance. I don't present knowledge in neat little chapters – themes overlap, crop up again later. It's all very cyclical, very organic. I also say what I think and I'm not afraid of pissing people off. But I don't do it deliberately or cynically, I just think you deserve my honesty. If we sat down for a cup of coffee together, this is how I'd talk. So I write it that way. I'm not hiding anything from you. And, interestingly enough, that means you can't hide from me. I don't set out to offend. But I call it as I see it.

I wrote the last book, and this one, for one reason only – to be of service. If anything in my writing entertains you, inspires or motivates you to further study and practice, if it helps at all in any way, I'm happy for both of us.

If there is any difference between the two books it's that this one is slightly less irreverent. I got a lot of stuff out of my system with the last one. This book is also more unashamedly Tantric. I had lots of interesting questions from readers of The Real Rasa, some of which are answered within these pages, but mainly people wanted more inspiration - prayers, techniques, ideas to kick start their personal spiritual practice. So I've tried to include a bit more of that stuff. Not that I feel I have much control over what comes through my fingers onto the keyboard. It's more accidental than intentional. And you have to find your own way.

Some of this book (not too much), inevitably, overlaps or even repeats material from The Real Rasa. Never mind - it's always good to be reminded of key concepts and ideas that may prove inspiring, and I've tried to give a new spin on stuff that, by necessity, has to be repeated. I guess what I've tried to do here is to dig around Tantra's roots, which come mainly from Stone Age Shamanism, take you walking briskly through Paganism, through Tantric principles, avoiding (hopefully) a lot of oriental and cultural hocus pocus on the way, arriving at a worldview and practice that's very, very ancient, embedded in every fibre of our being, yet relevant to religious practice in this Kala Yuga, Dark Age.

I believe that Tantra needn't necessarily be perceived, or practiced, as an eastern religion. Tantric principles and practices can be applied within (or outside) any culture. At a high level both Tantra and Shamanism are wonderful vehicles for self healing. I hope you find something in this book that will help you.

Make the material contained in these pages your own. Practice. Enjoy.

CHAPTER ONE - CLOUDS, RAIN & MOUNTAIN RETREATS.

First commandment of writing – thou shalt not bore thy reader! So a very, very quick look at basic ethics before we get to the juicier stuff...

I had an unusual and interesting experience the other morning. The weather was pleasantly mild but it was raining and I was sitting in meditation just inside the door of a friend's conservatory, enjoying the sound of the water hitting the glass roof. I opened my eyes at one point, which I sometimes do when the inner dialogue gets too noisy and I need to cut short the mind's incessant conversation with itself, and I found myself gazing at the doormat outside the conservatory door. It was like a shallow rectangular rubber trough with soft rubber spikes to clean the underside of muddy shoes. The trough had filled up with rainwater but you couldn't see this at first as the water was clear and the rubber was black. As a raindrop hit the surface of the water it obviously caused a small circle of ripples. But because you had to look really hard to see the water covering the doormat, the effect was actually that of a solid object rippling when hit by a raindrop. It was a fascinating optical illusion.

As I was in a reflective mood I immediately connected the phenomenon with a spiritual aspect, namely that of karma, the universal law of cause and effect, a favourite discussion topic of mine. It seemed to me that karma was like the visual event unfolding in front of me. Every word, every deed from us causes ripples in those around us. Usually we can't see the effect unless our perception changes dramatically. But it happens anyway. We go around causing ripples, some small, some catastrophic, in other people's psyches. And most of the time we're oblivious.

In fact, most of the time we're also oblivious to the ripples happening inside us, caused by the actions or words of others. Only occasionally do we have the necessary time or sensitivity to process what's happening inside. Most disturbances, especially the minor ones, have to be overlooked. But ignoring them doesn't mean they don't have an effect. They do, but the busy quality of modern life means we have to just carry on regardless.

The problem is that we're then acting a lot of the time in response to messages and stimuli we're not even aware of, like robots obeying an electronic code that would sound like chattering gibberish to human ears. We're being subtly manipulated by our own unconscious mind, which in turn is being manipulated by the collective karma of those around us.

We've all heard of those experiments where a volunteer is manipulated into agreeing with data or information that his own eyes and ears tell him is faulty. The peer pressure of the others in the group causes him to eventually doubt his own senses and follow the group's dictates. We do this all the time but no one ever tells us when the experiment is over or what we've been deluded into accepting!

It's difficult to be perceptive enough to sense the ripples of other people's karma impinging upon us. For one thing, we have to be possessed of a certain level of toughness, ie- insensitivity, numbness just to survive. Secondly, it's hard to be that perceptive when our very process of perceiving the world around us is also conditioned. We're conditioned to not knowing we're conditioned! Argh!

The long and short of it is that we're very, very conditioned beings. We like to think we're free, have our own impeccable opinions on a vast array of subjects, and know when we're being manipulated. Unfortunately this isn't true. Anyone who doesn't believe he or she is a product of their time is self deluding. For instance, fifty years ago smoking cigarettes was perfectly acceptable. You'd even get offered one in a doctor's waiting room! Asbestos existed for our own protection. A woman's place was in the home. All perfectly acceptable. It was the norm, and anyone who said differently was a dangerous subversive. These days we have our own culturally accepted norms, our own received wisdom, which we believe to be the truth. How quaint will we look in fifty years?

Our unconscious conditioning causes our egos to work overtime, protecting us from that which it senses could harm our self esteem, unknowingly putting others down, presenting ourselves in the best light, justifying our behaviour to ourselves and others. After all, that's the ego's job and it does it very efficiently. But by carrying on this process of self delusion we harm ourselves and others too. To wake up from this hypnotic state is very difficult. The teachings of Buddhas (Awakened Ones) will always go against the grain, so to speak. To listen to voices other than one's ego takes a lot of courage.

Shiva Shankara, that's a peaceful aspect of the Hindu/Tantric God Shiva, says (as I understand it) that we suffer because we see and experience a distorted view of reality. For example, if a group of people held you down and stuck a sharp needle in your arm, you'd be kicking and screaming, wondering what the hell was going on! But if you'd made an appointment for an inoculation that would save you from contracting some awful disease, you'd sit quietly through the temporary sting and even thank the doctor afterwards. Knowledge of the big picture would make an enormous difference to the experience.

If we were able to see the big picture always, knowing the effect we were having on others, and being able to sense where the actions and words of others was subtly leading us, we'd have a different appreciation of each interaction. If we could see the ripples, we'd maybe adjust our behaviour and our reactions accordingly. We would probably even reverse some of our opinions about which situations were helpful and which were harmful, both to us and to others. Knowledge would change our perception.

I was intrigued to read in Ajahn Sucitto's book "Kalyana" (usually available from Cittaviveka or Amaravati Monasteries in the UK) that the Buddha sometimes taught a supplement to the Eightfold Path. He would add two extra elements. Correct knowledge and correct release. This makes perfect sense. Correct knowledge, an extended ability to know what was happening at any particular moment, a perfect insight into the core of events and counter-events, would lead to perfect release, a freedom from perceptual conditioning, a freedom from conditioned action. When our practice, our experimentation if you like, reveals the truth and relevance of the spiritual path, be it Buddhist or otherwise, our faith can grow and our knowledge increase. And faith and knowledge bring release from doubt and anxiety...

Ajahn Sucitto is a Forest Sangha monk, disciple to Ajahn Sumedho, himself the author of many fine and helpful books on Buddhist wisdom. These two bhikkus (monks) have added much to western resources on Buddhist philosophy and practice. As westerners themselves, their observations and insights resonate strongly for many Buddhist practitioners in the modern world. This is particularly helpful as our spiritual practice shouldn't be removed from everyday life. It should be present in every aspect of our existence, including work, shopping, recreation, relationships etc. Real practice involves our whole being.

And real practice is done in the "real" world, not in some romantic misty mountain top retreat. As tempting as that location sounds, we'd still encounter the Buddhist nivaranas, "hindrances" of desire (attachment), aversion, mental torpor (boredom, depression), inner restlessness (anxiety) and sceptical doubt (ignorance) wherever and whenever we tried to turn our attention inwards. Even in the snowy vastness of the Himalayas!

I study Taijiquan, the Chinese martial art, and Qigong (working with Qi, our vital energy) and have been a serious practitioner for almost twenty years. I train hard every day. These physical disciplines afford me a lot of challenges, a lot of coming face to face with myself on many levels, bodily, mentally, emotionally and even spiritually. It's an ongoing process of unfolding, of growth, setbacks and revelations.

There's an exercise in the Dayan Gong, the Wild Goose Qigong form that I practice regularly, called Looking for Clouds in the Mist. There's an exercise too, in the Healthy Living Qigong series, called Separating Fog to look for the Clouds. These "cloud" exercises usually refer to our qi, our vital energy, being separated into heavy and light qi by our movement and breathing. In the same way that fog, mist, and clouds are all composed of water vapour, yet clouds are light and fog is heavy, more condensed, so too can our qi be experienced in many different ways, for example as Hao Qi, clean fresh energy, or Bing Qi, heavy, stagnant, turgid energy.

And of course our minds can be experienced that way too, as light and clean, clear and serene as a white cloud drifting in a blue sky, or as heavy as grey fog, bogged down with irrelevant chatter or emotional turmoil.

And thinking of clouds reminds me that as a child I was fascinated by Chinese landscape paintings. Their mysterious, muted tones of grey ink, evoking dragon clouds, mountain mists, craggy rocks, crooked pine trees, enormous distances and the solitude of nature, stood in stark contrast to Western style paintings, which I found almost brash and vulgar by comparison.

The human figure was treated differently too. Chinese paintings were like exercises in perception. You had to look hard to find the one tiny, solitary, almost insignificant person on a mountain pass or in a boat on a lake, whereas in Western paintings the human presence was much more central. To my childish eyes it seemed almost intrusive. In the Chinese paintings humans were given space to move, landscapes to measure themselves against - and nature was vast!

And poetry was endlessly inspiring too. What a wealth of feeling and insight a few lines could hold! The first time I read Lewis Carroll's "Alice In Wonderland" I was moved to tears, not by the story, which was great fun, but by the poem on childhood's passing, which ends the book. The Persian religious classic the Rubaiyat of Omar Khayyam, with its wry, fatalistic, almost Daoist overtones, has been a lifelong favourite too. I have many different translations in my possession.

There is a famous collection of poems by Han Shan, a Chinese Daoist who lived ago in the Tang Dynasty (8th Century CE). His poems really resonate with me. Han Shan means "Cold Mountain" and the poems are full of the bitterly cold, singing winds of high altitude, the ringing emptiness of the mountains. Though superficially sad and rueful, the verses, on deeper inspection and reflection, brim over with a deep, deep stillness.

"Climbing up the Cold Mountain path
The Cold Mountain trail goes on and on
The long valley choked with rock
The wide stream, the misty blurred grass
Even without rain the moss is slippery
Even without wind the pine sings
Who can escape the world's ties
And sit with me among the white clouds?"

The reclusive monk Han Shan has obviously left the clamour of the world far behind in these verses and has elected to spend his remaining years in quiet solitude, with only the mountains, the wind, birdsong and the clattering of icy streams for company. He's left the heaviness, the burden of society's demands, and ascended. Gone up into the mountain, up into the quietness of his own, purified inner being. The stillness and the cold emptiness fill him up completely, and his words evoke a profound inner quiet. He is at rest with himself.

To be at rest in oneself! That's quite an achievement and quite an aspiration too, isn't it? Many people never find that peace inside. Many more don't even know they long for it! To be at rest in one's body, in one's mind, in one's life, is hard. Most of us can't run off to the mountains for too long, and to be honest, just a little Spartan rustic solitude probably goes a long way! Too much being alone and the average person starts to go a little crazy!

But we do need to dip into that quietness sometimes, either in meditation, performing our Taiji or Qigong forms, or just reading a book on a rainy Sunday. Many people have told me that they really appreciated learning the Heavenly River Monastery Hard Qigong, which is a form of Shaolin body conditioning. Not because of the intense physical demands of this discipline, but because they had to learn to meditate as part of the practice. They really enjoyed it and the meditation became part of their daily routine. That's great!

So close your eyes for a moment. Ascend with Han Shan. Picture the vast, snow covered mountains, stretching off into the distance. Smell the cold air, the frozen resin of pine trees; hear the bright sound of a melt water stream, distant birdsong. Feel that chill misting of the mountain clouds on your face, on your eyebrows, on the backs of your hands. You can almost taste the chill, the freshness on your tongue. So, relax, drink in that spaciousness, that deep stillness. Forget yourself for a while...

Ah! That was nice! But like everything else, I suppose too much of anything gets to be routine. But a little peace and quiet is wonderful. We need some down time to rebalance ourselves occasionally. And the world desperately needs as many sane, balanced, calm and patient inhabitants as possible. All these desirable qualities can be by-products of regular meditation. We may feel like those figures in Chinese paintings sometimes, small, lost, almost insignificant, but actually we form an integral, important part of our, and others' environment. Just carrying a little of that Cold Mountain stillness inside can refresh those around us.

The gift of being calm, tolerant and patient for those you come into contact with is a precious gift. We can change negative to positive, turgid to flowing, stagnant to bright, just with our attitude. We can transform any situation, actually. It's a combination of our ability and our attitude. It's turning lead into gold. We have to want to do it and we have to be able to do it.

By turning lead into gold I mean acknowledging, accepting and then owning all our dross, all the stuff we've crammed into that giant rucksack of the psyche that we call our "shadow". We spend much of our lives stuffing all the qualities that society, our parents or our peers deem undesirable into this rucksack until we're almost crippled, dragging around this shadow burden of shame, guilt and anxiety. Sooner or later there comes a time when we want to haul some of this baggage into the light of day again, examine and process it. The trouble is that often there's so much garbage in the bag that just the act of opening it causes an avalanche, an outpouring of memories, complexes and psychic knots. When we finally get round to tidying up all these accumulations, dusting them off and giving them a new display shelf in our hearts, we find that some of these qualities aren't bad or undesirable at all! The lead paint has worn off to reveal the gold underneath! They may have been inappropriate at the time they were bagged, but that was then – you, and circumstances have changed. A lot of this stuff you don't need to drag around any more. But – the process of tidying and dusting can be tedious – and traumatic.

A spiritual practice, whether it's Buddhist, Hindu, Daoist, Pagan, whatever, will slowly change our hearts and minds. We can learn to be more sensitive to others, see the world through their eyes and become more cautious with our words and actions. The reverse is true too. We can become more sensitive to the way others push and pull us in different directions, often totally unconsciously. We may not have to stuff so much of ourselves into our shadow bag.

As a child (and by the age of ten I already had a huge shadow rucksack!) I used to love watching clouds, fantasizing about the magical castles that I could imagine built into their white slopes. Aah! Bless! And watching clouds teaches you all about impermanence, the fleeting nature of form, shape and substance. I wrote this poem when I was nearly fifty, when I'd had many years of Buddhist practice and a few years of shadow practice under my belt...

"Hooded and heavy-eyed against the cold
Hawk-high on the hills' wind-heaved horse hair steeps
I wait and watch, half envious, half exultant, banks and bulks of clouds
Getting torn to rags over the sharp prowed peaks
Buildings and beasts, castles and great ships
In their small eternities of roll, boil and flux
All dissolve and reform endlessly, and under the deep sky tipped
Drip and embrace impermanence upon the rocks

Wishing, like two moons ago, I was burrowing groin deep in warm clover
And tongue deep in love under an arch of summer stars
Clutching at the aching moment and holding it under my shaking chest
Until, inevitably, my moving breath reeled it out and away

Down into the long grass and the waiting stone womb beneath
Where all my snatched moments lie
Jawbone to jawbone jammed and clenched
In uneasy sleep with the black, howling hours
How dramatic the wound times
In this coldthorn cave of my huddled, hurting powers!

Oh the times I have burrowed, with alarming ease,
Into women's warmth, in bland untruths and blanket conspiracies
In the admiration of other men
As I sell them the hero's mask that hides the leaden cast of my own dread
In the bought silence of my children and their unanswered needs
Unknowing, uncaring of their be-coffined deeps
Where the fat and fierce worm of woe, having fed, now sleeps

Every man must tear himself from the cross
And redeem his body from the rock
Every man must untangle himself from the past
The harsh words that separated and castrated
And awake at long last from the hurting shock
And though his new shadow be sinister and unwelcome
Like a stranger at the wedding in a small country church
Whispered about and wondered at
That bulging bag of darkness must stain the church floor first
And we will grow, swell and burst
And from our glad wounds will ooze
The blood that feeds the winter rose
Fingers in the cold, clear stars, our anointed body still swells
Rooted in heaven, we can flower in hell
And where our hills and hollows meet to celebrate eternity
Eternity opens its gate and we can embrace
The father-mother becoming
And believe undefiled our true face
The gold beneath the lead"

Phew! Well, there's a few lifetimes' work right there. Acknowledging and accepting past sins against self and others, accepting and sorting out the shadow stuff, living a life in some sort of God (or Buddha) Consciousness. I think it all starts with an understanding and acceptance of the Buddha's teaching on impermanence, emptiness and suffering, and continues with a more mindful practice of how you and others affect each other...

The Buddha taught that everything, that's everything, you, me, antelopes, skyscrapers, situations, emotions, computers, galaxies, empires, apple trees and Scooby Doo, everything is impermanent. Everything passes. And everything is ultimately hollow, empty. A car is a collection, for example, the sum of its parts. Take some parts away and it's not a car anymore. Same with humans, take some components away and we're not humans anymore. Everything is a collective. And everything depends on everything else, no sun and moon, no life on earth, no flowers, bananas or human beings. No clouds, no rain, no water, no clouds. Everything interacts, leans upon the next link in the chain to make things happen. To try to find and rely on a solid, ego based self in this shifting, interacting world is to invite delusion and heartache.

So, knowing that we all need each other to a certain degree, we can relax our preferences a little, accept things as they are, treat all living beings, and that includes ourselves, with a bit more respect, even love. We can make all our interactions with others a little more positive. Using the language of alchemy again, we can try, on a daily basis, to turn lead into gold. To quote my beloved Rubaiyat of Omar Khayyam...

"Oh love! Couldn't you and I with fate conspire
To grasp the sorry scheme of things entire
Shatter it to many pieces and then
Rebuild it closer to the heart's desire?"

Oh yes please! If we could strike a bargain with Buddha, God or Goddess to remold the world the way we think it should be, wouldn't that be cool!

But Lao Tzu, another favourite, the author of the Dao De Jing, "The Way and its Virtue", or as my Tai Chi Sifu (teacher) succinctly calls it, "The Nature Morality Classic", thinks differently. Lao Tzu isn't passionate like Omar Khayyam. He's cooler, more detached. He asks, "Can you improve the world? I don't think it can be done. The world is perfect, holy."

"Those who would take over the world and bend it to their will never succeed for long
The earth is a mysterious entity
Dishonourable hands will pollute it
Those who try to seize it will lose it"

Now Lao Tzu isn't just referring here to evil men, or the Hitler, Stalin or Bush inside each and every one of us. He's referring to the intellectuals, the reformers, the meddlers. Those that think they know how the world should be run. This kind of arrogance stretches from the nosey or interfering neighbour at one end of the spectrum, right through to religious fundamentalists, who think it's ok to bomb, shoot and kill fellow human beings in the name of their faith.

But does this mean we shouldn't be involved in the world at all? Does it mean we shouldn't try and improve material conditions or medical treatments? Does this mean we shouldn't try and improve ourselves? Does this mean we should leave the busy workings of the world to others and retreat up into the cool, peaceful mountains? As tempting as that sounds, the answer is probably no. The world needs intellect, the world needs reformers. Maybe it doesn't need meddlers though! The world needs caring people trying to make a difference. Maybe not on a global scale but just in the way we treat ourselves and others. That can make a huge difference. If in the course of one day you positively affect say, just six people, that's six people whose lives have been made marginally better just through your actions. On a world scale maybe not so significant but to those six people, that one day was their world, and you just brightened it a little. It's significant then, isn't it?

I think what Lao Tzu is warning us against is the tendency to interfere, to think we know better than others what's right for them. This is arrogance, and it's true on a personal level and on a national level, when a government over-legislates until its citizens feel they can't even function without infringing some new law! It just breeds resentment. Lao Tzu likens the governing of a country to frying small fish. If you keep poking and prodding you just end up with a mess! This is true on a smaller social level too. So, as individuals, whether we're on a spiritual path or not, we need to be careful how we interact with others. If we're not humble, the tendency to be preachy and righteous can possess us, causing us to be either nauseatingly smug or downright overbearing. And if we can't be doin' with all this spiritual stuff, it's easy to scoff at all the tree huggers and cushion jockeys! And of course, with the best will in the world, sometimes we hurt people without actually meaning to. Even if the words aren't particularly harmful, sometimes the tone of our voice will betray hidden resentments, impatience, aversion. If we can't temper ourselves a little, then maybe we should take ourselves off to a mountain retreat, as an exercise in damage limitation!

Protect other people from yourself!

CHAPTER TWO - DARK & LIGHT, TWO RIVERS RUN.

Tantra is a gnostic, experiential spiritual path, containing elements of Buddhism and Hinduism, or more accurately, employing Buddhist/Hindu paradigms. Its techniques are a blend of classical Asian and ancient Shamanism. It's where esoteric Buddhism and esoteric Hinduism overlap. Actually, in this modern age, an era of cultural globalisation, Tantra needn't necessarily just employ Hindu or Buddhist symbols. As long as its basic principles are adhered to, there's no reason that I can think of that symbols from other cultures or religions, Celtic, Native American, African, whatever, can't be incorporated into daily practice.

Whereas Buddhism (and to a certain extent Hinduism) advocates the seeing of the body/mind complex as an impersonal bundle of physical, emotional and mental energies, resulting in an experience of anatta, non-self, and thereby freeing oneself, by detachment, from any suffering caused by the ego's conflict with the world and the way it works, Tantra (which means "to weave") seeks liberation of a narrow sense of self by identifying closely with all life forms and all energies of the world. Tantra seeks a deeper integration into all forms and energies and a cultivation of empathy and receptivity. As the boundaries between self and other dissolve, the hold of the ego is diminished. Both methods advocate "letting go", Buddhism by detachment, Tantra by cultivating "widened" states of mind and identification with one or more deities.

So one could define Tantra, together with Shamanism, as consciousness engineering.

One of Tantra's fundamental tenets is that no energy exists, however base or deplorable, that cannot be transmuted, through a spiritual practice, into divine service and ultimately into moksha, release, enlightenment. Of course this worldview lends itself to all sorts of misuse, deliberate and accidental, so one has to be careful. You can't use Tantric practice to justify committing negative or harmful actions. Stealing, raping and killing for God/dess (remember the Thugees, the murderous Indian cult?) is still stealing, raping and killing, and carries a heavy penalty, both legally and karmically!

Tantra is a path of passion, of turning base energies into holy ones, of riding the surge of emotion or enchantment into deeper, calmer waters of introspection, self knowledge and compassionate living. Its rasa, flavour, seems to contrast strongly with the serene and logical, measured feel of orthodox Buddhism. But Shiva, one of Tantra's chief deities, especially in the Hindu tradition, is a God of paradox. He embodies sensuality and abandon and also asceticism and discipline. He seems to embrace all seemingly disparate energies and gunas (qualities) without breaking a sweat.

The two streams of passion and detachment run through my spiritual life. Early on I learned to admire and emulate the cool serenity and otherworldliness of the Buddha and of other eastern sages such as Lao Tzu and Bodhidharma, the founder of Zen. But India is a vibrant and colourful culture, its music and art vibrate in my heart, so I couldn't not rock with it. I've been a fan of Indian culture most of my adult life. And when I first encountered Tibetan Buddhism, with its long rituals, complex deities and mind-blowing iconography, I thought it was just wonderful too.

So the misty mountain serenity of Daoism and Zen are balanced by the day-glo fervour of Tantra. I love them both. And I have no problem reconciling these two, apparently disparate currents. It wasn't always that way though. There came a moment in my spiritual evolution when I realised I was starving myself. I was trying so hard to be spiritually pure that I was in a downward spiral of denial. I needed colour, music, conversation, mental stimulation. I was trying to be a monk way before I was ready to even disengage from the world skilfully. I had to come down from the mountain top, as it were, descend down through the scrub and undergrowth and into the forest and a world of fertility in search of spiritual and sensual balance and ultimately, fulfilment. This is what I told myself at that time...

"I must deepen, and go back, and follow the ancient twisted track
The old cracked path, the gape-dark well
The sea of blackness, star seeded, shining
The overhanging lipswell, boundary of worlds, where soft holiness sings
And brings the balm of devotion's blossoming
To find shelter and warmth in the forest court of an older Lord
One who scorns narrow, ego-fuelled ambition
And instead gazes out, half imminent, half invisible
Breathing the scent of bull musk, pine and weeping earth
From every ancient, pregnant shadow"

I'm especially proud of the phrase "half imminent, half invisible". This was before I found out that one of the names of Shiva is Natha Kadavul, "The Lord Who Is Here, Now and Also Transcendent." The sea of blackness mentioned is the subconscious mind, the dark mirror that we can use to see our "real face", as Zen calls it, the face we had before we were born. This is the being we were before the world's conditioning bit into our psyche. The sea here can also represent the event horizon, the "black hole", the consciousness of God/dess that sucks everything back to it, in a final merging. Shiva's inner being is also said to be as black as outer space. The overhanging lipswell, where wave and shore meet, the boundary of earth and water, of solidity and flux, where soft holiness can be experienced, is that interface between our minds and a deeper reality, between the individual and the transcendent. It's where we can experience holiness. Without our mind, and without the universal mind, Buddha Consciousness whatever you want to call it, it doesn't work, the two have to meet, like question and answer. Then it becomes a mutual acknowledgement. Oneness can be felt. The fact that they were never two, never separate, becomes personal knowledge.

Another way to look at this meeting place, this mutual inspection and merging, is that God/dess uses YOU for a mirror! What do you think He or She sees in that mirror?

Now, I have to be honest. In trying to redress my spiritual balance, true to form, I went too far in the other direction, and created for myself a kind of Buddhist/Tantric circus, full of colour, spectacle and diversion. What I didn't do for a long time is work on any of my hindrances. So then I had to seek a balance again. I finally got it right, due in large part to the steadying influence of Lung Por (Grandfather) Ajahn Sumedho. I look at his picture every day and say thank you.

Speaking of question and answer and a meeting of minds, traditionally the Mother Goddess Parvati, the embodiment of compassion and phenomena, was the questioner. She would skilfully interrogate her husband Shiva, the embodiment of pure consciousness and wisdom, and it was His responses that are handed down to us in the Tantras and other holy writings. And they always boil down to two themes, or if you prefer, the two seemingly disparate currents of self knowledge and devotion. Know yourself, love God/dess. Then you can love all beings and know God/dess.

It's said that Shiva Shankara's skin is pure white. He meditates for aeons, unmoving, Bol Shankar, the Oblivious Lord, gleaming palely through the long succession of Himalayan days and nights. But inside, his essence is darkness, the darkness of vast space, the darkness of that fruitful womb the Tibetans called Tongpanyi – the Void. He represents both the root, undifferentiated consciousness and the ultimate, embracing inclusiveness of consciousness returned to the source. He shines darkly inside.

His dark starry self constellates into a knot of consciousness in every living creature. And by living creature I also mean that which we would normally term inanimate objects, like rocks, radios, aeroplanes and government leaders! These sparks burn in us all, unnoticed mostly, as it seems to take us virtually all of a whole earthly incarnation to recover from the squeeze of the Mother Goddess's womb, and to stop taking for granted the magical, bewitching world of Maya (illusion). Then we start to look behind the scenes, to see how things work. And to look inside ourselves, to see how we really work.

And what a shock that can be!

Anyone who meditates regularly will be quite familiar with all those incessant inner voices, chattering, slandering, scolding, fuming, sticking obsessively on a given subject, however much one tries to maintain concentration and inner quiet. It can be quite dismaying at first to realise that all this garbage has been spawning, warring and poisoning for decades without one even knowing! And be reassured, it's not just you. Every human skull is the container for this whirlpool of ill will and ego. Only those that have learned to discipline the "monkey mind" are able to detach themselves from its relentless broadcast.

So, like Shiva Shankara, we can be said to be white on the inside and black on the outside. But in a very different way! We try and present a mask of light to the world, an image of intelligence, warmth and generosity, but inside we can be a dark, seething cauldron of resentment, aggression, treachery and spite. I recently lost the company of a kung fu brother. Though a senior who should have known better, his behaviour had become increasingly challenging and self centred, so our Sifu, ever mindful of the big picture and how his behaviour could affect others, had no choice but to "evict" him. I have to admit this caused a great turmoil in me. Part of me was sad because he was an extremely talented and once-loyal companion. Part of me rejoiced because to be honest he could be a total pain in the ass, rude, aloof and over enthusiastic about discussing maiming and breaking techniques! But it was this rejoicing part of me that caused the turmoil. There was I, supposedly this patient and forgiving spiritual seeker, and I was happy that he'd been kicked out. How compassionate was that? The fact that he deserved it, having used up all his opportunities for redemption, was irrelevant, it was my own attitude that was giving me sleepless nights. I really had to work hard to own, acknowledge, accept and transform that horrible glee. Once I realised that its root was a selfish rejoicing that his behaviour had made me and the rest of my brothers and sisters look quite virtuous by comparison, I was able to use this as a positive development, thank him in my heart for this gift, wish him well and let him go. I was also able to moderate my own feelings and stop all the self blaming. Lead had been turned into gold, but only by wholeheartedly accepting the darker or negative elements of my psyche. If I had allowed myself to get stuck in the "His karma, he deserved it" position, or the "It's his fault I'm having conflict, not mine" position, then progress would have been impossible. I wouldn't have been able to evolve spiritually. I wouldn't even have been able to mature!

Humanity has to constantly evolve in an ever shifting world. A lot of our behaviour and the thoughts and instincts that drive those behaviours are biological imprints. Our survival has depended upon learning techniques and practices and being able to use them unconsciously. If a loud explosion happens behind you, you don't have to think about moving, your body will do it for you! Most of these patterns of thought and behaviour are useful and don't need tampering with, but to recognise and accept our animal self is not necessarily a backward step. Some of the elements of our inner being are straight from the Stone Age. But that doesn't make them shameful or irrelevant. Anything that we can examine, and acquire more self knowledge in the examining, is useful.

A friend of mine is really fond of the God Pan. I think He helps her connect with her physical body, the raw energies of the natural world and perhaps the fleet footed, elusive deer within her that helps her evade the hunters and traps of her own inner landscape. Sounds a bit fanciful I know, but she's not a new-age type, and it seems to work for her. She's very physical, very sensuous, trains hard, always sniffing herbs, fingering fabrics, always swaying to music, needs a lot of physical contact. But she's also very busy, sociable, civilised, quite intellectual, always hard pressed for time. Perhaps Pan lives out the parts of her life that she can't, the solitude, the shunning of human company, the timeless forest days, the basic, shameless physical urges. I don't know. None of my business!

Speaking of private business and apologies if you find the next couple of paragraphs distasteful... Go into any men's public toilet anywhere in the world and, it's more than likely, somewhere in a cubicle, someone has drawn an erect phallus, often spitting seed, and a pair of hairy testicles. The chances are that this graffiti wasn't drawn by a gay guy for other gays to admire, but by some heterosexual youth making his territorial mark. "This is my dick, and I'm a real man!" Primitive and pretty tasteless too, but obviously fulfilling some deep stone age need to mark his space and beat his chest in front of other males, possible rivals or enemies.

When the internet first exploded into the homes of Mr and Mrs Average, and everyone suddenly had access to webcams, before you knew it, every other women's public toilet was a website, and movie clips of women urinating, defecating and changing tampons were public property. All this is quite invasive. We're all entitled to a crap in peace. I often go to the loo just to get away from other people. The last thing I'd want is my morose face contorted in defecation posted on the net! So, putting my anger aside, what urge expresses itself in filming women in these moments? Well, I guess it's a combination of the traditional power of the voyeur, the invisible watcher, able to see all and not be held accountable for his actions, and the desire to see everyone as dirty, as animalistic as possible, ie – as dirty as the voyeur.

But of course there's something else beneath this urge. There's a desire, however distorted, however perverted, for intimacy, for closeness.

I know a couple who have a parting ritual that goes right back to the Stone Age. They told me this in good faith so I'm giving no clues about their identity. When they're not going to see each other for a while, and I'm not sure how delicately I can put this, he gently inserts a finger into her, sometimes vaginally, sometimes anally and she grips his testicles. They both murmur "Mine..." Now, these people are not weird. They're quite "normal" and I like them both. They've been together for a long time. It took a lot of courage to tell me something like this. I actually found this little ritual quite sweet and endearing. I may take it up myself! How primitive is that! I'd take a step backward if I were you! But they're not individuals with an overtly possessive or territorial nature, as far as I can see. This kind of animal bonding works for them, reassures them, connects them with some primitive need. They're able to embrace a very ancient part of their humanity in this way. And it doesn't hurt anyone else, so good for them!

And when they're apart for a few days, she packs a pair of her dirty knickers in his suitcase, and he sleeps with them under his pillow. She wears one of his unwashed t shirts to bed. Primitive but effective. A businessman I know spends most of his day dealing with abstracts, stocks, shares etc. I advised him to pick a few blades of grass from his lawn every morning before he gets into his car, and roll them around in his fingers, until they release their green onto his skin and he can smell that unique sharp scent. He told me he now does this when he gets home in the evenings too. It grounds him and that simple act of touching the grass, the realm of nature, acts as a bridge between his two worlds, the abstract, detached world of work and the human, connected world of his family. Again, primitive but effective.

I know another guy, with a new girlfriend. She adores him but was quite sexually active in her younger days. His initial fear of "not measuring up" was soon overcome - apparently everything proved quite satisfactory in that department – but a subsequent and more subtle jealousy arose. He didn't mind her having "conquests", he didn't mind her "wanting cock", it was the thought of her "giving" herself to another man that plagued him. The idea of her wanting to surrender to another man was quite painful for him, not the sexual act but the emotional opening and yielding. I advised him to think of these past surrenders as a loving and trusting act of a woman who wanted to please a partner, and to think himself lucky that out of all the men in the world, it was him that this experienced and sexually athletic woman wanted to spend her time with. He was a lot happier. But he had to accept his jealousy and insecurity long enough to see it for what it was, a defence mechanism to prevent future hurt and rejection. The Tantric version of this process would have been to imagine this woman as an incarnation of the Goddess. She is free to use any man for her pleasure, she is also free to surrender her physical form, what we call the nirmanakaya, the illusion body, to any other illusion body she sees fit. And this Goddess now chooses to bind her illusion body to this man's in the long term. He can exhibit his Godly qualities now, by caring for her wisely and by nurturing her trust and commitment.

In Buddhist Tantric art and ritual, the male is regarded as active compassion, skilful means, and the female as wisdom, arcane knowledge. In Tantra that employs a Hindu paradigm, the roles are reversed. In the case above, it would seem that the couple have an opportunity to embody the qualities of wisdom (the man) and compassion (his partner). Good luck to them.

So Tantra is all about employing our human energies, however base, primitive or negative they may appear to our ego based conditioning, and transforming them into something more positive, even spiritual or transcendental. But Tantra is not merely a collection of psychological techniques, though I fervently believe that self analysis, self knowledge and improvement are a big part of the spiritual path. Tantra is a full blown religion, and its pinnacle of achievement is also the goal of orthodox Buddhism and Hinduism, moksha – release, or nirvana – enlightenment.

So what are Tantra's main principles and practices? What symbols and techniques does it employ? How exactly do we turn "lead", negative energies, into "gold", positive spiritual qualities? Well, every negative situation is different in some way, and of course every individual brings something different, something unique, to the mix. So we have to identify a principle, and then find various ways of expressing that principle.

For example, in Taijiquan, we use an opponent's strength against them. When a fist comes in, we don't block at a ninety angle with our forearm. If the opponent is bigger, stronger, or "harder" than us, the result is likely to be disastrous – and painful! No, we block at an angle that favours the original direction of the blow, part block, part deflection. Let's say an opponent offers a straight punch with their right fist towards our nose. Depending on which of our feet is forward, ie- closer to the opponent, we can either block slightly inwards and towards our body with our left palm, deflecting the fist over our right shoulder, or block/deflect slightly outwards and over our right shoulder with our right forearm, thus passing through the classic kung fu "right wrists crossed, about to kick off" position. Either way, the result is the same, and we obviously, at the same time, try to manoeuvre the body "off line" to further evade the punch. (In fact, footwork is paramount, even more important than the block.)

So the principle, evade and deflect rather than block strength with strength, is fairly constant but can be expressed in many, varying ways. What I want to do for you is find a principle of Tantra, an underlying rule that can be interpreted and employed in various situations. Hmm...

Ok. Let's examine a couple of scenarios and see if we can trace the progress of the process so to speak, follow the trail left by the mind's journey from confusion and division to illumination and transcendence. Firstly, let's imagine it's the middle of the evening. You're lounging on the sofa watching TV in your living room. It's been a particularly trying day at work and you've been trying to relax and shed the stress since arriving home and having the evening meal. It's just beginning to leave your mind and body and a particularly absorbing programme is about to start. You stretch and sigh contentedly, beginning to feel better. Suddenly, there's a loud blast of music outside, followed by laughing and chatter. A glance through the curtains confirms your initial suspicions. The next door neighbours have gone out and their two teenage daughters are holding court, surrounded by what seems like a host of male admirers. You try to turn the TV up and block out the intrusion but it doesn't work. You can feel the tension knots tightening again. Grrr.

Now obviously you can just go outside and hurl abuse at the inconsiderate brats, threaten to tell their parents, call the police, and strike threatening kung fu postures. Depending on the circumstances this will bring various results, ranging from cooperation, ridicule, defiance or a brick through your window later that evening. But we're trying to do more here. We're trying to turn lead into gold, reach some kind of inner knowledge. And self knowledge is spiritual currency.

So let's first identify the primary emotion. Is it anger at the teenagers' lack of consideration? Is it depression or self pity that your hard earned evening of rest has been destroyed, because that's what always happens to people like you who work hard, try to make an effort. Someone always comes along to mess it up. Someone with no thought for others. Whoops! Anger and depression combined! And whatever it is you're feeling, you don't want it. You want to be able to relax in your own home. You want to live in a world where people respect each other. You want a world where parents raise their children properly. You want a world where young people are locked in dark cellars until they reach a responsible age...

Stop! Let's backtrack a bit. Step one of the process – identify the primary emotion. It may be anger, or resentment, it may be depression. Identify it. Step two- own it. It's your emotion, no one else's. Don't project. Don't try to justify. Don't blame the teenagers for your emotions. Don't try and justify those feelings to an invisible third party. The teenagers may well be at fault but that's irrelevant to this practice. Own your emotion. Don't use the thought patterns that contain the phrase, "They made me feel like this." Instead, employ the process that begins with "I have allowed myself to feel..." The emotion is yours, no one else's. Own it.

Step three. This is the hardest. Identify the quality those teenagers are exhibiting that you're denying in yourself. Because, wriggle as much as you like, this is the key. If that quality wasn't in you somewhere, you wouldn't be suffering so much. The chances are that it's their freedom, the lack of need to worry about the feelings of others, that you envy. They feel no responsibility. So suddenly it's a different vibe. The real problem is that you deny yourself this freedom so you resent it in others. Aha!

Now I'm not suggesting that you now go to the other extreme and become a selfish prick. But you may need to look at some elements of your life where you're ignoring subtle messages from your brain that all is not well. Maybe you're going along with someone or something you're not quite happy with, but hey, anything for a quiet life eh? Rocking the boat will be more trouble than it's worth...

See how this works? Because you've been denying part of your inner reality, God/dess has come along, in the shape of a bunch of unruly teenagers, to show you the error of your ways. And because we're so dumb, we have to endure extreme lessons in order to achieve that "Aha!" moment. So much of our intention is unconscious, we don't even recognise that we asked God/dess to intervene...

Shiva is often referred to as Pashupati, Lord of Animals. But this can also be translated as Lord of Souls. Compared to the er... cosmic consciousness of God (or Goddess), we're just like dumb creatures, cattle to the slaughter. A slaughter engineered by our own ignorance. And by ignorance I mean ignoring, turning our back on our own intuition, following the rest of the herd. Convenient of course, but ultimately self defeating. The spiritual path will often go against the grain, against conventional wisdom. The Buddha said quite plainly two and a half thousand years ago that His teaching would never be for the masses because it was "against the stream".

A female friend of mine, and one of the most dedicated students I've ever had, inadvertently made me look at the teenage scenario above. We'd just bought train tickets to travel to an upcoming seminar in London and as we were leaving the station, a train arrived with a loud, leaping load of night clubbers, eager to sample the cultural delights on offer in my home city (which consist of a wind-up gramophone, two coloured light bulbs and some drunk, underage slappers. Hey! Only kidding, ok!) My student, who didn't feel at all threatened by the laddishness, the boisterous behaviour, the swearing etc, just smiled fondly and said, "Ah! Boys! I like to see them having fun." She had a totally different attitude to those around her, who were glaring daggers at the revellers and muttering under their breath. Again, I'm not saying that people don't need to behave in public. As a lifelong Buddhist, long-time martial artist, and great respecter of my teachers' code of conduct, I have very conventional views on what's appropriate around other people. But our attitude, the way we involuntarily colour a situation, can impact enormously on our inner states. My student and the other onlookers at the railway station were obviously having very different experiences of the same event.

Let's examine another scenario. In your office, there's a job up for grabs, an internal promotion that would mean more money at the end of each month, and a little more clout. Let's say some kind of team manager's job. It eventually boils down to a short list of three people. You, Mrs Jones and Sammy Snide. Your strength is that you've been there a long time, you know the work inside out. Mrs Jones' strength is that she always gives it one hundred and ten percent. She's the first to arrive in the morning, last to leave at night, loves being useful, always volunteering to take on extra tasks. She's also (surprisingly) very popular. Sammy Snide is a fast tracker, a big talker, and specialises in getting other people to do the work for him and taking the credit. He's also famous for presenting other people's ideas as his own in committee meetings.

Well, surprise, surprise! He's the dude to get the promotion. Why? Because he can sell himself. He says what the bosses want to hear. This infuriates you. You see him as a pretentious parasite, who knows nothing about the work involved and who couldn't organise a melting competition in an ice cube factory without a blowtorch, an instruction manual and a note from his mother. So in your mind you rail against the bosses, you resent the system that rewards jerks like Sammy, and you fantasise the rest of the day about exposing him for the tosser he truly is! So... let's examine the emotions and we'll find that underneath the resentment and injustice, if we're honest, the real flavour of the day is good old fashioned jealousy. He got what you wanted. It's so unfair! But you have to own and acknowledge that jealousy. Don't blame it on Sammy, or on the bosses. It's your emotion, not theirs. Don't start mental sentences with the word "But..." Don't try and justify it. Just accept that you're jealous. It's the healthiest thing to do. Then identify the quality that Sammy is exhibiting that you're denying in yourself. What he's good at is using other people and taking the credit, in other words being the leader of a team, which is exactly what he was hired for! You weren't perceived as having those qualities, however deep your knowledge of the actual work. What you're denying in yourself are those perceived characteristics of a leader. You're not showing that you can round up ideas and energies and co-ordinate them. Sammy shows this (the bastard!) So you naturally resent him for displaying the gold that you can't access within you.

Again, I'm not advocating that you now become a user and exploiter of people. But maybe you have to learn how to know what you want and how to make it happen. You have to take charge more often.

Someone asked me how we know when "shadow" is operating. A good rule of thumb is that if something really gets under your skin, really causes internal abrasion, then it could be shadow. Of course, every day, there are endless opportunities to get annoyed. But shadow has a sticky, obsessive feeling. And if you react strongly to the idea that the other party, the person you're annoyed with, is displaying one of your denied characteristics, if the idea sounds preposterous! Well, it's probably true, it's probably your shadow. The more denial is involved, the more likely it is that shadow is at work.

So all of the above is basic "shadow" psychology, the art of discovering the denied (and therefore potentially destructive) aspects of yourself and rescuing them from their dark, internal bondage. But be careful! Like any caged beast, when first released, these energies can be wild and fickle. Use a bit of restraint and eventually the energies will calm down and settle happily into the community that is your collective being.

Someone asked how we can avoid cramming unexpressed inner material into the shadow rucksack. I don't think you can, certainly not in the early part of each life. One is still open to influence, one is still being moulded by the various influences of family, friends, society, culture. And quite often the conditioning is subliminal, not overt. You'd have to be supernaturally awake for this not to happen! It's in later life that we have the opportunity to become more resistant to conditioning and more likely to want to undo former habits and responses. And not everyone gets to open that rucksack. Most people, of any age, just don't want to, let alone know how to go about it!

Now of course, this is psychology not Tantra. But the mindset, the attitude of the Tantrist (or Tantrika) is paramount. It's all about turning lead into gold. So no energy is considered unworkable, impossible to surf on, impossible to transmute. Ultimately all energies, base and pure, apocalyptic and humdrum, are perceived as just variations on the background hum of the multiverse, the mother vibe. Every single energy in the world, whether coalesced into the form of a cabbage or king, or shapeless like a breeze or a passing thought, is part of the vibe of Shiva and Shakti's lovemaking. Um.. you're right. I'd better explain that a bit more clearly...

But before I get into that, I'll just finish the train of thought we were riding about the relationship between Tantra and shadow work. If, to the Tantrist, every energy is part of the same vibration that fuels and underpins the universe, it follows that there's no energy that isn't divine. So Sammy Snide, and the teenagers earlier, are God or Goddess turning up in disguise to help you achieve some kind of recognition, internal alchemy and self knowledge. If you think about it, if there are is such a thing as God or a transcendent force or being, whether you call it Pan, Kali, Buddha, Allah etc (and we'll probably discuss this too later), then there can't really be anything that isn't God. Everything in you, everything that happens to you, everything in the world, is God/dess in some form.

So what the practitioner of Tantra has in common with those who employ the techniques of Jungian shadow work, is an honouring of those energies that, at first encounter, seem undesirable, hideous, destructive. It doesn't matter whether you call them complexes, demons or wrathful deities. You have to honour them in order to work with them.

If I worship the Mother Goddess in a pure, loving mode, for example as Tara (a Tibetan saviouress), Sarasvati (the Hindu Goddess of learning) or Parvati (the peaceful aspect of Shiva's wife), but deny, in my Goddess, and by extension in every woman, anger, righteous fury, aggressive protective qualities, possessiveness, greed and lust, then it's those very qualities that the Goddess will eventually employ to bring me down. And it will be for my own good. How can She tolerate me half-worshipping Her? I have to accept Her in her totality. And of course, as soon as I learn to do that, She's usually happy just to show Her sunny side. Why? Because those darker energies are no longer caged and shunned. They're not going to lash out in frustration at "the life unlived".

That's why Tantric deities tend to be represented in art and literature in quite dramatic ways. They represent dramatic energies!

CHAPTER THREE - THE HUMMING WOMB.

Before we explore the techniques and goals of Tantra, let's look at its paradigm, the philosophical setting in which everything takes place. So we need to look at space, time, and how the world works. Hmm... so nothing too complicated then!

Space, the universe and t'ing. A kid on a TV commercial asked, "If the universe is expanding, what is it expanding into?" A good question but a very western one. It's not like there's a sea of nothingness into which our universe is expanding like an ink stain in a bowl of water. That implies a merely mechanistic worldview, where time is linear and space is just an absence of matter. Time is actually a product of matter, of entropy, the decay of matter. Time and matter are linked. Time is also, in part, a product of our mind. Please allow me to try to explain the Tantric take on all this.

Well, first of all, matter and space aren't separate entities, so to speak, nor is space merely what you're left with when matter is abolished. Space and matter are two ends of a "spectrum" of energy vibration. Shit! Sounds new agey doesn't it? Sorry. Let's try again. Imagine a really tight guitar string vibrating. At that high a frequency it's quite a force. It could cut a piece of paper easily. If it's slackened off, we hardly hear a sound. But if we touch it, we can just about feel that the vibration is still there. So that's like dense matter and a less dense state, like space. I'm not saying space and matter are like a guitar string, y'dig? I'm saying they're both vibrations of energy, but at different "speeds".

The groundbreaking book of the '70s, The Tao Of Physics by Fritjof Capra, used more or less the same language to describe "the dancing universe", different manifestations of energy, all melting into one another. It's an ancient wisdom, hard to describe in lay language.

I suppose another analogy is light. A candle flame is light, but quite nebulous, quite fragile. In a huge warehouse, it's hardly there. But a laser beam! You'd notice it, I think. It's almost solid, the way it can punch/scorch through stuff. But it's still light. So even light can be more or less dense, like matter and space. It's a question of intensity of vibration. Same for matter and space, it's just a question of intensity of vibration. But it's really hard to figure out, and my explanation may not help much so don't beat yourself up if you can't understand it.

As far the birth of the universe is concerned, there wasn't a big bang a few hundred million years ago so suddenly there was matter, which meant that time began then also. No. The universe is a heartbeat, pulsing once every kazillion years, a big bang, expansion, contraction, implosion, big bang. Again and again and again for ever. It's continually being born. And where the universe expands, it expands from itself, retaining an internal balance. It doesn't expand into anything. There's nothing for it to expand into except itself. There's no edge to the universe. Hard to grab hold of, isn't it, with our minds that can only conceive of either empty space or matter? But there isn't an "empty space or matter" either/or, only more condensed or less condensed waves or vibrations of energy. So actually, however "big" the universe is, it's always infinite. You can't get outside it to measure it.

This vibration, the pulse of the universe, the single holy vibe, the coarser or more refined (but still single) vibe that can be "light", "space" or "matter", is known to Hindus as Om (pronounced aum), the most sacred of syllables. More on this in a mo...

And time has no meaning here, in this cyclical event, this eternal folding, unfolding, thickening, rarefying, internal balancing. No beginning, no end.

There wasn't a first big bang. Time doesn't have beginnings, middles and ends in the mind of the Tantrist. Time is an eternal now. Millions of nows, all happening at once. If you've read my first book "The Real Rasa", you'll remember the concept of Indra's Bubble Bath. Indra is a Hindu deity and I likened time to a million bubbles in His bubble bath. Each bubble is separate, a now, an eternal moment. But being close to one another, each bubble also affects other bubbles. If you pop one, you may pop another without meaning to. If you pour green shampoo through a bubble, you'll notice that the bubbles around it reflect/contain the green hue. If you blow on the bubbles, you may distort some, destroy others. This is temporal dependant origination. Each bubble, each moment reflecting and affecting other moments. And as these bubbles are all experienced as "now", they could be a "now" in the "past", or a "now" or in "the future". In this worldview, it's even possible to perform an action in the future which will change your past, or to be reborn into the sixteenth century. Eternal nows radiate out from one another. The bubbles stack up on top of each other, behind one another, they even sometimes penetrate one another. What they don't do is march in an orderly single file, from past to future.

I've just read, in the Daily Telegraph (very respectable!), that scientists are now coming round to this "time bubble" paradigm. Hah!

A friend of mine recently had some aromatherapy. Not a perfumed massage, though I'm sure she would have been up for that. The real kind, where you sniff different basic scented oils from the end of a swab and they bring up, evoke buried memories. She wasn't expecting much from this, to be honest, but much to her surprise, one oil brought up a past life memory of death by drowning. And though one could say this was an occurrence from her "past", it was experienced very vividly, very unpleasantly as a present event, not a memory. So is it past or present? It's the present I think.

And who hasn't had a flash of intuition, a certain knowledge of the outcome of an event, or a visual flash of someone that they haven't met, but subsequently encounter? When it happens to you, is it present or future? It's the present I think.
So the past and the future can impinge upon the present. And the present is all we can ever know. The eternal now is all we have. But we have potentially millions of nows, being affected, as we've just seen, by the past and the future. Each "now" is one bubble in Indra's bubblebath. And there are millions. And we potentially have access to all of them.

I would imagine this view of time is a little like the Aboriginal dreamtime, where we and ancestral memories merge, where God can be a 'roo and you can heal hurts that haven't even happened yet. I know it takes a bit of a headstretch to take this in but that's how it feels when I'm temporarily free of my internally constructed temporal gravity. Of course, when I'm eating, watching TV, listening to heavy dub, then time feels linear. The meal ends, the programme ends, the music ends. However, sometimes even though the cd comes to an end, I can still hear the music. I can relax in bed and summon up any song by any artiste, clear as a bell, even ones that don't exist. I can listen to Bob Marley or Hendrix playing tunes by other artistes that weren't even around when they were alive. Mind you, I still prefer real cd's! And no, I can't do it with food, I still have to eat in the old fashioned way...

So time is a radiant mandala (a sacred geometrical symbol. More on this later), a star burst of "nows". Pick anywhere in the pattern. Any bubble. That one? Okay, that's the first moment, the centre of the mandala, the secret heart of the rose. This is the womb of the Dark Mother. From this one moment, all time springs. So all matter also springs from this one point. Now pick another bubble. Ah yes! That one. That's the first moment, the centre of the mandala, the secret heart of the rose. This is the womb of the Dark Mother. From this one moment, all time springs. So all matter also springs from this one point...

The womb of the Mother Goddess, and She has many names, Kali, Parvati, Durga and to most Tantrists Shakti, is everywhere, every single point simultaneously, giving birth to matter from Her womb. The sacred sound Aum, the humming of the universe, issues from her vulva, condensing into various life forms. The seed, the essence, one might say the true nature of her consort Shiva, pure consciousness, is injected into all matter as it's born. All life forms are born of Shakti and carry Shiva, God Consciousness within. Cool, eh?

So having looked at where these nows come from, and also from where matter originates, ie- everywhere, simultaneously, it follows, logically, that matter is constantly being born and decaying, being reabsorbed. The original big bang is still happening, a million times a second. The universe is constantly being born, not only, in one sense, every gazillion years, but also every single second. And the end of our universe is happening as well, constantly. There's not one single big bang, a period of hanging around, cooling, growing limbs and brains, learning to walk upright, becoming beings of pure energy then collapsing back into ourselves, along with the entire universe. Well, actually there is, but it happens all the time, every moment. If you could travel from bubble to bubble in Indra's bath (and with training, you can), you could witness the birth of the planets as many times as you like, maybe with some interesting variations. For each bubble can be a different now, a now in which something different happens from the bubble next door (though probably affected and coloured by it). It would be possible to witness a thousand variations of any single event you could imagine.

Any given bubble can be the very centre of the universe, the birthplace of matter and time. And there are an infinite number of these bubbles. This of course makes a nonsense of "reality". Yep. So?

Reality is another name for a consensus, a majority decision based on the best available evidence. So we tend to treat science as a religion, looking to scientists for reasonable answers. And they do their best with the mental equipment and technological apparatus at their disposal. And they do come up with decent by products, like non-stick frying pans, electric blankets and antibiotics. But try and find two scientists who agree completely on how the universe was born and how it works. Good luck.

Another way to look at this time t'ing is to imagine parallel universes. You know the old Twilight Zone concept. There are other worlds, other realities, where you didn't catch that bus and ended up meeting the love of your life and having a beautiful baby boy together. You named him Adolf! Whooo... spooky! Or there's another world where you decided to give up trying to invent x rays and instead gave the world its first full length accordion symphony. So if you can conceive of parallel universes, parallel time streams, all we have to do is take away the "parallel" bit. Imagine all these continuums piled up one top of one another, coiling around each other, nudging each other, even penetrating each other. Like copulating snakes (Ugh!) And you'd never even know if two streams met and you wandered off in another direction. It would seem normal to you...

This concept of time isn't quite like the Tantric mandala of eternal nows. But at least it's not quite as mechanical as the standard western linear model.

In Tantra, time is the great devourer of all things. The deities Mahakala (male) or Kali (female) are portrayed with black skin, dark and forbidding, like the howling gulf of outer space. But if we honour these deities, try to hear their lessons, something curious and rather wonderful happens, they shine forth a clear white light from their inner being, and we realise that, if we can hold that insight into the nature of time, that it consists of an infinite number of eternal nows, then the inner nature of Kali or Mahakala is a white light, pure being, pure consciousness. It's the reverse of Lord Shiva.

Kali and Mahakala, the great devourers, also represent rage, destruction, blind fury. But their alternative inner nature is compassion, protection. We could say that their love, their nurturing abilities are the golden shadow of their anger. Shiva Shankara's shadow is Bhairav, the Terrible One. Tantric deities are soooo extreme! So if we honour our anger, and the anger of others, without drowning in it, we can see it for the protective tendency that it wants to be. More lead into gold, more inner alchemy, the trademark process of Tantra.

While we're in these physical bodies of ours, with their decaying appendages, Stone Age impulses and limited intellects, we're in the realm of Kali, and in her grip too. Men are at a disadvantage here, they can't identify too strongly with the archetype of the angry crone, of the murderous mother, of the frustrated female warrior, the repressed sexual maiden. So they have to learn to honour these aspects of the Mother Goddess in women. Then they won't be castrated, intimidated, brought low by these dark forces.

And maybe women can't identify very well with the pointless destruction, the gleeful rending, the sheer ecstasy of the brutal impulse, the male strength at its most primitive. A lot of men have problems with it too. Yet we admire it in lions and tigers. We allow them their true nature. Mind you, if we lived in the savannah or the jungle and had to interact with big cats on a regular basis, we may think differently! So we cheer at boxers in the ring or rugby players, even WWE wrestlers, savouring every physical collision, knowing that we're safe in the audience. We honour our primitive need for combat and territorial confrontation. But anyone who's been caught up in a real scuffle between violent football supporters of opposing teams will know how very, very different it feels!

So, it's good for us as individuals, as members of society, and as Tantrists, to find safe and positive ways of honouring our primitive, Stone Age instincts and urges. Then those urges can evolve, transmute and transform.

Okay, back to the big bang thread...

The Mother Goddess gives birth to all matter, everywhere, simultaneously. From between her legs emanates the primal hum and crackle of the universe, condensing, as it were, into various life forms (and inanimate materials too). Every living creature also carries the seed of Shiva, Shakti's lover, partner and co-creator, like a small spark inside. This seed is pure consciousness. When we evolve enough we start to feel that spark glowing somewhere deep within and if we choose to examine that glow, that inner burning, and realise, at least intellectually, that we carry that reminder of our own divinity at our core, then we want to find our way home again, we want to reunite with the source.

As men, we want to reunite with the alpha male, God, who carries all our gold for us, all our worthy qualities. As women, we want to unite with the Goddess, the alpha female, the source of power, the holder of our internal treasures. And even this is part of the illusion. At this exalted level, once we discard the physical body, male and female are redundant concepts. In fact there's a famous representation of Shiva as Ardhanarishvara, the Lord who is half man, half woman. And to be fair, we could call this a representation of the Mother Goddess, Parvati in this instance, as half man, half woman. This image of a united duality can be seen as any "two-in-one" you care to imagine – male/female, wisdom/compassion, energy/matter, consciousness/physical being etc

Tibetan Buddhist art and sculpture, in a reversal of the Hindu scheme, concentrates mainly on the intertwining, the conjoining of a male Buddha or Bodhisattva, representing compassion or skilful means, and a female consort, representing wisdom. Tibetan iconography contains some of the most beautiful and meaningful images I've ever seen.

By the way, a Bodhisattva (lit – enlightenment being) is a fully emancipated being who has elected to postpone their final merging into the void in order to help sentient beings. This concept, common to all later schools of Buddhism such as Tibetan, Zen, Pure Land etc contrasts with the early Theravada Buddhist (Way of the Elders) definition of a Bodhisattva as a Buddha-in-training, an "almost there".
In the Theravada tradition, the Buddha was a man, reborn many times, purifying His inner nature, until attaining full nirvana, enlightenment. After ascending to the very peak of human achievement, He spent His remaining earthly years teaching the dharma (the Law) to others. He claimed to be the latest in a long line of Buddhas (Enlightened Ones). Then He passed into final extinction, one might say merged with the rest of the universe, never to be reborn into a world of suffering. In later schools, the concept got a little bent out of shape. It was thought that only His material form was extinct and that the Buddha consciousness, the current of enlightenment still existed. Bodhisattvas were "invented" to bridge the world of sentient beings and Buddhas.

Which begs the question, is any of this real? Who's right? The Theravada or the Mahayana (Great Vehicle) schools? Do Buddhas, Bodhisattvas, Gods and Goddesses exist?

Well, yes, they do. But not in a "sitting on a lotus up in the sky" kind of way. They don't live "out there" in a material form. It's only rarely that such powerful bundles of energy take physical shape, though most mythology and literature is quite clear that Bodhisattva, Gods and Goddesses, Devas (Shining Ones) etc can more or less do what they wish, and are quite capable of assuming any corporeal form they think fit. A quick glance through the vast body of Greek mythology, with its numerous anecdotes of rape, abduction, backstabbing and courtship, will soon confirm this.

The Gods and Goddesses are huge archetypal repositories of energy, wisdom and power. They hold various aspects of humanity's collective psyche. Because they each hold a different mix of the collective golden shadow, they all have a different feel, a different rasa (flavour). They're as real as greed, compassion, love or hatred. These energies are real, aren't they? We can feel these forces intellectually, emotionally, even physically. They impact enormously on our lives. And if we know how to put ourselves in the mood, we can almost make ourselves feel greed, compassion, love or hatred. We can, with practice, access these energies. The difference is that the energies of the divinities are independent, they have a life of their own. And we can also learn to access them, interact with them. So, in a way, the Buddha does live on! Not as the guy who lived and taught in India all those centuries ago, but as the current of energy towards enlightenment, the wisdom, the compassion, the aspiration for liberation. Bodhisattvas are split-offs, rays of light bouncing from this energy. So they really do exist too. But not often as flesh and blood entities.

If we do all the necessary work, realise God/dess within us, or Buddha within us, then He/She/They will be able to hand some, if not all, of our gold back into our hands. We can own our godly qualities, in the same way that we have to learn to own our dark shadow self. We can flower in any realm then, we can give up caring which body we inhabit, which situation we find ourselves in, which relationships we maintain, which disease is going to finish us off. Why? Because it all happens in that transcendent, shining inner state that we call enlightenment or liberation. There isn't a cramped, ego mind to do the worrying. And that's moksha, release, freedom. Way cool!

But of course there's a lot of work to do before that happens. Maybe many lifetimes' worth. It's up to you. Before we can determine the sadhanas (efforts/practices) we need to employ to make this happy state occur sooner rather than later, we need first to finish examining the Tantric paradigm. We've looked at how the world, or worlds, are born. Let's look at how we, as individuals, are born, grow spiritually (or fail to grow) and die. Let's look at the processes involved. Only then can we discuss our working methods.

So... the Mother Goddess gives birth to all life forms, everywhere, simultaneously. The rocking of Her lovemaking with Lord Shiva penetrates Her entire body. This vibration, at different wavelengths as it were, will shape the life forms issuing from her humming womb. His inner fire, in the form of seeds of consciousness, pulses into the life forms being formed. Thus sentient beings are born of matter and consciousness. To be born in this world we need Shiva's spark of consciousness and the material body to hold it, the matter being formed from Shakti's power, the primal vibration.

So what determines the make up, physical and mental, of each being? Well, if you're a human now, the chances are that you'll be a human again. It takes an enormous effort to change the hardwiring, as it were, of the human being into a God or Bodhisattva, or into something much worse. One would have to be real pig for a long time to be born as a real pig (for a long time). But in rare cases it can be done. So be careful!

But, human or not, one's behaviour in this life will determine one's physical wellbeing and ability to practice a spiritual path further in the next. The law of karma, the principle of cause and effect that permeates all of existence, except the absolute highest, rarefied states, of which I know next to nothing, holds sway and is implacable and relentless. It's also extremely hard to understand. You'd think it would be simple, wouldn't you? If I do something good, then that's good karma. But what if I do something with a good intention but screw up somehow and hurt someone? Is that good or bad karma? And what if I say something nasty, hurtful, to someone but they misunderstand me and feel happy? Good or bad karma? The karma of any situation will depend upon the intention, the perception, the physical situation and the ultimate outcome of all participants. Intention, contrary to orthodox Buddhist thought, is not the main determining factor.

And the "outcome" of any given situation may, in turn, become the cause of the next set of circumstances. One may as well point a finger arbitrarily into any chain of events and say "Good." "Bad." It's hard to say. It's not over 'til it's over. And there isn't an end in sight, so you might as well start to abandon notions of what's good and what's bad. A lot of it is culturally conditioned anyway, not universal.

But there are some clearly defined rules. Don't deliberately kill or injure living beings. Don't steal, or borrow stuff without permission. Don't lie, gossip, brag or slander. Don't sexually exploit others, or use your body sexually in a way that will cause hurt for someone. Don't wreck your mind with alcohol or drugs. These are the five basic precepts for Buddhist lay people. Make of them what you will. Interpret them how you like. It's your karma!

Now these are all moral rules, designed to help communities, countries and cultures to get along with a minimum of conflict and harm. Following these rules won't get you enlightened. But living this way settles the mind, reassures people around you, makes you feel good about yourself and lays a nice, peaceful foundation for that most basic of practices – meditation. More about meditation later.

Trying to follow some kind of moral code will give you a challenge every day. It'll bring you face to face with the gap between who you are and who you want to be, between the way things are and the way you'd like them to be. It'll help you understand karma a bit better too. You'll realise just how strong a karmic current can be, how strong some karmic resistances can be, how there's no escape from karma's grip, how subtle or blatant karma's workings can be, and how deeply profound the whole subject really is.

Now, none of this is about repressing ordinary human desires. A world without a little bit of desire, whether it's for the next door neighbour, a new pair of shoes, or for enlightenment, would be a little dull. The difference is whether you can experience the desire as an energy flow, something to be enjoyed, processed in meditation or reflection, and then released (in other words – let go of!) or whether you experience it as a torment, something that keeps you awake at night, turns you into a stalker, an obsessive or a criminal, the kind of person you really don't want to be. And because we all have stuff in our "shadow", a lot of our hardwiring, the reasons we have these various desires, are not going to be easily accessible to us. It takes a lot of work, over a long period of time. Anything not worked through will get reborn into another existence. And depending on your karma, the set of circumstances within which you get to work this stuff out, will be good or bad.

Karma is way complicated. The Buddha Himself once reprimanded His favourite disciple Ananda (Bliss or Joy) for thinking that karma was easy to comprehend. "It isn't", He said. Quite firmly. So there.

So our karma in this life, how we play the role allotted to us in this birth, will determine what we become when we die and are reborn from Shakti's womb. Unless we do something really, really bad, or really, really outstanding, the chances are that it's a human body for us again. But how healthy and strong that body is, how keen the intellect, how fortunate the material circumstances, how loving the parents, will all depend on one's individual karma.

So, it's important, ok?

CHAPTER FOUR - NAKED TO THE DANCE.

All life comes from the yoni (vagina) of Mother Goddess, in the form of Parvati, Shakti, Kali, or actually any Goddess form you prefer. You might term our phenomenal world the yoniverse! (How I wish I'd thought of that first, but I found the term on the "Yoniverse" website. Way cool pun or what!) And all life eventually returns to the Goddess. After all, it's her energy we borrow to create a physical body from our karmic impulses. Our unfinished business, anything left in the shadow (good or bad), our unconscious tendencies, all accrete around themselves a new physical vehicle. All life is like walking, it's a (barely) controlled lurch forwards. "All life forms exist on borrowed energy," as one of my most astute students remarked, "And eventually the energy runs out and has to be renewed in another form." So the Goddess takes back what's Her's.

When we die, after an initial sensation of heaviness, being buried or drowning, followed by lightness, disembodiment, we often see a brilliant white light. This is the pure, shining consciousness of Shiva (or the Adi-Buddha, the primeval consciousness "before creation"). You'd think it would be comforting wouldn't you? But actually, in our befuddled, bewildered and vulnerable state, it's quite frightening and most folk "run away" from it, as you'd run away from something scary in a dream. And this white light is the only non-conditioned state available to us. Every other realm, good or bad, is conditioned, subject to karmic laws and processes. So then what happens, if we fail to abide in that state, is that we get visions, dreamlike rays and clouds of other colours, representing different parts of our consciousness. You could even stretch a point and say we see the strongest colours of our auras, or our chakras (energy wheels of the inner body). If we can pursue one of these currents successfully we end up in a fortunate birth in a non-earthly realm. Again, all too often, we fail this test as well and undergo more dream experiences. At first these are benign and heavenly. We see friends and loved ones. If we can rest our mind here, that's the realm we'll inhabit for a while, or rather that's where our basic consciousness will rest for a while. If we fail yet again to see these visions as products of our own dying mind, the picture turns ugly and we see monsters and demons, experience storms and earthquakes. All this is usually enough to send us squealing and bleating, like cattle, to the nearest womb compatible with our karma.

Incidentally, the bright light and visions of angels or loved ones experienced in near-death situations are real. These people aren't making it up. But. It takes a while for the brain to die thoroughly so these experiences aren't quite the same as a prolonged and irreversible demise. The whole process takes more than a few minutes, the usual duration of these reported events.

So the real thing's not very pretty. We panic. Like being naked in a dream, we don't have much control over the process once it begins. We can only go where the process, and our training, or lack of it, will take us. But like an expert competitive canoeist we can pick our best route through the rapids before we enter the water. Once we're in we have to go with the current and hope for the best. It's all in the preparation, the work we put in before we die.

And usually what happens is that our shadow gets reborn and mixed with a new inherited set of tendencies and characteristics. Off we go again. Another round of worldly existence...

I need to make it clear. This is a traumatic experience. And we're not talking about being able to think about it rationally. Though the body/mind complex will be dissolving, there's still a sense of "I", as there would be in a powerful dream or nightmare. The dying consciousness will be throwing all sorts of unprocessed material up. That's why it's important to do the work now, not wait until you die! Start training, especially in meditation and devotion, now. Start the process of stripping yourself of negative emotions, ego illusions while you have the chance.

The person that you are now will die. That's a certainty. It's not "you" that will have these experiences. It's the fading consciousness that goes through all this inner turbulence, like a small boat caught in heavy seas. But. Big But. It will feel like you. The confused awareness that will experience all this stuff is being created, trained or not trained, prepared or not prepared by you right now, in this earthly life. And it's this blank awareness that'll get reborn, and get imprinted with the physical and emotional characteristics of the earthly parents. These new parents will be important. And we get the parents our karmic momentum creates. We fall into the womb our karma merits, for better or for worse. In that sense we're our own parents – we give birth to ourselves through our parents!

It's the internal karmic momentum, the shadow, the unconscious predispositions, that undergo death and rebirth, not your personality. Shiva's consciousness, polluted by unconscious psychic material, will be moulded by Shakti into a new material body.

And it's not like Shakti gave birth to you, through your earthly mother, a few decades ago. If we take a Tantric view of time, She's constantly giving birth to you through your mother, continually, second after second, moment after moment. And She's doing the same for your mother too, through your grandmother. You're all being born, simultaneously, moment after moment! So every single second is an opportunity to try and stop the heavy, heavy roll of karma. It's an opportunity to be reborn with a new initiative, a new orientation. Not easy of course, but achievable. And we all have to be reborn many times before we achieve clarity and the ability to change our karma. The difference is that some individuals are reborn several times within a single lifespan and some are seldom reborn, however many lifespans they undergo!

People ask me, "Well, how did it all begin? Why did it all start in the first place? I couldn't have any karma before my first birth! I couldn't have karma before I came into existence, could I?" Well, that's a very profound question. If you have a Tantric awareness of time, it's not a problem because there wasn't a first birth. Just lots of simultaneous ones, linked by your karmic stream. You could be clearing up several incarnations' worth of karma right now – or even creating good or bad karma that's going to affect you in the past! Argh! If time isn't linear, then there's no beginning or end, only points in infinity.

Many philosophers cite God as "the first cause". When their logic runs out they use God to explain themselves. Fine, except that there isn't a first cause – because there wasn't a first moment. Only this one – forever. Oh, and that one over there...

But if time is linear, and if God is the first cause, then your first incarnation was as God. So you tell me why you decided to keep the whole process rolling...

Yeah, I know. All this "eternal now" stuff gets a bit freaky (or tedious) after a while. And time is such a subjective beast anyway. Even if you can only conceive of time as linear, it's still so goddam flexible! Two minutes in a warm, scented bath or having your shoulders rubbed, two minutes in mabu (an excruciating "horse riding" stance in martial arts), two minutes at a red light when you're in a hurry – all very different experiences of what should be a standard unit of time.

Anyway, getting back to Shakti – She's the queen of matter, and we live in her realm, the world of phenomenal creation. And she's so good at what she does! She uses human wombs (which she gave birth to) to create human beings. She uses mouse wombs (which she gave birth to) to create mice. She uses smelly oozing bags of pus to create politicians and boy bands.

Myriads of life forms, all interacting, often mutually dependant. And we're one of those life forms, dancing in the whole cosmic ebb and flow. It's pretty overwhelming. So we have to take it seriously. And we forget where we came from, that formless pure consciousness that is Shiva's essence. And the whole death process is so traumatic. Our consciousness is crushed, ground into tiny pieces. We become frightened and confused, like sacrificial animals, and we run to the nearest compatible womb, one that our fear and ignorance has created. And so we begin another life, forgetting all that's gone before, learning the ways of the world all over again. And we don't usually realise it's a bit of an illusion at first. We take every individual life form at face value, not seeing them all as the play (lila) of the Goddess, imperfect reflections of her glorious creativity. We don't see her face, feel her power at all!

It takes a few hard knocks before we start to question the way things are, the way they appear to be. It's usually suffering, the existential uneasiness, the unsatisfied, disillusioned feeling that Buddha called dukkha, that prompts us to start looking behind the scenes, wondering if there mightn't be more to life than we suspect, answers somewhere to why things work the way they do.

"Seeds must sunder and break apart to burst into blossom
Perhaps too the human heart
But for how long and alone down through the years?
And what must change in the heavens or in man
In time and tide
Before any green shoot appears?"

Sometimes perhaps only a broken heart can flower. And we all have our hearts broken by the world at some point...

The Buddha said that all life is conditioned by three influences. Firstly, everything is anicca, impermanent, nothing is going to last forever. Secondly, everything is eventually unsatisfactory (dukkha). No matter how much money you earn, sooner or later you'll want more. However gorgeous your partner is, sooner or later, someone even more stunning might make them look commonplace. However good your health is now, however reliable your body, the chances are that sooner or later it could betray you, through illness, injury or defect.

Thirdly, all phenomena are what the Buddha called anatta, which literally translates as non-self. What this means is that everything is revealed to be hollow. For example, we talk about a car as if it was a nailed down entity, a concept beyond question. But what if we remove the wheels? Is it still a car? What if we remove the engine? Is it still a car? How much can we remove and still have a recognisable car? We talk about marriage, and everyone thinks they understand, but what if one person goes to live in Cardiff or California for ten years? Is it still a marriage? What if both partners sleep around but still love each other and one day, one of the partners changes their mind? Where is the marriage? What if you live together for twenty years and then discover the priest that officiated over your wedding ceremony was a fake? Do you still have a marriage? What's a pen? Is it just the wriggly plastic bit that seeps ink? What if you find a golden pen, but without that wriggly central seeper? Do you still mentally label it a pen? You don't have to actually answer any of these stupid questions, I'm just trying to illustrate that everyday concepts break down quite easily when analysed.

None of this nonsense about anatta really affects us much. We can simply live together "in sin", catch the bus and use a pencil. No big deal. And the Buddha's message can come across as just existential pessimism, an excuse to run off into the misty mountains and hide away from life. No, the really interesting problem comes when we apply anatta to ourselves. Then it gets a bit weird. What is a human being? In other words, what exactly are YOU?

The Buddha's teachings are very clear on this. A human being, the dharma (law) asserts, is comprised of physical form, consciousness, sensations, perception and mental phenomena. These are called skandhas (lit – heaps or bundles) and they all rely on one another, prop each other up. A body without any sensations or perceptions is dead meat. A brain without sensory apparatus is just as screwed. A body and a brain that can't form coherent thoughts is still just a member of a boy band. Each component needs the others to form a functional human being. Take any one skandha away and we become less than human. In fact it's the combination of the skandhas that makes a human being. So a human being is a collective, not a single entity that can't be reduced. This is one description of anatta.

There doesn't appear to be anything solid within us we could label an eternal soul, something that will get reborn or return to heaven. What there is however is our shadow, all the caged energies, all the parts of us that are condemned to the life unlived. All that unfinished business, all that unworked out karma. That'll get reborn, so you could call that your soul if you wish. And it's not really you, 'cos you disowned it. You chose to identify with the ego mind instead. This bundle of shadow impulses is the closest we get to a soul. And you disown it. You're a stranger to your own soul!

I had a vivid dream long ago, where a young, immature "me" wandered through a strange, gloomy city. There I encountered my soul. I was made aware of the damage caused by carelessness...

"Like a child through the dark towers winding
Pale and dazed through grey streets gliding
By these grim stones lost
Over the old metal bridge
Where the dirty water is tossed
Careless, discoloured froth
You never know who waits at the next crossroad's edge
You never know whose hatred your presence will encourage
Who would be so bent and bowed?
Who would seek to bend me so?
Until my distended mouth bubbles liquid distress
Careless, discoloured mess
Let us pray for no hard feelings

Then a faint clamour from a dim doorway stirring
A gathering crowd, curious, murmuring
A young girl huddled lay
Limbs limp and pale
Sprawled, as if from a fall
Careless, discoloured, frail
Her fevered eyes met mine and she blinked her dying
Recognised kin and whispered, "It's ok, just move on."
Who could see her dreadful injury?
Who would relate the whole sad story?
Whose mouth would dare render blasphemy?
Oh careless, discoloured history!
Let us pray for no hard feelings

The burdens we lay upon one another
The words we use to bind and sunder
The deeds we do live on in secret parts
Of our careless, discoloured hearts
Our own thickening thoughts will bring a reckoning
So let us pray for no hard feelings"

I still hate the way that poem makes me feel, even after twenty years.

So there's no indestructible, eternal "you", no irreducible part of "you". Only an ever changing complex bundle of karmic energies. The more karma we create, the more the bundle "thickens" and gets harder to work with. We are not a pure soul imprisoned in karma, we're the karma that encrusts the pure, empty consciousness, the essence of Shiva. We're the knot. That's another way to look at anatta. The God/dess or Buddha consciousness within the knot is eternal, unchanging, but it's not "us". When we finally realise/reclaim it, again we're no longer "us". We've merged and become that consciousness.

Some orthodox Hindu texts will urge you to investigate and identify with the feeling of "I", that feeling that was there when you were a kid and is still there, even now, especially in those moments just after you wake up in the morning and you're in that drowsy, semi-conscious state. There's a feeling of "just being", of a "self", but this feeling is before you're awake enough to remember what day it is, or even what your name is! So it can't be anything to do with your personality, your character, the everyday "you". It's more of a blank consciousness, the kind we're born with, or achieve in meditation. It's worth investigating of course, but it's not "you". It's not even "yours".

The base consciousness of the mind is clear, cool, spacious, but it's not contaminated with a notion of "I". So the "unchanging, just being" vibe is almost there, but not quite. Once the base consciousness is experienced by a mind disciplined by meditation, insight and detachment, the feeling is very different from that semi-awake consciousness. Consciousness seems to open out, become vast, not personal at all.

If we identify with the material world and/or our ego mind, we allow the forces of dukkha, anicca and anatta to wreak havoc with us, sending us spinning, confused, unhappy and deluded, into lifetime after lifetime. We have to learn to see behind the scenes, so to speak, figure out how things work. This is the classis Buddhist stance on suffering and the way out of suffering.

Shiva Shankara has a simpler way of expressing the dilemma. "You suffer,"

He says (as I understand it), "Because you chase an illusion." If you identify with the world of phenomena, and that includes most of the perceptions of your clever little human mind, you end up chasing phantoms, and you keep chasing them until you grow disillusioned with the whole pointless pursuit. Then maybe you can take stock and think about reorientating yourself.

If you reset the compass of your life, make Shiva consciousness (or any holy consciousness) your spiritual magnetic north and keep everything else lined up with that, you won't go far wrong. Everything can be analysed in terms of your relationship with God/dess. This becomes your sadhana.

Even the simple act of praying every day can be an opportunity for investigation and reflection. I have an altar in my living room, with some pictures, some flowers and some candles on it. To be honest, it's not really a "working" altar, more of a sacred space, a reminder of my aspirations, like a photo of one of your heroes hanging on the wall, to inspire you every time you look at it. Most of my worship is performed outside. After training every morning, I meditate to settle my qi and my mind, then I say prayers for the wellbeing of all sentient life forms. After this comes my more private, intimate puja (ritual of worship). I find a space in the garden, a patch of sunlight, or under a tree if it's raining, and there I squat down on my haunches and light an incense stick. In touch with the earth, and nature, I make namaste (the hands in praying position), and surrounded by sunshine or raindrops, by birdsong, neighbours' radios and passing traffic, I recite...

"Aum Namah Shivaya

Aum Namah Shivaya

Aum Namah Shivaya

Honour to the Highest

The Auspicious One

The Lord of Souls

Dancer of the Worlds' Destruction

Seed of Shakti's Power

Spiritual Goal Beyond the Known

Lord of all Possible Realms

The Ash Covered One

Devotee of Devotees

God of Energy and of Supernatural Stillness, Oblivious to the World

The Highest Ground of Being

Whose Limbs Are the World

Sorrow's Destroyer

Conqueror of Ignorance and Delusion

The Lotus Presence

The In-Dwelling One

The Giver of Grace"

(An explanation of this prayer can be found in the last book – buy it, it's cool!)

Then I pray "May I be of service to you and to all beings. May I and all beings in all worlds receive your blessing and protection and be freed from our suffering." Then I add the more private stuff, the health of a friend, a relationship problem, how I'm feeling about a particular situation etc, and I finish with thanking Him and closing the prayer.

"Aum Namah Shivaya Hum"

This is a communion very dear to my heart. It's personal, private, intimate, just me and Him. It's one of the highlights of my day. The world shrinks to the plume of incense smoke and my inner voice reciting the prayers. Fantastic.

But the things I ask for are a reflection of my inner state. They tell me what's on my mind and what kind of emotional flavour I'm bringing to the prayer. And if I'm being totally honest in what I'm asking for, and my reasons for asking. If I'm scrupulous in analysing and processing my prayers, I can learn a lot. This kind of investigation of my own inner material is useful. If you can uncover, sometimes painstakingly what you really want, as opposed to what you think you want, you're a step closer to self realisation. Remember, I said self knowledge is spiritual currency. You can get rich quick by investigating yourself.

It's a bit like what happens when a fruit bat sends out a sonic blip to find out where it's flying. It hears the echoes of trees, buildings, other bats, insects, and knows the appropriate action to take. Investigating your own inner states is like that. You send out a signal into your desires and watch to see what comes back.

If pays to be careful too, because God/dess will often give you what you ask for and it may not be in the form you envisage. You'll get found out by your own unconscious urges. You may ask for one thing with your ego mind, and quite another thing unconsciously. God/dess may grant the unconscious wish. Then you won't understand what's happened and wonder why God/dess has forsaken you! So absolute honesty and purity of intention are vital. You can't hoodwink God/dess! You have to come naked to the dance, so to speak.

And if you can stand before your holy image, be it God/dess or Buddha, stripped of all ego-driven vanity and hypocrisy, then you're showing sincerity, true devotion and humility, you're opening yourself to the healing truth of God/dess (or Buddha). As the ninth century Sufi mystic Mansur-Al-Haiiaj so eloquently puts it, "Love is to stand before your beloved, stripped naked of all attributes, so that His qualities can become your qualities."

He's absolutely right of course, and it's tragic that his message wasn't appreciated by his home crowd back in Persia. He was executed for heresy after returning from India.

Actually, even the Buddha started out as a devotee of Shiva. He practiced lots of self mortification, as was the custom in those days. But this is a crazy, unskilful way to try to subdue our earthly body. Self torture and starvation achieves little apart from a very strong willpower. So the Buddha-to-be was quite right to reject that as a way to one-ness with God. Those earnest practitioners just simply missed the point, and they hadn't "felt" Shiva, hadn't tasted His flavour. Yes, Shiva loves sincerity and humility, that's why we should try to stand before Him naked, stripped of pretence and ego's delusion. But self torture is actually an ego demand – look at what I'm doing to myself! Pay attention to me! Shiva's not going to be impressed! So when the newly enlightened Buddha returned to visit His former religious brothers, with an obvious spiritual glow about Him, Shiva's disciples felt impelled to follow Him. And I can't blame them. Results count!

Many Tantric deities are depicted naked, whether meditating, dancing or in sexual union. They're often called Shiva/Shakti, the union of consciousness and form, or of wisdom and compassion. Buddhist depictions are called yab/yum – Tibetan for father/mother. Their nakedness symbolises their transcendence of social norms, their liberation from earthly ties and their absence of illusion. And to understand these wonderful, ecstatic naked divinities, we have to become naked too. Spiritually that is, though what you do in your own living room is your affair! We have to strip our conditioned minds free, try and see things anew, including ourselves, the deities, the whole process towards enlightenment. Try not to let your practice become habitual. Stay naked!

Returning to our earlier theme of twin currents of detachment and passion running through the spiritual life, I'd say that orthodox insight meditation, vipassana, would seem to be the ideal candidate to stand for the detachment ticket. Vipassana means to see things as they are. In this kind of meditation, we sit comfortably, with a straight back, either on a chair (thighs parallel to the floor) or on a cushion just high enough for us to sit cross legged with a relaxed tummy slightly higher than the knees. Shut your eyes. Relax down the body. Loosen the forehead, the face, the neck and shoulders. Relax down the back to the waist. Do the same at the front. Relax your arms and fingers. Relax your legs, ankles and feet. Ok, well done. Now let's feel the breath...

The body will rise and fall slightly as you breathe in and out. You may feel it in the tummy or in the chest. It doesn't matter. You don't have to count the breath. You don't have to change it, make it slower, deeper, more meaningful. Just relax and be natural. Breath is always changing anyway, so forget it. All you have to do is keep your attention gently on that slight rising and falling.

Then we allow the mind to settle. That can take a few years, right there! I have to warn you now, you'll be dismayed at the contents of your own mind. It'll yap and chatter, do anything to distract you. Before you know it, you're lost in thought. Then you have to gently bring your attention back to the breathing until it all goes quiet in there! Your body will also complain. You'll get cramp, itchiness, twinges. You'll want to cough, sneeze, swallow, fart. Just do it and forget it. If you have to shift position to remain comfortable, then do it. But if you're constantly fidgeting and not settling, the chances are it's your mind, not your body that's uncomfortable.

Most people prefer to meditate with their eyes closed. I find however that, if the mind is chattering too much, opening my eyes stops the noise. I can then shut them again, if I wish. I've trained myself to disengage that part of the brain that process visual information so I can meditate quite happily with my eyes open and not get distracted. In fact, if I let go enough and allow shape, form and colour to just be shape, form and colour without labelling every phenomenon as "cat", "bird", "leaves" etc, these shapes become almost transparent and begin to lose their individuality. The energy trapped in every form starts to shine through. It's like a stained glass window lit from behind, though slightly more fluid, or like an oil painting on transparent tracing paper.

Anyway, eyes closed or open, sitting on the floor or on a chair, try to relax, let the body settle (though the chances are it'll constantly demand attention) and let the thoughts settle too.

Then the contents of the mind itself become the objects of meditation. We notice thoughts coming into view, so to speak, trying to stick themselves onto our attention, eventually fading away again, only to be replaced by others. If you engage with the thoughts, it can get really sticky and before you know it, you're engaged in a whole dialogue with yourself again. If, however, you can steer clear of this entanglement and identify with the clear, shining space between the thoughts, it's a very different vibe...

"The calm space awaits
Thoughts arise, are witnessed, and then retreat
The calm space awaits..."

That shining space, that empty clarity, that dwelling in the unformed, that faculty that witnesses and recognises the nature of phenomena, whether inner or outer, is called Buddho, the One Who Knows. We could also call it God/dess consciousness. It's not the same as the blank consciousness we experience in our waking moments. Buddho has a serene, detached "knowing" feel. It just observes, witnesses. Perhaps it's just that the "blank" consciousness has to be witnessed by an aware mind to take it from "blank" to Buddho.

Most of the time our Buddho is smothered in mental processes, drowned out by the ego's clamour. It takes practice, perseverance and persistence to find that calm pool in the middle of the mental jungle. But it can be found. And as you watch by the side of the pool, as the late, great Thai meditation master Ajahn Chah explains, "All manner of strange animals come to drink at the pool." We don't have to engage with any of these animals, whether they're fluffy and cute or vicious and deadly. We just watch them, leave them in peace and eventually harmony will reign over the entire forest. In other words, as we meditate, there'll be happy thoughts, loving thoughts, resentful thoughts, malicious thoughts, all manner of mental beasts. Leave them be, just observe, and eventually you and the mental beasts can co-exist in peace. You won't bother each other!

So meditation is one way to strip the mind naked. In the next chapter we'll explore other, perhaps slightly more dynamic, methods...

CHAPTER FIVE - DESIGNS ON DIVINITY.

WHEN I was a flower child in the '60s (in East Anglia for fucksake!), strange as it may seem, yantras were everywhere. Usually just drawn in black line on a white background, these Hindu Tantric diagrams, consisting of interlocking geometric shapes, could be found on album covers, in magazines and on posters. No one really seemed to know much about them - only that if you stared at them long enough, groovy, psychedelic things would happen to your mind. What usually happened is that people got stoned, stared at the yantra, listened to Quintessence or Ravi Shankar and then got bored and got up, looking for biscuits or breakfast cereal with a bad case of the munchies!

I didn't know then that yantras came in full colour too (far out, man!) and that different designs represented different energies, different deities. It wasn't until slightly later, the early '70s, that I began to appreciate their complexity and value.

The best way to describe a yantra is as a two dimensional drawing of a multi-dimensional concept. If you look at a cubist painting, where the artist has painted three sides of a garden shed, overlapping on one plane, like a collapsed transparent box, you'll see the yantra vibe right there. Another way to explain it is like looking at a stepped pyramid from the air. All you'll see is a series of squares. But you can imagine the physical reality of the pyramid from those shapes.

Yantra takes this a step further. Within a containing square, each yantra employs mainly downward pointing triangles (the female principle) and upward pointing triangles (male principle), and miraculously, somehow manages to capture the whole flavour, the core, the energy of a God or Goddess. The word yantra literally means "tool" but it actually implies "to transcend by holding the essence of a deity". Some yantras are simply line drawings but colour can also reinforce the rasa (flavour) of each rendition, blocks of colour, red for fire, blue for water, saffron for earth, black for space or emptiness etc. There's a central dot (bindu –seed), sometimes visible, sometimes not, which is the focal point of the yantra.

So how is it used? Well, us hippies were half way there in that whole staring at the wall period, but most of us didn't take it far enough. Physically staring at the yantra (but without straining, you are allowed to blink and breathe!) is only the first step. The point of this close study is that, next, one has to know the yantra by heart, be able to reconstruct it, in every detail, in the mind's eye. This constant assemblage and meditation upon the yantra can take a long time. Practice looking at it, memorising it, on a daily basis, even if it's just for a few minutes. Practice holding it in your inner vision for longer periods of time. Eventually, when the whole of your consciousness is suffused with it, you'll see the yantra everywhere. Let's take the Kali Yantra. It's a simple enough shape, in fact one of the simplest yantras around, but its energy is extremely powerful, as you'd expect from a diagram that holds the core energy of the Dark Mother. Its main colours are black, yellow and red. It's quite striking. If you meditate on this yantra long enough, if you can know it inside out, carry it in your mind at all times, two things will happen...

Firstly, you'll begin to see its shape everywhere. That powerful downward triangle will make itself visible in all phenomena, everywhere. You'll see the Mother's form in clouds, in trees, in the walk of women, the shoulders of men, in windows and on every face. You won't see anything that isn't the Mother! And secondly, the Mother will begin to reveal Herself to you more and more as you become attuned to Her energy through the yantra. You'll be able to understand Her role, Her functions, Her energies, Her essence. You'll feel Her everywhere.

Mucho fabbo, of course, and a goal worth pursuing. But not for beginners maybe. Kali is a very strong current, dark and deceptive sometimes. She'll gobble you up for breakfast if you're naïve, arrogant or careless. This is why I advocate studying Jungian Shadow Work. If you can accommodate your own demons, you'll be better equipped to deal with any potentially destructive forces encountered in your spiritual practice. Not that this isn't the aim of Tantra anyway, to assimilate and transcend base urges, negative emotions. But you can't leap into anything new foolishly, particularly unpredictable pursuits such as hang gliding, crocodile wrestling and tantra! So be warned. If you're harbouring stuff you haven't dealt with, the Dark Mother will reflect it back at you. In spades. With a grin. Better to start with a more obviously beneficent deity. Ganesh, the Dumbo headed God of Thresholds (who is such a way cool dude, He ought to be the God of surfers), or Parvati, the smiling face of the Mother, are much better first steps.

It's possible to create your own yantras, or customise the more traditional ones, but the problem here is that too much tinkering diminishes or even corrupts the energy of the deity. A yantra is far more than just a piece of art, it's more like a drawing of the wiring inside a tv. To the expert, through the wiring diagram, the workings of the apparatus are laid bare. So too, are the workings of God/dess to the Tantric adept who's worked well with a yantra. So go your own way if you must, but you'd be better off printing a traditional pattern from the internet or photocopying a picture of a yantra from a library book.

Tantra with a Buddhist flavour tends to employ mandalas rather than yantras, so we'll examine these next. Mandala also implies "holding the essence", though both the Sanskrit and Tibetan terms can be translated simply as "circle". Both yantras and mandalas are visual tools. The yantra, though simpler in design, is said to hold the core energy of a deity (and there are planetary yantras too, for the star gazers among you), whereas the mandala is much more sophisticated to look at. Though originally of Hindu origin, mandalas find their full flowering and deepest complexity in esoteric Buddhism. Mandalas hold the body, or technically the sambhogakaya, the body of shared bliss, of a deity.

Quick diversion. There are three levels of the presence of a divinity. Three bodies. The nirmanakaya, the "illusory me" body is our flesh and blood frame. It's rare that Gods, Goddess and Buddhas use this vehicle, though of course, when it happens, it's very special. The sambhogakaya is that point where our minds and the divinities meet, in meditation, in dreams and visions etc. Mandalas are a journey to this kind of encounter. Lastly there's the dharmakaya (law body) which is formless. Yantras hold this body for a deity.

So, mandalas are like a maze or a labyrinth. They lead us, in a circular and progressive manner, into the heart of the mandala, where we encounter the central divinity. One has to be able to read a mandala like a map, so there's more intellectual understanding involved. Each mandala is surrounded by a symbolic protective border, often of a red colour, symbolising fire. So before anything else can happen, one has to surrender one's body and mind to the mandala, be purified as it were. It's the price of admission. Then there will be other symbolic challenges, walls, mountains, guardian spirits. All these have to meditated upon, committed to memory, before one can move on and begin work with the image of the central deity.

So, just as with a yantra, one begins by learning the mandala, studying it on a daily basis, committing every detail to memory. And one should be familiar with the symbology of the mandala too, know why the central divinity wears skulls, carries an axe or a cup, why they're depicted as green, red, white, blue, black or yellow in colour, what they're sitting or standing on, the attributes of their consort (if one is depicted). There's a lot of work involved. But it's worth it. You'd be amazed at how much detail you can reproduce in your mind with a little practice.

Ok, let's say you have a good working knowledge of the mandala and can carry it in your head at will. Well done, right there! That's an achievement in itself. The next thing to do is begin your journey through the mandala. It helps to know the mantra of the central deity as well, in case you feel the need to chant (more on mantra in a mo). Do whatever little ritual you're used to, say your prayers, sit in meditation and settle your mind. Then try to see the mandala as a three dimensional landscape, a central mountain, or maybe a courtyard that shelters the central deity. This central core is guarded by protective deities, by the lay of the land itself (mountains, rivers, fire etc), by walls or by ghosts and demons. Each mandala is different. The mandala of Manjushri, the Bodhisattva of Wisdom, and that of his "shadow", the buffalo-headed (and scary) Yamantaka (Conqueror of Death) have quite a different vibe.

So, it's like a guided visualisation – except that no one's guiding you! Traditionally one makes an entrance from the eastern side of a mandala, like a sunrise I guess. Look for the portion of the mandala that has a white background. This represents a mirror-like wisdom. That's your eastern sector. Other sectors may be coloured red (compassion), yellow (a jewel-like enlightened mind, openness and generosity), green (perfect action) or even blue/black (the primal consciousness). Don't be in a hurry with all this. Take your time. On each successive visit, learn more about the landscape of the mandala, slowly moving inwards, bit by bit. In fact, what you're actually doing is moving in, little by little, through a depiction of your own mind. You're slowly coming face to face with, and learning to work with, the forces of your own inner terrain. And of course, some of these forces are scary and forbidding! Or treacherous and deceiving. But eventually you'll arrive at the desired state of insight and transcendence symbolised by the mandala's core deity. You'll arrive at your own Buddhahood, or enlightened consciousness.

As with yantra work, this all takes time. And being able to put yourself through this internal three dimensional map isn't easy. But progress can be felt so it's very encouraging if you stick at it. A mandala may be viewed as the pathway to a deity, a ground plan of enlightenment or simply a map of the mind. Any way you look at it, it's still an object of meditation. And of course, it's a culturally conditioned piece of art. We may hold demons in our mind that look nothing like the Tibetan version! Certainly I know that the Shiva Shankara I sit and rap with, and get scolded by, bears only a superficial resemblance to the traditional or "authorised" version. He doesn't wear all the Hindu bling to start with, though some of my students still see Him that way. If you're the devotee of a non-eastern God or Goddess, feel free to create your own mandala. Use your own symbols, your own colours and shapes. No one can tell you you're wrong.

There's another set of two rivers running here, isn't there? The currents of tradition and what we'll call Gnostic or "self-discovered". Both have their value. We need stability and roots but we need innovation too. Too much stagnation or too much chaos. Neither are good. For example, I train in taijiquan, qigong, "hard" qigong and Chun Yuen, a form of northern Shaolin kung fu. But taiji is my mother style. Though I practice all these styles now, I didn't start learning them all at once, that would have been silly. One thing at a time, get a handle on one before starting another, that's the way forward. When in doubt, traditional stuff is best but it may have limitations, misinterpretations, or it may actually have depths of meaning and relevance that you can't fathom at this moment. So by all means strike off on your own in matters spiritual, but you'd better have an understanding of what you're turning your back on, otherwise you could be accused of laziness and arrogance. I sincerely think that the spiritual path, though it can be made much more pleasant by like-minded company, is essentially an inward, solitary pursuit. You have to follow your own heart. But you have to know your heart first, which means an extensive period of hunting around and trying things out. By all means reject anything that doesn't work for you, though my experience has taught me that what we reject in one decade is often the one thing that redeems us in the next! The spiritual path will take us alternately to join spiritual communities (even if they're only cyber-tribes) and lone retreats, to exotic alien imagery and to home grown symbols, from eye-popping colour and excitement to lonely jaw clenching and reproachful self improvement. It'll take us a lot of places. And what we need for the journey will change from time to time. So don't be too quick to reject stuff. You might need it later!

Having said that, ultimately, you MUST go where your heart leads you. It's the only way to learn. Yes, you'll make mistakes, make detours, make a dickhead of yourself. Again, that's how we learn. If you find something that works for you, use it fully. If it stops working, try something else, or have a break then get back to the tested and true.

Chanting is one method that's been employed successfully by many for a heightened state of consciousness or simply to harmonise their inner energies, calm themselves down, put themselves in a spiritual frame of mind. It can work well in a group too, everyone tunes in to the group vibe and the energy is stronger and smoother. Chanting has been used by so many different religions and cultures for thousands and thousands of years, from Africa to the Americas, from New Zealand to India. Especially India. And despite what many learned Hindu pundits might say, not all the magic is in those groovy Sanskrit syllables. Tibetans and Chinese seem to get on fine even using their own language! I'm sure many western individuals have had successful results with chanting, even if they're blissfully unaware that they're mangling their Sanskrit pronunciation. Some people today still chant Om as omm rather than aum but it doesn't matter.

A mantra is a string of sacred syllables that holds the essence of a deity in the form of sound, though the written version is felt to be sacred too. The famous Om Mani Padme Hum mantra crops up on numerous bracelets and roadside rocks in Nepal and perhaps still in some parts of Tibet. Let's explore how mantra works...

Firstly imagine that you're a budding guitar player. You've bought a book of guitar classics and you can just about fumble your way, scraping from chord to chord, tongue sticking out the corner of your mouth, through Lynyrd Skynyrd's "Free Bird". You think you're pretty cool! But when you try and play along with the cd, it sounds like small mammals being tortured at a barbed wire convention. Your guitar isn't in tune with the guitars on the cd! So after some cussing and plonking, some tightening up and loosening off, you're at least in the same post code area as the Skynyrds. You can bang along and even throw some cool shapes. But this couldn't happen until you retuned your instrument.

Now imagine Free Bird being sung by a trained opera soprano, to a rippling harp accompaniment. Bizarre. Now, the tune is correct, the words are correct but it's not the song you love is it? It's very er... civilised. There's no

Southern Rebel vibe, no guts, no manly regret, nuddin'. The singer is in tune but she doesn't have the feel, the flavour of Free Bird. How could she? Her training, her background, her conditioning all lead her miles away from that kind of sound. Talented she may be, but rock & roll it aint!

So to use a mantra, we need to tune our mind into its vibe and we need to feel its flavour. Most mantras have a bit of a tune and some rhythm, they're not all one level of pitch and not all the syllables are given the same amount of time. You know how a robot speaks? "How-are-you-today." All syllables given the same speed and pitch. Well mantras aren't like that. So you have to give it a bit of a lilt. Again, it doesn't matter if you make up your own little tune. Don't use Free Bird though! And don't make it too bloody elaborate either. Let's take Om Mani Padme Hum. For a start, it should actually be pronounced a little differently to the way it's written – aum marnee paymay humng. You can chant it "Aum" for two beats, "Mani Pad" (actually mani pay) for a beat each, "Me (may)" for two beats and "Hum" for three. Just as a rough guide though, don't get anal on me with this stuff. As far as pitch goes, just dip down a little on "Me" and come up again for "Hum". In other words, they can all be the same pitch except for "Me". "Auuuuum marneepay maaaayy humng" Got that? No? Don't sweat it. You won't go to hell if you get it a bit awry. The magic is in your mind, not in the mantra.

Om Mani Padme Hum (the jewel in the lotus) is the mantra of the Tibetan bodhisattva of compassion Chenresig (Sanskrit - Avalokiteshvara – He Who Hears the World's Cries). He is said to manifest in all worlds, all realms of consciousness, to help suffering beings. Shiva Shankara's mantra is Aum Namah Shivaya (the name of the auspicious one). Shivaya is pronounced Shiviya. One of Kali's mantras (there are a few) is Om, Krim Hum Hrim, Dakshinah Kalike, Krim Hum Hrim, Svaha, "She Who Faces the Darkness for Us." Svaha means "(May it be) Well Done, or Successful. Krim means a fee to be paid to Her and Hrim means Her heart. So a workable translation (and be warned, I'm no Sanskrit scholar!) could be "capturer of our hearts, She who faces the darkness for us, may it be well." A further connotation of "facing the darkness" is "preventing us from falling into hell worlds."

The mantra of the Tibetan deity Hevajra (more on this groovy Tantric dude and his consort later) is Om Deva Pichu Vajra Hum Pah! Svaha. Deva simply means Shining One and Pichu can mean "Face of Disease" (presumably because His face is dark and distorted, as in anger or passion, or "Drinking Simultaneously (of kisses)" Guess which I'd prefer to go with! You'll see the relevance of the kiss in the next chapter. Vajra can be translated as thunderbolt or diamond but actually refers to an adamantine, unshakeable level of awareness. Hum and Pah! (often written Phat) are both syllables one closes a mantra or "spell" with. Pah! especially has an expelling, projecting or banishing feel.

The mantra of Vajra Yogini, the central female deity of Tibetan Tantrism, is Aum Sava Buddha Dakiniye Vajra Vananeyi Vajra Vairochanaiye Hum Pah! Svaha. Rough translation – Sky Clad (Naked) Consciousness of All the Buddhas, Diamond Family of Clear Light. Vajra Yogini is another fascinating divinity, an inspiring blood-red sky dancer, first worshipped in India and then exported to Tibet in about the 11th century. We'll be having a closer look at Her soon, but let's finish off this mantra t'ing first...

In case the above paragraphs put you off the whole idea of chanting complicated mantras, I feel honour bound to tell you that the name of a divinity is sacred enough to use, with opening and closing syllables, as a workable mantra. To use the above mentioned deities as an example, you could try chanting "Aum Avalokiteshvara (or Shivaya/Kali Ma/Hevajra/Vajra Yoginiye) Hum Svaha."

We've established that we need to "feel" the mantra, which can be aided by knowing a little about the chief deity of the mantra, the goal of the mantra, its "point". We've established that we need to be familiar, at least to a certain degree, with its pronunciation. We've established that it works a little better within the mind if there's a bit of a lilt, a little up-and-down in pitch, if not an actual tune. Now we have to chant it. Don't be too clinical about this. When I've been around chanting masters, they breathe when they feel like it and bugger the mantra! Their heavy conviction concerning the mantra's efficacy and their total commitment to the inner processes associated with chanting seem to far outweigh the importance of "beauty", of chanting prettily.

So we chant for as long as possible, or at least until it gets tedious! It's important to do this regularly and diligently for a while until the practice becomes automatic, commonplace. Then the real practice begins, and that's the internal chanting. The mantra has to be internalised, so it's heard with the inner ear, the mind, constantly. Chant it silently as often as possible. Let it soak into your bones. Then every sound becomes the mantra. The traffic, the birds, conversations, all hum along with the mantra. Every sound becomes praise of the deity. Every sound will carry the essence of the deity. Every sound will refine your mind to the vibration of the deity. Then you'll hear the deity talk back to you! Eventually your senses and the essence of the deity become one and the same thing. Way cool!

So just who are these divinities, these Tantric Gods and Goddesses? Let's examine the form, flavour and function of four typical Tantric deities...

CHAPTER SIX - CAUTION! HIGH VOLTAGE DEITIES!

In which we examine four principal players in the world of Tantra - two from the Hindu tradition and two from the Tibetan Buddhist schools. Two of these deities are male, and two female. So hopefully a good balance! The aim here is to get an idea, an overview of what Tantric deities are all about, the kind of energies and principles they represent, the symbology used. We want to catch their flavour, as it were.

Tantric deities are high voltage. Whereas non-Tantric Gods and Goddesses shine with light and warmth like the sun, the Tantric divinities are more like lightning bolts, an enormous power travelling from heaven to earth, a force that perhaps can be harnessed and channelled by the skilful but that can also blow up in your face and reduce you to ashes if you don't know what you're doing ...

We'll begin with Shiva. Shiva is regarded by many as the creator of Tantra. Once the world became too corrupt, too materialistic, for the pure, original teachings of the Gods and enlightened ones to be practiced, Shiva gave mankind the gift, the blessing of the Tantric path. Now those very energies which could drag us down further into materialism, sensuality, greed and anger, deeper into conditioned states of existence, could be used as stepping stones to higher insight and liberation.

I guess the historical setting for this went as follows... Buddhism created an enormous challenge to Hinduism. Until the creation of the Buddhist sangha (religious community), the chances of a non-Brahmin (upper caste) Hindu achieving any kind of depth of religious study was virtually non-existent. Suddenly, with Buddhism, the religious life was open to all. Buddhism gave a short cut through all the Gods and Goddess, the rituals, the caste system, intensive intellectual study, straight to contemplation and liberation. Hinduism responded with some clever reformations, cleaned up its act a little, cut down on the animal sacrifices, beefed up (no pun intended) the common approach and fought back. After a few hundred years, Hinduism had regained a lot of ground. So I think Buddhism began to incorporate some of the qualities of Hinduism that appealed to the common man, more ritual, heavenly beings etc, and widened its formerly quite narrow field of practice. The chanting of mantras, the contemplation of visual representations of deities, all blossomed again in the Buddhist arena. There's a lot of evidence that Buddhist mantras are older than the Hindu ones. Hinduism responded again by stealing back and refurbishing these practices. And by this time Shiva had become a much more important deity within the Hindu paradigm, hence His association with all sorts of colourful practices and techniques. Buddhism eventually all but died out in India, though it blossomed beautifully in various forms throughout China, Tibet, Japan, Korea, Thailand etc.

All of the above is just a guess on my part so take it with a pinch of salt. It seems reasonable though. Maybe it was just that Hinduism, being an older and (in terms of numbers) greater religion, just exerted a stronger gravitational pull.

Anyway, back to Shiva. From a simple weather God of great antiquity, through a role as the Protector of Animals for the hunter-gatherers of old, maybe even the Horned God of the "pagans", through being a consort to the Mother Goddess of the farming communities that settled the Indus Valley, through being part of the mainstream Hindu pantheon, Shiva has come to represent at some point the more esoteric yogic practices and austerities. He wears three horizontal stripes on his forehead to symbolise His mastery of the three worlds.

Most people are familiar with His function as the destroyer in the Hindu trinity of Brahma the creator, Vishnu the preserver and Shiva the destroyer. Most people are also familiar with His role of Nataraja, Lord of The Dance. It's His peaceful aspect, Shankara, though, that most accurately represents yogic aspirations. Shiva Shankara is usually represented as peaceful in appearance, seated in meditation with a huge snake coiled around His neck (shudder!). This snake (Visuki Naga) is a complex symbol. Its ability to shed its skin can represent reincarnation, cyclical time and eternal renewal. Serpents often allude to a dangerous, alluring power with erotic, fascinating, bewitching undertone. And of course their venom is deadly. Shiva's use of the snake as an adornment symbolises His transcendence of time, worldly passion and "poisonous" attachments.

Shiva is the snake charmer par excellence. It's Shiva who awaits for Kundalini, the serpent Goddess, as She ascends our spine, causing bliss and torment as she rises. It's Shiva who calls forth our inner serpents, our rage, our envy, our spite, our poison, our lust, and offers us, through devotion to Him, the opportunity to transform these snakes into streams of compassion and insight.

Often a crescent moon is shown in His hair, calling to mind the myth that His spiritual power is so advanced, so "hot" that the other Gods gave him a "cooling" moon to wear. The heat from His "third eye" once reduced Kama, the God of Love, to a cinder! There is another story that Shiva was suffering from a burning throat after drinking some poison that sprang up from the ocean and threatened to flood the world, so the Gods rewarded Him by granting Him the cooling presence of the moon, which is also associated with the ocean.

A further hair ornament is the tiny figure of Ganges, the Goddess of the sacred river. She was afraid that her descent from heaven to earth would be too much for the planet, leading to widespread flood and destruction, so Shiva offered to catch the deluge in his long, matted, tangled locks, releasing the waters in a more controlled fashion. Sometimes a thin spout of water can be seen springing from His hair! He often wears large earrings, a symbol of prosperity, but what's striking is that the earring in his left ear is that usually worn only by females. This tells us two things! Firstly, Shiva is happy with His feminine side! And secondly, that He wears at all times a symbol of the yoni, the vagina and of Shakti, the female power. Shakti is also the name the Mother Goddess is known by when locked in embrace with Shiva.

Shankara is often seen accompanied by a white bull called Nandi (joy), which symbolises strength, loyalty and happiness. Bulls have been venerated for their power, virility and regal appearance in many ancient cultures. A deeper interpretation of the appearance of this vahana (steed or vehicle) is that the Mahayogi, the Great Lord of Yoga, has transcended worldly power, his base need for earthly sovereignty

Shankara is often depicted as naked, his skin covered in a pale, blue-grey ash. This symbolises humility and purification, a rejection of materialism. Sometimes a deity is shown with many arms or legs, but however many arms are shown in any particular representation (and having many limbs is a visual Tantric shorthand for supernatural powers), in any depiction of Shiva, one hand will almost always be shown in the Abhaya Mudra, the "don't worry" gesture. This is a palm-out shape, like a policeman or a lollipop lady asking you to "stop". This gesture says "Whooh! Calm down! Cool your jets. I'll fix it, don't let it worry you." It's very reassuring!

One of Shiva Shankara's chief "weapons" is the trisula, the trident, itself an ancient symbol of power. It appears also in a lot of Tibetan Buddhist art. It represents mastery of the three worlds. And what are these three worlds? Our old friends nirmanakaya, sambhogakaya and dharmakaya, in other words, form, immaterial phenomena, and ultimate emptiness. Or we could say the three worlds are firstly the natural world of (in descending order) men/women, animals, plant life, minerals and boy bands, secondly the world of energy, myth and inner experience and thirdly that non-conditioned formless state we call nirvana, enlightenment or Shiva Tattva (the state of being one with Shiva).

Shiva is sometimes shown with a drum (damaru) to show his mastery of sound, associated with creative and destructive vibrations. The hourglass shape of the damaru is significant – it relates to the shape of the star constellation we know as Orion – The Hunter, one of Shiva's attributes. It also depicts a double funnel shaped tube or tunnel, which in Shamanism is thought to be an entrance to an underworld of spirits. More on this later.

And of course, as well as Shankara and Nataraja, Shiva comes in other guises too – Lingabhava (God of the cock, ie- worldly energy and spiritual ascension, Rudra the storm God, Pashupati, Lord of Animals or of Souls, Digambara, the Naked dope head, Bhairav, the Terrible, a multi-limbed demonic form - the list goes on and on. Shiva is lord of all those who wish to apply themselves to spiritual endeavour, to work towards liberation and transcendence, and yet He's also a friend and a lord of refuge to all the abused, the reviled, the rebellious, the stoners and weed smokers, the outcasts of this world (and demons and monsters of other worlds too, as we shall see).

Ultimately though, what Shiva represents is pure consciousness, an awareness that's not contaminated by or conditioned by space and time. Some schools prefer to think of this level of consciousness as pure white light, some as the pregnant darkness of deep space. But whatever description one hangs upon it, it's beyond that, beyond all labels. So I'll shut up about it!

Second thoughts – one comment I'd like to make. Though Shiva is a transcendent deity, defying category and convention, and though He's a huge figure in mythology, at home in many different worlds and settings, He's also quite intimate and er... close at hand. I find Him under leafy hedgerows, in wet earth, in art and music, in the skin of a drum, in clay pottery, in the bare branches of winter trees, in the athleticism of cats, the power and grace of bison, in the colour blue, in the starry night sky, in neon lights, in the noise and bustle of a market. He's not removed from the natural world at all. In fact, the natural world is just the skin that holds Him. He feels very intimate. Though a Tantric deity, in the sense that He doesn't despise or reject what orthodox religion would term our "baser" nature, Shiva usually appears in human form.

From this short description we can see that the symbology surrounding Shiva, and indeed all other Tantric deities, is rich and complex. As a God of spirituality and eroticism, Shiva holds all paradox and apparent contradiction quite happily. There's a Shiva to suit every personality! His popularity shows no sign of diminishing, in India or here in the west. In fact the internet, a form of group mind, is probably Shiva's natural new home. There's a whole Shiva cyber tribe out there right now, either chanting Aum Namah Shivaya or getting stoned off their tits – maybe both!

It's interesting how sometimes the past and the immediate future are so close. Modern houses, with accentuated security features and independent power sources, are getting more like caves. The internet is the equivalent of talking drums. And speaking of drums, I love that whole techno-tribal dance vibe. The best tracks are those where cutting edge technology enables the keyboards to sound like slightly edgier versions of ancient instruments like drums, more drums!, didgeridoos, bull roarers and bone flutes. Even though the sound is harsh, immediate, obviously electronic, it speaks to something ancient in me. My whole body twitches. And that's the point of course. Though a lot of good music is meant to be listened to passively, and though an awful lot of dance music is unlistenable, when stirring sounds and a pounding beat combine, our bodies know what they're supposed to do – move!

We've seen that Shiva represents a certain higher consciousness, a one-ness with all form and yet simultaneously transcending it. Kali, the Dark Mother, a shadow of Shiva's consort Parvati/Durga, would seem to be the face of rage, of the blind destruction and hunger of madness. Phew!

Kali is a devourer, a witch, a vampire, the curse of the mummy. She's black, naked and very, very pissed off! She's got fangs and Her tongue lolls out most disconcertingly. Her usual adornments are skulls and severed body parts (She wears a skirt of hacked off arms. Nice) and carries a machete. She's one of the most recognisable deities in the Hindu pantheon. The story of Her birth is fascinating.

A certain demon was a devotee of Shiva (even monsters love Him!) and by strenuous and sincere ascetic practices and penances won from Shiva a certain boon – that of being almost invulnerable in battle. The deal was that every time a drop of the demon's blood was spilled on the earth, a fresh demon would spring up fully formed. Armed with this most unusual of battle defences, the demon set about terrorising several villages, secure in the knowledge that not much harm could come to him. The villagers sought the help of the Gods, who flew in like conquering heroes, only to discover the awful truth – nothing they could do was going to work, every time they thought they'd vanquished the beast, showering his blood all over the place, a thousand more would spring up, fresh and ready to fight. Slightly alarmed by now, the Gods called in Durga (Hard To Get To), a wrathful form of the Mother Goddess, another emanation of Parvati, Shiva's wife. She rode in on her tiger and set about her with a will, hacking and slashing. Guess what? Same result!

"How could this be?" the Gods wondered and, as one, all looked at Shiva, who was whistling sheepishly, scraping his toes on the ground and desperately trying to avoid their gaze. Well, the truth came out eventually but it wasn't going to help much, there were still thousands of demons like a plague of locusts, all of them invulnerable. Fortunately, Durga became thoroughly pissed off, and as the Gods gazed in awe, her brow grew blacker and blacker in anger, until suddenly, another Goddess appeared from the darkness. This was Kali, and what a sight she was! And there was no fooling this Goddess! She quickly sussed what was going on and split herself into thousands of Kalis. Every time a drop of the demon's blood was spilled, Kali would catch it before it could touch the éarth, lick it up and swallow it with relish. Before too long all the demons were gone. So, was peace restored? Er... not quite...

The problem was that Kali was now in an insatiable blood lust and wasn't going to stop the carnage just because there were no demons left to slaughter. She turned her attention onto the surviving villagers, even the Gods, and fresh killing and devastation erupted! She was dancing, destroying and dealing out doom! The Gods turned to Shiva, Her husband. Once again, He was whistling sheepishly, scraping his toes on the ground and trying desperately to avoid their gaze! "Well, do something!" the Gods demanded. Shiva had a brilliant idea. He threw Himself under Her feet as She was dancing among the severed limbs and crushed skulls. Now, according to Indian culture, the feet are a lowly part of the body - to point your feet at a person, let alone touch someone with your feet, is quite rude. You traditionally show respect to a guru by touching their feet, symbolically placing them above you. So Shiva let Kali dance all over His body with Her feet. When She realised She'd touched Her husband in this way, Kali was ashamed and calmed down.

There are many, many depictions of this scene in Indian art. Kali is dancing on Shiva's chest. They both looked turned on by it. Her tongue lolls out in lust (some say embarrassment) and He looks ecstatic. Let's leave them to it.

So we can see that Kali was born from rage. Also perhaps from impotence and frustration. So She's a powerful bundle. This isn't the kind of energy you want to play with lightly. Of course there's much more to Kali than just anger, but it's the charge of madness, the electric howling, that fuels Her. Kali is the dark devourer, like time itself, eventually She swallows all. If Shakti, the Mother Goddess, is the wellspring of all beings, then Kali is the other end of the tunnel, so to speak. All returns to Kali eventually.

And of course, her inner nature is one with Shakti, and with all the other forms of the Goddess. She's another form, another face, of the loving, embracing Mother. She receives all life forms eventually, devours everything. Reabsorbs everything, back to primeval darkness. That's Her job. She can be fiercely protective, impatient of hypocrisy and pretension. She is of the blood, ancient as blood itself. She's the night time, the dark cave, the touch of something on the back of your neck, the unidentified noises in the distant forest. If life is a carnival, Kali is the ghost train. Her very presence is thrilling to the point of rapture or hysteria.

One of the most shocking of images associated with Kali is that of the Goddess Chinnamasta (The Headless One), another emanation of Durga/Kali. She's shown, with two young women in attendance, trampling on Shiva, who in turn is reclining on a corpse. One of Her four hands holds a sword, with which She's just cut off Her own head! Blood is spurting out from Her neck. Her severed head, held in another hand, thirstily drinks the blood from Her own body! Not only that, but Her two acolytes are also being refreshed in this macabre fashion! Shiva rests beneath her, serene and absorbed, not a bit phased by the whole grisly scene.

That's a hell of an image, isn't it? And so rich with symbolism. But for the whole, life, death, nurture, destruction, renewal and transformation vibe of the Mother Goddess, you'd have to look a long way to find something more breathtaking and worthy of study.

So, as you can see, unless you're Shiva, you have to be careful with Kali! Great power is there but so too is the opportunity, the possibility of going off the rails a bit! The main thing is respect. If you honour and acknowledge the rage and the madness inside yourself, you're less likely to be knocked off balance by Kali's vibe. She'll reflect what's inside the devotee. Anything that hasn't been acknowledged, processed, assimilated, will come as a big shock.

You probably won't even know it's yours, so Kali will appear even more fearsome, unknowable, unstable.

"So," I hear you ask, "Why the hell go near the bitch?" What possible reason is there to want to worship Kali, to work with Her?

Well, Kali is an important energy. She's as relevant as the more benign forms of the Mother. There's an enormous amount of energy locked up in Her current. If you can learn to access Her safely through regular puja (a ritual of worship), get to know Her a little, learn to understand the way She works and why She does things that way, then you can learn an awful lot about the nature and properties of time, the importance of impermanence, the way you interact with others unconsciously, your innermost hopes, dreams and fears. Remember, personal knowledge (as opposed to book learning) is spiritual currency. Her anger, madness, bloodlust, cruelty (which is also yours, don't forget) can be transformed into protection, passion, honesty. If you can see your face in Hers and Hers in all beings, you might have a better understanding of how we're all in this together, all Her children, trying to make our way in this world of illusion, desperate for love yet trying strenuously to avoid gazing into the dark face of one who loves us anyway, irrespective of the world's opinion. Even the misfits, the outcasts, the addicts and criminals, She'll receive us all when we enter Her presence. It's up to us whether we do that gracefully and thankfully, or kicking and screaming like the kid that doesn't want to go to the dentist!

And like that kid, the short term pain and fear is better than denial, avoidance and enduring a different kind of pain and fear for much longer and then still having to go through the ordeal again anyway!

So to sum up. Firstly Kali is meant to be scary. She's a Tantric deity. They're not renowned for picking flowers and playing with butterflies you know! The whole point of Tantric divinities is that they represent huge energies, awesome forces. They're meant to look the way they do. You wouldn't expect a Tyrannosaurus Rex to be pink with yellow polka dots would you?

Secondly, Kali is a form of the Mother Goddess that though initially appears terrifying and repulsive, actually just reflects back what's in our psyches, buried and repressed, dishonoured. Everything we're ashamed of, or perhaps inordinately, inappropriately proud of, she'll show you. Change yourself and your ability to see through to the core of Kali, your ability to see beyond appearances, will be enhanced. She'll look different.

Like Mahakala, Her Tibetan Buddhist counterpart, who is the shadow side of Chenresig, the bodhisattva of compassion, Kali's inner nature is mercy and kindness. She is love.

Gaze into the heart of darkness to find the light. You'll find that Kali is definitely a Goddess of transformation. And let's not forget, we're living in Her time, Kalayuga, the Dark Age. We're all children of darkness right now. But there's an upside to this. It's relatively easy, I stress relatively, to attain some kind of insight, transcendence and liberation in Kalayuga. If we lived in another age, where great psychic powers, unity of being and a cosmic consciousness was the norm, imagine how much more we'd need to attain in order to achieve enlightenment! At least in this murky time bubble of the Dark Mother, we poor crippled cattle-souls don't have to do too much to achieve some kind of breakthrough. All we have to do is turn our minds towards the divine. Of course, every age has its good and bad points so it probably all works out the same in the end, but in a way we're lucky to be born under Kali's shadow – the tickets outa here are cheap!

Moving on, then. Imagine, if you will, what we'd look like to God's eyes, if He can see our past, present, our future. Imagine one day in our life as seen through God's eyes (or the eyes of a Buddha, if you prefer). It wouldn't look like a home movie, because God would see each moment seamlessly, from start to finish of the day. We'd look like a multi-limbed caterpillar or millipede crawling through a film set. Each and every one of our moments would be linked to, and arising from, its neighbour. Using the analogy of a string of beads, God would see the whole thing as a necklace rather than separate, isolated beads. Am I making myself clear here? Sorry if I'm not. Let's try again. You know that photographic/cinematic technique they use to show tennis shots or a golf swing, where each micro-second of the action shows a separate image? With this process, a hurdler clearing a fence seems to have multiple arms and legs as he or she approaches then jumps over the hurdle. The action is cut up into slices, as it were.

Well, God would see our day like that. We'd look like a multi-limbed being, getting up from bed, going to work, coming back home again. There wouldn't be gaps between His (or Her) perceptions. The morning you, the afternoon you and the evening you, even the past, present and future you, would be completely connected. In God's view, no separation. Same for each and every action – deed and consequence completely as one. From this viewpoint it's easy to see where we're coming from, where we're going, and the forces that impinge and influence that process.

But of course, most of the time we don't have the advantage of that viewpoint, do we? But we can imagine it. And we can depict that principle in art. Imagine painting a supernatural being that represented a mind, a consciousness unfettered by time and space. We'll call it the Buddha Mind. Ok, so we'll start with that idea we had about seeing things as one continuum. We'll give this being multiple arms and legs to show His non-separateness through time, His multi-dimensionalism. Multiple heads too, to show His awareness shining in all directions, into all worlds. We'll colour Him a dark blue-black to represent outer space, the void, a consciousness uncluttered by worldly phenomena yet rich with infinite possibility. We'll give Him a fierce face to show the illusory nature of appearance and the passion of His mercy for all living beings. We'll give Him a .... Oh! Hang on! Someone's beaten us to it! And the supernatural deity in question? Enter stage left, the striking! The compelling! The fascinating! The Earl of

Enlightenment, the Duke of Dakinis, the Nabob of Non-duality! The one, the only... Hevajra!

Hevajra means heart of diamond. "He" is a syllable that relates to heart, to compassion. "Vajra", which translates as diamond or thunderbolt, represents wisdom, a state of consciousness as hard, as bright and as indestructible as a diamond. So Hevajra is the non-dualistic union of compassion and wisdom.

Interestingly, the whole concept of vajra, which is also the name of a Tibetan Lama's ceremonial sceptre, can possibly be traced to Neolithic times. Stone Age shamans prized quartz crystals highly, as they seemed to hold light within them. Traces of quartz crystal have been found in innumerable Stone Age sites. Quartz would have represented something hard and virtually indestructible and yet also fluid, shifting, ever changing, like the light trapped within it. This dual quality came to represent, in the Tibetan tradition, which is very influenced by pre-Buddhist Shamanism, an awareness that was unshakeable and yet responsive, flowing, like the mind of all the Buddhas and deities.

Hevajra was a key component in the conversion of Kublai Khan to Buddhism in the 13th century. The Hevajra Tantra, which gives details of Hevajra's iconography and methods of worship, combined with the deity's fierce countenance and dramatic symbology, must have made a great impression! The Hevajra Tantra also contains one of the key quotes of Tantric principle – "By passion is the world bound, by passion is it released."

Hevajra represents the naked Buddha Consciousness. As a male deity, he also represents active compassion, skilful means, so to complete His being, He's shown in passionate embrace with His equally dark and fierce consort Nairatmya. Nairatmya, like most female deities in Tantric Buddhism represents wisdom. Her name indicates a lack of self, a freedom from a limited identity with nama rupa, name and form. In other words, with anything in the mundane body/mind complex. She clings to Him so tightly, wrapped around Him, impaled upon Him, perhaps absorbing Him, so completely, so ferociously, that they're inseparable. Their lips suck hungrily on one another in a deep kiss. Wisdom and compassion drink of each other, feed one another. The Buddha Mind will always comprise of both wisdom and compassion, they can't be separated in the Buddhist worldview. Buddha Consciousness is non-dualistic.

Hevajra is shown with four legs, dancing ecstatically, triumphantly on four figures which represent maras, "killers", obstacles to enlightenment. These are death, which is the ultimate no-no, the ultimate aversion, the skandhas (components of the body/mind, bits we identify as "us"), karmic hindrances such as negative thoughts and lastly the ultimate yes-yes, a blissful continuation of the life of the self. All these are trampled and subdued by the enlightened awareness that Hevajra embodies.

Each of Hevajra's arms (usually 16 of them!) holds a kapala, a cup made from a skull. These are sometimes used as offering bowls in Tantric ritual. They hold blood or wine, a blood substitute. The kapala represents both the impermanence of form and the emptiness of ego and also a mind dedicated to enlightenment, that wisdom which lies beyond the human world. Further skulls adorn His body. This whole victory dance takes place on a dramatic background of darkness, roaring flames and accompanying dakinis, female knowledge-holders, inspirers of the faithful. Quite a picture, eh? And let's be honest, just a tad reminiscent of Shiva as Nataraja, Lord of the Dance. To give Hevajra the benefit of the doubt, maybe they grew up together! Whatever Hevajra's origins, possibly in the 8th century, and influenced, one suspects, by an early connection with the development of Nataraja's cult, He's still a way cool dude and a Tantric deity par excellence.

Hevajra's sixteen arms also represent what the Tibetans call the sixteen voidnesses. These are negations, the ultimate emptiness of the physical body, the emptiness of time, the emptiness of individual ego, the emptiness of duality etc. Shiva Shankara says actually there's ultimately only one voidness, one thing to negate, and that's the separateness of Him and us. When we understand His qualities, His being, His essence, and when we realise that these are our qualities too, in Shiva Tattva, Shiva Consciousness, then that separateness disappears, becomes void.

The image of Hevajra is very striking, very unusual if you're not used to Tantric art. Of course, peaceful images of the Buddha, of enlightenment, of transcendent awareness, abound, and most of them are quite beautiful, serene and inspiring. Hevajra represents the urge to enlightenment, that whole aspiration to release, the fire and passion of commitment, the total involvement of every fibre of one's being, the incredible energy of the multidimensional insight that freedom from illusion grants, the victory over deluded narrowness that we associate with spiritual liberation. So the imagery has to be dramatic. Hevajra is loaded with meaning. If Tantra was just about sex (and it isn't!) Hevajra would be permanently in the throes of orgasm. He holds Himself permanently in that moment of dissolving into non-duality. What a dude!

The Hevajra Tantra places great value in the female principle. The female genitals are described as the triangle of origin, which of course they are, but here the triangle is held to mean the source of wisdom and insight as well as the origin of human beings. It's revered as a symbol of the unity of the devotee and "his" wisdom. This reminds us of the cult of Shakti and of the downward pointing triangle of Kali's yantra. The triangle of origin is described also as hanging in empty space, to remind the devotee (and us) that it's not just about getting your rocks off, or confusing sexual contact with the human female genitals with freedom from illusion. Relying on sex for wisdom, however pleasant a pursuit that might be, will, in the end, probably prove to be self defeating. The Hevajra Tantra tells us that "we must rise by that which would drag us down." In other words, use our lust, our greed, our anger etc as the energies that will fuel our spiritual endeavours. They become the nectar of enlightenment rather than the poison that will kill us or make us insane. It's that turning lead into gold again.

So Hevajra, adorned in skulls, surrounded by flames, dancing on demons, clutches His wisdom tightly, swallows Himself up in it, becomes one with it and glares ferociously out as us. In comparison, we're pale, fragile, impotent little beings, aren't we? His compassion and commitment burn like a flare in the darkness of delusion.

Phew!

Well, we've now got thumbnail sketches of three Tantric deities, two from the Hindu tradition and one from the Buddhist. Two male, one female. As we've seen, it's important, central, to Tantra that female energies and principles are honoured and revered as much as the male, so, to redress the balance, we'll look at an important female figure from Tantric Buddhism – Vajra Yogini (Tibetan Dorje Khadroma).

If Shiva can be said to represent a certain consciousness that is at one with all life and yet transcendent of form, and if Kali may be described as mercy disguised as anger and madness, in other words, the dissolution of the ego and all matter, and if Hevajra represents a mind dwelling in non-duality, we can begin to see the common thread here - a freedom from fear that insight into the illusory nature of form and self can bring about, a liberation through a transcendental viewpoint. Abhaya! Don't sweat it.

And Vajra Yogini represents the call to arms for the spiritual seeker. She's the inspirer, the guiding light, the red hot passion of spiritual striving, the inner flame. Her fire can help burn away inner obstacles to enlightenment. She's the waker-up!

She is queen of all the dakinis. What's a dakini (Tibetan khadroma)? They're female divinities, vidyadharas (knowledge holders). They're traditionally depicted as naked, representing freedom. Well, naked that is, apart from the usual Tantric "bling" of skulls and stuff. The term dakini also has connotations of sound, calling down by sound. So a dakini is like a heavenly guru, a source of wisdom and inspiration that we can invoke and embrace.

Vajra Yogini (yogini is simply the female equivalent of yogi) is bright red in colour, the colour of fire and passionate energy. She looks fierce, ready to fight and conquer any ignorance and attachment! She literally burns from inside, with bliss and compassion. She scorches away delusion and doubt, dispels fear. Her traditional accoutrements are a knife to cut away attachments and a skull cup (kapala). Like the old Zen story about "the full cup", the kapala reminds us to empty our minds of our own cherished opinions and prejudices and allow Vajra Yogini to flood us with Her higher wisdom and knowledge.

So, look at this hot chick! (Sorry, bad taste, I know. I always manage to sound disrespectful but actually I have great reverence for all Gods and Goddesses. I just can't pretend to be all pious and prim. Doesn't mean I don't love and honour this stuff. I do.) She dances on two figures that represent ego and illusion. She tramples these poisonous delusions underfoot, Her bone ornaments clicking and clacking, Her long hair wild and dishevelled. Her scarlet body burns with spiritual power. She looks completely abandoned to Her dance, free and wild. She's deliberately showing us our comparative stiffness, inhibition and insipid lifelessness.

Over one shoulder appears a khatvanga, the Tibetan term for a trident (where have we seen this symbol before, kiddies?) adorned with severed heads in various states of decay, showing the gradual dropping away of worldly attachments. She's often accompanied by a retinue of other dakinis and the Citipati (Lords of the Graveyard), a strange couple of dancing skeletons, one male, one female (some say brother and sister), said to be protectors of the Buddhist doctrine and a protection against thieves. If you study a good rendition of Vajra Yogini, you can almost taste Tantra! You can feel the urge to enter into the strange and wonderful world of dreamtime, myth and religious passion. As an inspirational divinity, She weaves Her magic well.

So, if you feel the magic of all the above deities, by all means use them. Get a picture, study their attributes, what they stand for, give offering and prayer to them every day. Meditate on them. Use their image as a doorway, through which, like Alice in Wonderland, you enter into a strange, fascinating, sometimes dangerous but rewarding world. Listen and look for their wisdom in daily life. Honour them, and they'll honour you. And inspire and instruct you.

If you have a local temple or monastery, I feel it's only fair to point out that they will have their own way of doing things, and you should respect that. Their methods are tried and true and work for the majority of most people. If however you're not a natural joiner, or you live a fair distance from any relevant source of teaching, then read books or use the internet for something other than e mails, porn, downloads and games! Do some research. Look at websites. Talk to the hosts. There's a lot of crap out there of course, and a lot of weird freaks. But there's also a lot of sincere, intelligent, committed and generous folk too. You might find something that suits you through them.

Take just one step towards the deities and they'll take one step towards you.

CHAPTER SEVEN - MORE BULL ABOUT GOD/DESS.

As I intimated before, I see no reason why Tantric techniques and principles can't be extended to non-eastern deities. The rest of our earthly history, myth and culture is rich in Tantric opportunity.

Let me just spell out the principles again before we carry on. By Tantra I mean the religious and psychological process of inner alchemy. A process of taking our "lead", our base urges, that's our anger, our fear, our greed, our lust, and by employing common sense, introspection, devotion, meditation, study, practices such as chanting or visualisation etc, turning them into the "gold" of insight, compassion and transcendence. When we look at the Gods and Goddess of antiquity, whether oriental or western, we see archetypes writ large, a language we can understand and employ in our quest for enlightenment and freedom. We see their "good" qualities and their "bad" qualities, we can see both the shadow and the golden shadow. We can relate that to where we are now.

To take two extreme examples, we could say that the Hindu God Vishnu is the gold. He preserves, He protects the material world and all knowledge and learning, all law and order within it. He's upright and just, holds all that's holy. On the other hand we have a deity like Baphomet, supposedly worshipped by the Knights Templar, who looks like an ideal candidate for Satan. He has a goat's head, female breasts and looks like He should be the God of Lust and The Father of Lies. This is a little unfair on Baphomet though, who's actually a composite God representing all life forms, human, animal and reptilian, in one. And He's not the only Goat God around, as we shall see below. And this short-sightedness of symbology is unfair to Vishnu too. He has many guises, some of them fierce and demonic, some in animal form. Appearances can be misleading. Symbols have many levels of meaning, great depth.

So the Gods are a useful language to learn. Mythology is a useful tool. Tantra is a useful tool. Jungian Shadow Work is a useful tool. And these subjects are not mutually exclusive either. Far from it. They're part of the same movement, an urge to understand, an urge to become one with the mysterious, the awesome, a tribal dance that began long ago, in the fire lit caves and moon silvered forests of our Stone Age ancestors and is still going strong even today, accompanied by the pulse, the drumming of the human heart, in the shared mind, the group mind we call mass communication or the internet. Daubed in ash grey or electric blue, we've been doing this dance for millennia. So let's not cut off half the world by limiting Tantra to India or Tibet!

So before we follow that drumming back through time in later chapters, let's have a quick look at a couple of "western" candidates for the Tantric approach.

Pan is a deity, half goat (the hindquarters and the horns), half man, that's been largely marginalised or diminished by civilisation. We don't seem to need Him much now. But if you've ever been lost in the mountains or in a forest, you'll have felt His presence. The word "panic" doesn't do justice to the overwhelming, irrational fear that His proximity evokes! He's still around, under the trees, under the hedgerows. And He's not like the charming little satyr statues you find in garden centres! He represents wildness, the natural world, with its own implacable laws and processes. And wildness, "out there" or within ourselves or others, can be frightening.

Pan's cult seems to have been well established in Arcadia, southern Greece by about 600 BCE. I suppose a rural community of shepherds and keepers of livestock would naturally appreciate a God that was half animal. But Pan isn't actually a cosy little farmyard deity. "Pan" means "All", so Pan is the divinity of all nature. And the natural world creates some awesome forces – lions and tigers, elephants, sharks, forest fires, storms, tornados, volcanoes, tsunamis, earthquakes. It's not all sunflowers and kittens out there!

And "Pan" or "Paon" also means shepherd. In some ways, Pan, as one of many "Horned Gods", has come to represent the shepherd and protector of Paganism, which is the worship of nature's principles and processes. We'll look at that subject later. For now, let's take a closer look at the Goat God.

Though He was adopted and adored by the Arcadians, most literature states that He was actually older than the classical Olympian Gods and Goddess such as Zeus (The Bright One, Chief of the Gods), Artemis (the Huntress, Queen of the Beasts) and Apollo (the Sun God and God of Medicine). In fact Zeus' mother Rhea hid Zeus from His ghastly father Cronos (Time) by fostering Him out to Pan's mother. So Pan and Zeus grew up together!

You wouldn't think it now. To most classical mythologists, Pan is a side note, a minor figure. The mysterious and disturbing cry that echoed across the ocean from the island of Paxi in the first decade of the Christian era, proclaiming that "The great God Pan is dead!" was a little premature though, Pan lives on in the hearts of many modern Pagans. He still seems to be going strong! It's possible that Pan's horns and cloven hoofs became useful tools for the Christian mythologists, highlighting as they do our "shameful" animal nature. And indeed to some people our animal nature, with its appetites, urges and instincts, is alien, unknown, uncomfortable, shameful, repressed. As a teacher specialising in Chinese exercise systems, I'm often amazed at many people are not at home in their own body. The first thing I try to get them to do is relax and then start from where they are, not from where they want to be. That's true of all spiritual endeavour too – relax and then start from where you are. By all means have a goal but you can't start from anywhere other than here and now!

Some say that Pan is the son of Hermes, the Greek prototype of Mercury, God of crossroads and trickery. They also say that Hermes taught Him the art of masturbation, which He in turn taught to the shepherds. I think they could probably figure that one out for themselves, Pan!

But Pan is indeed a lusty God and will quite happily prong anything with a pulse. It's His job. Nature will seed anywhere it can, even in the most inhospitable locales. Why expect the God of Nature to be any different?

Nature is multi-layered though, and so is Pan. A student of mine, who has a very strong connection with Him, experiences Him almost as a protective deity. He comes sniffing, snuffling around her when she meditates. He can be small and as quiet as a rabbit or as vast and awe inspiring as a great storm. He also has connections with music, being a master of the syrinx (so-called pan pipes). In fact He even bested Apollo's lyre virtuosity in a musical competition. Though a bit of a bad boy by reputation, He can take the role of protector, teacher and mentor.

As a child I was surprised and captivated by Pan's appearance in the children's book "The Wind In The Willows" and Rat and Mole's worship of Him. Pan is described as "The Piper at the Gates of Dawn", also the title of Pink Floyd's first album, an acid-drenched psychedelic masterpiece. I never forgot the book (or the record).

Ultimately, and especially today, Pan represents the wildness within us and the wildness of a planet under siege. Pan's world is fast disappearing, as forests get axed and mountains become littered with dead tourists, but we'll never get rid of Pan, He'll inhabit the dark forests and wild places of our psyche for as long as our collective unconscious has uncharted areas.

And you can sense Pan in this world, even as you step outside your door. The smell of wet earth, the tang of pine trees, the musk of cats, the hint of sea on the wind, the lift of your hair when you turn the corner into a breeze, the heat of the sun on your arms, the scurrying sound at the bottom of the garden, the surreal glare of a full moon through your bedroom window. He's around.

Here's a poem, set in the wintry Norfolk countryside at night. A long way from Arcadia, yes, but they have bad weather there too! I used to loathe winter. In Norfolk we sometimes have to endure the cold east wind that blows straight from Siberia. And being flat, in Norfolk, there's nowhere to hide! I hated the bleakness, the bare trees, the cold, implacable stars. To be on a North Norfolk beach in a storm in winter is to feel the fragility of warmth and humanity in the face of such cold, destructive power. I had to learn to love my area's cold wildness and the wildness and the ferocity inside myself before I could find peace. Ultimately I found that wildness can be inspiring and even soothing, comforting. Hopefully you'll feel Pan's full power in these verses, The Song of the Flatlander ...

"I was born in the flatlands
The wet darklands
Salt-lashed and edged by blackened ditches
Where the bitter coffinwood trees lean crab-sailed away from the howling coast

I steal through the sucking fields in rags, fur and feathers
Stitched in scarecrow shadow
Past the splayed stiff crows' wings
Past the rats and vermin strung up on wire
Past the wind-whipped sullen cattle
Past the old forgotten milestones
To the salt marshes bleached by moon
To the coastline under siege
To the haunts of something nameless, terrible
That walked these pocked, corroded dunes
Ancient, even before the people came

I hear its passing sometimes
Under the keening stars
Desolate cry
When the north wind whines through the wire
When the sea feathers
And sucks the shingle down with a cold and hungry kiss

Who does this land belong to?
Something in me is divided
And doesn't know where to stand

This is the first year ever
I do not fear winter
Under the wild skies
At the edge of some frost-scarred field
I face something inside myself

It has a hungry voice and a cold touch
It has a dark face
But from that darkness
A light in me answers."

Before my breakthrough, my own wild nature felt cold, implacable, inhuman. It wore a dark face. But when I accepted it, it felt almost nurturing, supportive. Then for a while I felt distant, removed from the world of man. I didn't know where to stand, whose side I was on, only that the fear had gone. Of course, in the end, it all balanced out again, I adjusted. But it was an interesting, if disturbing, time in my life.

Pan makes an appearance in my previous book "The Real Rasa" (buy it!), in a poem about panic and the opening of the first chakra, the energy centre at the base of the spine. That was an even scarier time! And interesting too, that He was the first deity that sprang to mind when I started that whole scary trip.

As with all the more familiar Tantric deities from the cultural wellsprings of India and Tibet, Pan can be approached as an object of worship. He can be invoked, meditated upon, studied, identified with, in exactly the same way as you would with Shiva, Kali, Hevajra, Vajra Yogini and all the others. The fact that He has so many different facets to His personality makes Him eminently appropriate. Why not? If a westerner is able to invoke Shiva or Buddha, then shouldn't a westerner be able to invoke a classical Greek deity too? History shows that geography is no barrier to religious fervour!

As many of the notable Greek, Roman, Celtic and Germanic Gods and Goddesses are worshipped under the umbrella of beliefs and customs we call modern Paganism, I'd like to find another, less well known figure, preferably female, to finish up this discussion on non-oriental candidates for Tantric-style devotion and practice.

And for the first time, I'm discussing a deity I know little about, except peripherally. We're staying in the same neck of the woods, the Mediterranean world of yore, and visiting the mysterious island of Crete. Here, the Minoan culture flourished, and eventually fell when a massive volcanic eruption on the nearby island of Thera in 1500 BCE destroyed most of their buildings and artefacts. Until that point though, the Minoan culture was truly sophisticated. The lack of fortifications around royal buildings seems to indicate their lack of concern over would-be invaders and conquerors. The palaces had baths and even a flushable toilet! The Minoans society has been dubbed the oldest European civilisation. It was the home of Daedalus, inventor of the forerunner of the modern hang glider. Unfortunately, his son Icarus perished in the test flight! Knossos, the main palace of the rulers of Crete, was also said to be the lair of the Minotaur, the sinister half man-half bull creature that haunted its underground labyrinth, demanding an annual sacrifice of a tasty young male or female Minoan. And what a wealth of symbolism waits to be sifted from that story!

The writing and language of the Minoans differed greatly from that of the ancient Greeks, and the absence of many surviving artefacts renders the workings of their society a mystery, even today. However, the discovery of two figurines, one intact, one that had to be partially reconstructed, affords a tantalising glimpse into a fascinating culture. A female figure, known today as "The Snake Goddess" stands wearing a seven layered robe. Snakes coil around her waist and neck. She wears a small type of sleeved waistcoat, which is opened to reveal, even to accentuate, her bare breasts. Another female figure, similarly attired, was reconstructed from fragments and appears to show a disciple of the Goddess, holding aloft a snake in each hand. Both Goddess and acolyte have long hair and wear a hat. The acolyte's is cushion shaped, surmounted by a seated cat. The Goddess wears a taller headpiece, similar to that seen on Egyptian Pharaohs. These figures could be the predecessors of the modern witch and medieval man's fear of unleashed female sexuality and power. Snakes represent wisdom, power and transformation. Cats are notoriously independent, roaming where they will. It's even possible that the seated cat could represent something much larger, more regal, such as a lioness or a leopard (There is a faint suggestion of spots on the cat figure). Other artefacts found at the main excavation of Knossos in the early 1900s feature cows and goats suckling their young, another traditional female attribute. It seems entirely possible that the religious power of Crete was female based and that these figures and symbols are all that remains of a long standing cult of female wisdom.

We know that the young men of Crete practiced bull dancing. Depictions on vases show fine athletic figures leaping and somersaulting gracefully over powerful and no doubt enraged and perplexed bulls. Not the sort of activity you take lightly! What's even more amazing is that the figures shown in this dangerous ballet obviously belong to both sexes. Again, it's possible that this was more than mere sport. It could have been a kind of ritual competition to see who was to be the chosen consort of the priestess, or perhaps even the High Priestess herself, for a year. There are parallel myths from around the world, where a young man would jointly rule as consort for a year and then be slaughtered ritually to make way for another, thus ensuring fertility and plenty for the community. The young man would represent nature's annual cycle of birth, renewal, growth, fruition, harvest and death.

All this is conjecture, yet entirely plausible. Eminent archaeologists and historians, far more erudite than me, have put forth similar theories. Certainly, figurines and representations of fertility Goddesses from the Stone Age have been found on Crete, indicating a long history of female divinity. The general name for a Goddess seems to have been "Potnia", which means "Mistress".

Bulls, snakes, underground labyrinths. Animal-headed deities. Nurturing. Sacrifice. All sounds a bit Tantric doesn't it? So maybe this mysterious Snake Goddess, who lacks even a name, yet foreshadows other, similar female deities such as Hecate (Goddess of crossroads and darkness, the old crone) and Anaitis (Greek version of Anat, Egyptian Goddess of nature's powers, hunting and sexuality), would seem to be an ideal candidate for investigation.

Remembering that Gods and Goddesses hold our gold, our latent, unrevealed divinity for us, there's bound to be a God figure that draws you, that speaks to you, that holds something for you. The Toltec (Mexican) tradition is full of fascinating Gods and Goddesses. There's Smoking Mirror the shadowy and capricious Trickster, Jade Skirt, the Goddess of dreams and imagination, Lady Filth Eater, the forgiver of sins, The African, Australian Aboriginal and Polynesian traditions are all rich seams of myth, legend and divinity in all its myriad forms. So why not follow these trails for a while - there's nothing to lose and you never know what you might discover...

MINOAN SNAKE GODDESS

CHAPTER EIGHT - TO THE BEAT OF AN ANCIENT DRUM.

Science and religion are two ways to investigate ourselves and the world around us. All too often, though, science and the study of religion and mythology seem to be mutually antagonistic pursuits. Science has become, for many, the new religion, the paradigm that explains the origins and workings of the universe, the origins and workings of mankind and the way the two interact. Science of course is invaluable and has led to vast improvements in knowledge and the human condition, especially, many would argue, in the field of medicine.

It can be argued also that religion, religious persecution and inter-religious conflict, have all caused an awful lot of suffering in this world of ours, for century after century, and that science and technology have vastly increased the number of ways we can damage each other! Both science and religion, ways to explain the world, have brought comfort and misery in equal measure.

But any study of any field of science will quickly reveal that an awful lot of scientists are like devotees of a religious cult, which I suppose in a way they are. They can be as narrow minded, cliquey, blinkered, hostile, dismissive as any high priest. Contrary to popular belief, scientists don't usually play well together, and will quite happily ignore evidence that doesn't support their pet theory. In the field of archaeology, it was only a hundred years ago that an eminent scientist dismissed the find of the first skeleton of Neanderthal man, claiming it was the body of a soldier killed in the Napoleonic war!

And scientists and archaeologists, like the rest of us I must add, are deeply conditioned by their expectations and by the current scientific climate. As someone who is, to all intents and purposes, at the other end of the spectrum, being a self-confessed council house mystic, I have to be aware of my own perceptual conditioning when making interpretations of ancient finds, such as cave art and rock carvings.

Bearing all that in mind, let's take a journey back in time and examine what are, for me, the ancient roots of Tantra, Paganism and indeed, of the religious impulse itself.

Throughout France and Spain, ancient and beautiful, breathtaking images of animals, geometric shapes and handprints have been discovered on cave walls. These have been dated to the Palaeolithic Age. This takes us back to about 45,000 years ago. By this time, Neanderthal man was beginning to perhaps feel the strain of living in competition with the newly arrived "modern" man. Food resources, cave locations, access to animal migration routes, even limited trade – these were all up for grabs and inevitably, Palaeolithic man began to dominate at the expense of the Neanderthals, who all but died out over the next ten thousand years or so. There exists evidence that Neanderthal man copied some of the perceived "advances" of Palaeolithic man, such as body adornment, jewellery, slightly better tool making techniques etc, but it was probably a difference in brain power that doomed the Neanderthals to eventual extinction. Palaeolithic man shared with us an ability to think in three dimensions as it were, to be able to resurrect dreams, memories, past experiences, and bring them back into the present. They were able to predict, by this faculty, when certain species of migrating animals would visit certain locales. They were able to target certain species at certain times, instead of scavenging and hunting with the prehistoric equivalent of crossed fingers!

So Palaeolithic man became the dominant species. But not simply by virtue of having a more varied diet, a greater resource of animal species as food. As David Lewis-Williams confirms in his excellent book, "The Mind in the Cave", it was because of their ability to extend awareness from the present to the past or future, and from the past or future to the present, in other words because they had the faculty of imagination, and a spoken language that was sufficiently sophisticated to communicate ideas, memories, dreams and plans, they were able to bind "families", tribes or social groups together under a totem or tribe emblem for mutual benefit. They were able to share, not only information but hopes and fears, common problems. And because any tribe or community has non-members, potential enemies, that perceived enemy, real or imagined, stimulates a further evolution in thought and planning. The stimulus of belonging to a tribe, reinforcing those ties and defending that tribe against "others" must have created a further deepening of awareness, perhaps also an appreciation of social living and the individual's responsibilities towards the community. It seems likely, also, that among the "other" tribes, some were perceived as friendly, some as neutral and some, of course, as hostile, dangerous. So man began to develop the concept of his place in this world, and how to improve his place in this world.

And the faculty of imagination would begin to extend that concept from the immediate environment into a larger landscape, including the experiences of more than one generation, which could be handed down, become received wisdom. This imagination would include other worlds too, including the world man felt he inhabited when dreaming. The concept of ancestors and spirits, of the life force of people and animals, became important. Individual identity, lineage identity, tribe identity, the beginnings of "religious" identity, all would become central to Palaeolithic man's daily life.

When religion becomes an identity, rather than a private practice, as we can see all too clearly in our modern world, it's a recipe for separatism and conflict. When we define ourselves by our religion, we automatically exclude all non-members of that religion. They become a sub-species, inferior and dangerous. The true faith has to be defended from these people! It's amazing how the worship of a God that's supposed to represent all the goodness, knowledge and truth of the universe can entail slaughtering anyone that does exactly the same thing but uses a different symbology to delineate their practice.

For Palaeolithic man, as with other so -called primitive societies, there would have been no difference between sacred and secular, between holy and profane activities. The religious impulse and the hunting impulse, the artistic impulse and the breeding impulse, would have been inextricably entwined. In that sense their lives were holistic. However, this would later change, as we shall see.

It seems very likely that the origins of all religions, at least in terms of trying to explain this world, some kind of imagined world of spirits or invisible energies, and the relationship between the two, began with some kind of shamanic worldview or mindset, which gave birth to religious practice. Or perhaps the two, the mindset and the practice, were mutually creative and supportive. Either way, the roots of this early religion, and "religion" means to re-tie, to re-ligature, oneself back to something greater than oneself, such as a God, were to run throughout human history, and show themselves most vividly in Shamanism, Paganism and Tantrism. In these three collections of belief and practice, the early roots of religion lie close to the surface and can be seen quite clearly.

So, for me, the journey back in time to examine the caves and the artwork of ancient man, and to postulate his religious paradigms and practices, is a religious pilgrimage, a spiritual journey, rather than a historical or archaeological exercise. I need to get myself into the right frame of mind for this or it'll be a bland recital of "perhaps" and "maybe's". I need to "tune in" to ancient man's vibe. So, in the shamanic equivalent of taking one's shoes off before entering a temple, let's take off some of our modern, patronising "superiority" before we enter the cave of the ancients. Let's lose a little of that rational, cynical attitude.

To do this, we need a prop. I can think of nothing better than the sound of a shaman's drum. So close your eyes and take a minute. Prepare yourself for an amazing journey, not only back to the past, but deeper into your own roots, into the world of spirits and animals, into dreamtime, into the world of the shaman, a time and place that still lives on, somewhere inside you.

Listen! The drum. In your skull. In the warm darkness behind your closed eyes. Let it fill you up. Boom, boom, boom... BOOM! Boom, boom, boom...

BOOM! Feel that tingle of the skin, that ripple in the belly, that tells you something "real" is happening? Feel your hair stir, as if with electricity? That's good, we can start. Open your eyes...

Here we stand in the dying of a summer's day in the middle to late Palaeolithic era. It's obviously been a lovely day here. Lots of tall trees, aren't there? Many pines and ginkgos too. The soil is dry and sandy, quite lighter in colour than ours. A big cloud of birds, a bit like rooks, circling around, over to the west. Isn't it quiet though? My ears are ringing. We spot what looks like a small roundhouse, half underground and with a turfed roof. The Palaeolithics don't just live in caves then. Look! People! Just down the hill. It's ok, we don't have to whisper. Those two can't hear or see us. They're wearing animal skins, like a kilt around their waists, and a smaller skin, just covering their shoulders. Just like we imagined them. No shoes though. And no furs. Probably a winter thing. And they both have bracelets, probably teeth or seashells. They look kind of Spanish or Italian, don't they? Olive skin, sharp faces. Somehow we both thought they'd be a bit more pug nosed, strong in the jaw, but no, they look absolutely modern in that respect. And they actually look bright, not primitive at all. They've both got matted dreadlocks, that must be the Palaeolithic style! One has their hair tied back from their face. No bushy beards either! Not sure if it's dirt or paint but one of them definitely has some dark marks on their arms. Let's edge a bit closer as we follow them down this narrow valley and see what's shakin'...

We can see a little more clearly now. They're both males, one about twenty and the other, with the tied back hair and the thicker beard, he's about thirty at a guess. The older guy's wearing a cord threaded with teeth on his left wrist, the younger dude has what looks like a mixture of shells and pebbles, also on his left wrist. Neither of them are carrying weapons so we assume they're not coming home from hunting. We can smell them now, a little like cooking fat and a lot like sweat. They probably don't wash much, if at all, and they probably smear themselves in animal fat, and perhaps ashes too, to keep warm in winter. Actually though, they don't smell as bad as we thought they might. The arms of the younger guy are definitely covered in paint. It's a rust colour and the shapes are like inverted sergeant's stripes. I think it represents either the scales of a snake or lizard or, more likely, the patterns you see in animal fur. They look fit and athletic, if grubby. They're both about five feet high, maybe just a little more, but not much. Actually, I don't know about you, but I feel quite weird being with them. They're as human as we are, but some kind of gulf seems to exist between us, probably because our experiences of life, the way we perceive the world around us, are radically different. They wouldn't understand electricity or continental drift. We wouldn't be able to tell the difference in smell between a deer and a tiger. To be honest, I wouldn't be able to smell any animal until it trampled over me! I think the sense of smell has atrophied enormously for modern man. On the other hand, our deodorant, or any city street, would probably choke these guys. We'd smell really bad to them!

Boom, boom, boom... BOOM! We've threaded our way down a dirt path to the centre of the valley. I can see four... no, five cave entrances. Look! That one with a level area outside seems to have some kind of hide cover, like a sun canopy, propped up by tree branches. Cool! Round the corner and here's another cave. That's where we seem to be heading. There's some artwork right at the entrance, just inside. Yep, it's a stag of some kind. This is either their emblem, like a family coat of arms, or maybe it was a stag or a spirit stag that indicated they should use this cave. Look how the artist has used the sticking out part of the rock there to make it look like the stag is hunching up, looking over his shoulder at us. Did you know the artist Picasso was a huge fan of cave art? Apparently he said it was better than anything any modern artist could achieve. I know what he means. Just a few lines and smudges and this animal is breathing, twitching. It must look even more impressive in flickering firelight. Hopefully we'll see more stuff inside.

Boom, boom, boom... BOOM! Wow! This is eerie! Just a few feet into the cave and it's already pitch dark. Our city eyes aren't used to this. I hope they'll adjust before too long. Ouch! I also kind of assumed the cave floor would be level. It isn't. There's all kind of bumps and ruts. Double ouch! You ok? Trust you to find the one stalactite! It sounded like a drum. Maybe they use stalactites as some kind of musical instrument. The whole ceiling is getting lower. There doesn't seem to be anywhere to actually live in this place, do you think it must be set aside for other purposes? Yeah, me too, feels more like a place to visit than a home. Let's keep up with the other guys.

Boom, boom, boom, BOOM! We're both getting a bit claustrophobic. The ceiling is only about four feet high and the passage is getting narrower. There's a dim light ahead. Ah, we've come to a corner, the passage turns left, and there's a ledge with a guttering lamp, like a small stone bowl. It contains animal fat, but from what animal I don't know. I read somewhere that bears have a lot of fat, so maybe it's bear. Bears' teeth are also highly prized for bracelets and necklaces because they're big, strong animals. They can walk on two legs, like humans and they live in dark caves. This makes them a bit special. So they're believed to hold a lot of energy. Wearing bears' teeth is like a protection from other animals, and especially from anything that might be hiding in the dark. Really, bears are almost like a protective deity. Wanna bet that we'll find a painting of a bear at the back of this cave? Ok, you're on. I bet you two pebbles!

By the flickering flame I can see some more paintings. Aren't they beautiful? Another stag, a horse and some kind of deer. All three animals are superimposed on one another. Possibly they were all painted at different times, to claim ownership of the cave, but there seems to be no attempt to eradicate, delete or paint over any of the images, so this probably indicates a kind of alliance – the people of the horse and the people of the deer are buddies of the stags. Or at least neutral, which is good enough for trading and for perhaps sharing this cave for special occasions. It could also be that this is the way the animals appeared to the artist, in some kind of trance brought on by chanting or dodgy mushrooms! By lamplight, these animal paintings float supernaturally on the walls of the cave. Or more accurately, they emerge from the walls. The cave is a kind of halfway house between the outside world, the world of animals and weather, and the inside world, the world of dreams, spirits and of the human community. The walls of the cave are where spirit animals can come through and where offerings to the invisible world can be taken through to the other side. See, here by the lamp? A string of pebbles, all painted with coloured dots. These paintings on the wall aren't meant to represent real animals at all, they're spirit animals. Again, more accurately, they represent the essence of animal, the essence of stag, horse and deer. Already, these people are beginning to make a distinction between the mundane and the spiritual. That would mean that whoever claimed to have greater access to the invisible world, and could back their claim up by explaining dreams, knowing where good hunting was to be found, or by curing illnesses, would automatically be perceived as special, set apart, of high worth. The first case of religion causing social division!

There's another lamp, just around another corner, this time to the right. Just before we turn, the cave passage gets really tight, only three feet across and it starts to slope downwards quite sharply. Look! On this wall. You can see the marks of finger trails. People coming down here dip their hands in the mud of the floor and leave a wavy trail on the wall. Maybe it's like dipping your fingers in holy water before you enter a church. Maybe it's a way of confirming your right to be here. I want to do the same. I don't feel at home here but I feel like I'm in a church and I really respect their space. So, dip dip, daub, daub. You too? Feels good, doesn't it? The mud is cold and gritty. It's like we're adding to the wall, acknowledging the entrance to the other world. We're touching their religion, joining it. It feels like a privilege. Did I ever tell you I once visited the "Temple of Diana" in Sicily? I had to climb up this really steep hill, covered in pine trees, for about half an hour. When I found this tiny place, almost like a Neolithic settlement, it was in the heat of the day and there was no one else around. I said a prayer to the Goddess and left an offering. It felt a privilege to be able to spend some time alone in that small, hot, sticky, claustrophobic, almost dreamlike place. This cave brings out the same feelings in me.

Yeah, I know I'm rabbiting on. I'm over excited. Still a bit nervous too. I'll try and calm down a bit.

Boom, boom, boom... BOOM! Boom, boom, boom... BOOM! And suddenly – nothing! The drum has stopped! That's dramatic. What happened to our soundtrack! Why did it stop?

Ah! Listen. Just round the corner. We exchange glances. We can hear voices. Way cool! I think this next turn is the main chamber and it's being used! We're getting to the heart of everything now...

We have to get down on hands and knees to get round the corner. It's worth the discomfort of a skinned knee or two. The chamber opens out, big enough to hold a lot more people. And there are about twenty five individuals here right now! There are four more lamps so we can see quite clearly. Our two "guides" have joined a gathering that now consists of six men and ten women. All the adults look to be about twenty to forty years old. No older. There are six children, aged from two or three to about ten.
Oh, and one teenager, maybe fifteen, sixteen. The mixed crowd tells us that this isn't to be a male or female puberty initiation. That would have entailed a single-sex gathering. They're all either squatting on their haunches or sitting cross legged, and looking up at another guy. He's quite impressive! He's about thirty five years old and wears the same skins as the others but a lot more body paint. Like some of the other men, his arms and face are covered in geometric shapes – dots, circles, wavy lines. These are the kind of patterns you see behind your eye lids if you cover your eyes from light for long enough. Did you ever play with that as a kid? I used to press my palms tight over my eyes and watch all these greeny-grey circles like smoke rings. The marks on the men's arms show that these guys have had some kind of significant spiritual experience, either an initiation or a close escape from death. The marks also allow spiritual energy to enter their bodies from the walls of the cave. But this guy, some kind of leader or priest, is absolutely covered from head to foot in markings. He's wearing a lot of bone ornaments too. Very Tantric! He's greased his hair so it stands up, like someone being electrocuted. A telltale bulge in his kilt tells us he's very, very excited!

It's possible that he uses some kind of mushroom or psychedelic substance to excite and agitate his system, or maybe he has some other way of charging up into ecstasy - drumming, dancing etc. He's chanting now and then the others chant back at him, like a call and response. The language sounds a bit like a mixture of Sanskrit and Hungarian or Romanian. There's a lot of up and down tone to it, but that might be just because they're chanting. There's the occasional click and whistle too, and a low pitched "urr", but whether that's their normal way of communicating or whether it's meant to represent animal noises, we have no way of knowing at this point. They slap their hands on the ground to keep time. We're surprised at the sound quality, the acoustics. Somehow we thought caves would be full of echoes but the singing is quite flat, just the same as it would sound in a modern room. It has the effect of somehow making the chant sound as if it's happening right beside your ear, rather than in a big space. Maybe their bodies soak up the sound. Oh! The priest hitches up his kilt, exposing his erect cock. It doesn't seem as lewd as it sounds. The erection seems to have more to do with a rush of energy than lust. Everyone else sits with their knees wide apart, even the women. So either modesty isn't an issue here, or they're deliberately baring their genitals to the priest, or more likely to the cave walls, the entrance and exit used by the spirit world. It's as if the energy is coming from the spirit animals on the wall, through the priest and into the rest of the clan.

There are more paintings here. More stags, more horses, more deer. And a big something that could be a bison or a mammoth. It's painted on a big piece of rock that juts down from the ceiling and the head is on the other side. All we can see is a hairy set of hindquarters! We can see more finger trails too, some of them seem to cut straight across the paintings of the "totem" or clan animals. Perhaps this is a further reinforcing of clan links, or possibly a kind of supplication, a plea to tribe guardians. There's a fantastic image almost directly behind the priest. It's a kind of half man, half stag and it's got several lines coming out from its body. Shamanic art from all over the world, and from every period of time, shows similar imagery. I think this one shows the spirit of the stag and the spirit of the priest as one and the lines are either spears, to symbolise a symbolic death to the external world and rebirth or initiation into the world of spirit, or maybe they're just lines of energy, power emanating from the shaman/stag hybrid.

There are handprints all over the wall behind the priest. All sizes. This is their version of "confirmation". They reinforce their link with the clan that's formed by birth or some kind of "marriage" or maybe a trade-off of personnel for a specific hunt or special event. Perhaps there are even enforced trade-offs sometimes - a child for a hunter, a hunter for a pregnant woman, we don't know. All members of the clan paint their palms and press them to the cave wall. They enhance their connection with the underworld too, by leaving part of their identity on the wall, like an offering.

The priest gestures at one of the women. She's carrying a baby wrapped up in skins. We hadn't noticed that. She brings the child to the priest, who unwraps the skins (it's a boy), paints his little hands and presses them to the wall. Predictably the baby cries. The mother looks as proud as you'd expect and the rest of the clan relax. If the baby didn't cry, it could be a sign that he is ill fated. Or that the animal spirits haven't come forth to touch him. If the child keeps quiet, it shows that the spirit animals haven't come to take a sniff at him. Or perhaps that he shows spiritual talents, in which case the child may have to undergo training and initiation, which would be inevitably have a dangerous element. We notice that the arms of the priest show great scars and welts under his paint. He's either been burned or mauled by something. But he survived. Maybe that was his initiation! He certainly seems to hold this crowd by force of personality. His erection and sticky-up hair denote a charge of spiritual excitement, possession if you like. Maybe that's why they were all flashing at him, it brings fertility. The energy can jump from him to them, or from the underworld, through him, to them.

Everyone's relaxing now, chatting among themselves. This is obviously a minor, or more informal ceremony. We think an initiation would have included some kind of musical instruments, most probably drums and bone flutes. The language they're using to talk amongst themselves still sounds a bit "flutey" but that could be down to excitement. The vowel sounds are quite soft and rounded, there aren't a lot of harsh consonants like "k" and "g" but there are definitely a few clicks and "urr's". Some lip smacking too, like an air kiss in the middle of a sentence. They use their hands a lot when communicating. There's the usual range of facial expressions but they use their eyebrows a lot more than we do. Those little caterpillars are up and down and contracting all the time. The smell of the people massed here together is quite overpowering. It's not a stale smell, or even that unpleasant, just really strong. The lamps reek a bit too.

We move through the chamber. No, I don't know why we're on tiptoes. They can't see us. We have an eerie moment though, when the eyes of the priest seem to lock on to us and follow us for a few steps. Then he frowns as if sensing something he can't explain and looks away. Phew! He's good!

The passage gets really, really tight now. The ceiling is only three feet high and the walls are only a couple of feet apart. Neither of us likes this at all. We crawl for about fifty yards, moving steadily downwards. It's getting damper but the rock feels dry, maybe there's a breeze from an underground stream or something. Maybe it's just nerves. We keep going, even though it's getting even more constricting, then sense another feeble glow of light in the distance. Just as we think we're going to have to turn back, and won't that be fun, there's no room to turn round, which means we'll have to crawl backwards, the passage widens slightly and takes a sharp turn to the left. We squeeze into a small chamber, about six feet wide. There's a guttering lamp and a few strings of animal teeth as offerings. But no painting of a bear. "Oh well," I whisper (why am I whispering? That's what this place does to you!), "I owe you two pebbles." I glance at you but you're shaking your head and pointing upwards. At first I can't see anything, then "Wow!" There's an incredible and very scary painting of some kind of big cat, like a lioness or puma, actually on the ceiling. It looms over us, flickering and snarling. It's very intimidating. The stag clan couldn't have picked a better protective deity to guard their sacred place from evil spirits. This big cat watches their back, as it were, and perhaps serves as some kind of tutelary animal for the shaman. If that priest back there survived an attack from a beast like this, he's going to have a strong spiritual connection with these predators. Maybe he uses this connection to pick hunting sites and protect his clan from real or imagined dangers. Just as all herds or packs of animals have a dominant male or female, so too do the stag people of the Palaeolithic. Good luck to them.

I close my eyes in that small dark space and feel the heartbeat of the cave. We're here, at the birth of religion. Of Shamanism. Of Paganism. Of

Tantrism. What an honour. We both take a moment to offer up a prayer. I want to leave something of me behind with my ancestors so I decide to leave my handkerchief buried in the mud of the chamber. I open my eyes and we each see how visibly moved the other is. You bury some coins deep in the mud, where they'll never be found. What an experience!

Can you hear something? Boom! Boom, boom...BOOM! It's our shaman's drum, calling us home. I wipe a tear from my eye. You don't look too bright either! We close our eyes again, follow the beat of that ancient drum, home, far away from the stag people. But actually not too far. We still have a lot in common. Coming home now. Boom, boom, boom... BOOM! You know, I'd love to have been able to talk with that priest...

CHAPTER NINE - THE DANCE OF BROK.

Shamanism is undoubtedly the oldest religion in the world, and it still survives, even flourishes, today. How did it all begin? How did ancient man arrive at the ceremony we witnessed in the last chapter? At the time we observed that "christening", Palaeolithic man had already evolved some kind of formal worldview and religious practice. It's possible that to find the roots of the religious impulse, and the moment of the division of the world into spiritual and mundane, we have to travel even further back, into Neanderthal times.

Neanderthal man had no such dichotomy of worldview. For him (and her) the world of hunting, breeding, animals and spirits was one indivisible realm. Perhaps it all began one morning before a hunt. The lads were bragging about how many deer they were going to kill and bring back to the cave. They were ribbing each other, poking fun at each other's hunting prowess. One of the lads, we'll call him Brok, did a little shuffle dance with his spear, stabbing invisible animals. So they all joined in, had a laugh. And perhaps the hunt went well that day. But the week after that – a bad day. No kill. The oldest hunter would have turned to Brok and admonished him, "You didn't do your dance!" Thus a connection is made between the ritual and the result. From then on, the hunters never neglected "The Dance of Brok"!

Or perhaps it was like this...

"Day one. Looked for deer. None came. Shit!" (Or the Palaeolithic equivalent)

"Day two. Cut finger. Jumped around and shouted. Red water fell from finger onto floor of cave. Deer came. Good"

"Day three. Neighbour's boy killed by bison. Neighbour jumped around and shouted. Much red water fell on floor of cave. Looked for deer. Many deer came. Very good. Hmm."

"Day four. Eyeing up neighbour's other son!"

Maybe it happened that way. A run of circumstances that led to a seemingly inescapable conclusion - that some kind of ritual brought good fortune. So, for the first time, some events could perhaps be influenced by prior actions. Ritual is born, propitiatory action is born, meaningful action that influences future events is born. And in the beginning there would be no need to explain this in terms of anything mysterious. There was no concept of a separate world of spirits that had to be appeased or prayed to. It was simply that "The Dance of Brok" made deer come to you. That's all you needed to know. So it would have become a regular ritual.

Inevitably at some point, Brok's Dance may not have been as effective as desired. So the next time it would have been performed with much more vigour, enthusiasm and emotional content, perhaps even with desperation. And if its efficacy was restored, the idea that one had to somehow "pay" for success with proven sincerity, with some kind of sacrifice, would become more popular. Perhaps this is how the idea of offering animal teeth or even a live animal before the hunt (or any important event) was born. And the idea that one had to be emotionally charged in order for a prayer or supplication to be successful.

An observant member of the clan would begin to notice that the hunt was more successful if Brok faced towards the (red) rising sun or wore red paint to represent blood. Perhaps this member was simply more sensitive, could "feel" unseen connections. Thus rituals were formalised and received wisdom appeared. The observant member of the tribe would begin to look for other signs of successful or negative elements of the dance. These would be argued about, adopted or rejected. This would have three effects...

Firstly, the observant clan member would begin to assume the role of spiritual advisor. This would give him social/political clout. Not only would his word and opinion carry more authority but he would almost certainly seek to further enhance his reputation. He would put a mystical spin on anything that happened. Elements of formalised appeasement may now begin to enter other areas of the clan's life, such as trade, childbirth, burials etc. Secondly, certain members of the clan could move in and out of favour if they somehow enhanced or marred the ritual dances and other, developing ceremonies, and by extension affected the prosperity of the clan. Even if the priest or shaman failed in some task, he could blame the failure on the insincerity or the baleful presence of any clan member. This kind of discrimination could lead to social division, could even eventually develop into a kind of caste system! Thirdly, as a cumulative result of the first two effects, we would begin to see the makings of a full blown religion. We can discern an authority figure that shapes and influences the daily life of the clan, not by physical domination, but by claiming to know what actions will bring success or failure to the community. He needn't have had a hundred per cent success rate either, to hold onto his position – he would have enough leeway to receive personal praise or apportion blame to others – he was in a no-lose position. Until challenged – then he would have had to deliver the goods!

At this point, there's still no hint that the world has been divided up into spiritual and material layers. The invisible and the manifest are still seamlessly linked. In fact, there's no concept of spiritual and mundane, there's only the world "out there". Even dreams would be regarded as just another journey, half remembered, half understood perhaps, but not disconnected from normal, everyday life.

I've heard it said that this is the dream of all shamans and mystics – to get back to that primeval unity. I guess in a sense that's fair comment, except that true shamans and mystics already live in that unity. They healed the divide for themselves by making a conscious decision to do so, to live in a world where everything had meaning, a world where a flight of swans meant that someone close had important news, or a world where the way leaves fell onto the pavement offered a clue as to what attitude one should take to the office that day. A world where the failure of the bus to turn up meant that the deity was telling them to contact a friend who needed help. Sounds silly to you? Well, some people see connections and some people don't. I was watching a friend solve a Sudoku puzzle. You have to fill in the blank squares on a grid so they all add up to nine. Or something. No matter how much he explained what he was doing, it was practically supernatural to me!

So being a shaman or mystic doesn't make you any better or worse than anyone else. It's just the way you choose to perceive, to experience the world. No more useful, no sadder that anyone else's reality. No better, no worse. Spirituality and psychic abilities are two separate animals – they can interbreed, and that's a happy birth – but they can develop, or fail to develop, independently.

And by spirituality I suppose I mean two things – firstly, some kind of moral code and secondly, some kind of immersion into something greater than the human world, or some kind of relationship with the divine, the sacred. A secular humanist works with the human world, with ethics and social, educational reform. A psychologist works with the human mind, probing its mysterious drives, seeking to re-programme damaging habits. A shaman works with the invisible world, with spirits, but is very much concerned with concrete results, on getting the job done. Spirituality is something that may grow around their personal experiences, working with ancestors, animal spirits etc. A mystic works with a relationship with a Buddha, God or Goddess, and perhaps develops psychic abilities as a result. Or perhaps they have latent psychic abilities as a child and naturally turn to religion to develop themselves further. And a person that works with ethics, the darker drives of the human mind, psychic abilities and religion, a relationship with the sacred? I guess that's a good enough description of a Tantrist.

At some point in our dim and distant past, during the whole Neanderthal, Palaeolithic transition period, the idea of the supernatural was born, the notion that there was another world, a world of animal spirits and ancestors, which ran parallel with the world of eating, sleeping and breeding. These two worlds could influence each other and the only person that really knew how this worked was the clan's shaman. It's entirely possible that this division of worlds came about solely through the shaman himself. By consolidating the idea of another world, that had to be acknowledged and appeased, the shaman would automatically consolidate his own position and authority. And it was probably the evolution of man, with the evolution of a mind that could hold the concepts of dreams, visions and art, and the evolution of a language that could communicate these concepts, that created the role of the shaman, the invisible world of the shaman and the religious practices of the shaman. In other words, it was getting smarter that created the first "trickster" figure.

The trickster is an ancient role of the shaman. He journeys between the worlds. He communicates visions. He heals sickness. He finds lost objects. He tells where plentiful prey is to be found by the hunters. He predicts future events. BUT. He also conceals his methods and knowledge in a tangled knot of misdirection, deliberate enigma and plain old bullshit! That's his job – to actually do what he's supposed to do for the good of the community, but to also protect the craft, the knowledge, from those that would misuse it (other than himself of course!). Only those that are sincere, are willing to undergo long study, are willing to submit to a painful, potentially lethal, initiation, would gain access to the shaman's inner knowledge and his techniques.

Maybe the ancient God Shiva Himself, often mischievous, always up for a laugh, decided to augment His repertoire from "Howling God of Thunder In The Forest" (though I'm sure He did enjoy that role, and the effect it must have had on mankind way back then) with the whole "God of Animals" routine. Certainly, ancient rock art (age unverified) has been found in Madhya Pradesh, depicting a dancing figure, possibly with a tail, armed with a bow and arrow, wearing the symbol of a horned animal in his hair, and featuring three horizontal stripes across the head. Sounds like Shiva! Maybe He influenced Brok! If so, Brok's account of the meeting would have been interesting! Here's an exclusive interview with the originator of Brok's Dance (patent pending!)

"Ug! Brok confused! Brok wake up on floor of cave not where he lay down to close his eyes in the black time. When Brok open eyes, cave has moved! And scrap of meat Brok had before laying down gone too! Brok ask Woman-belong-Brok but she say she see no meat. Brok ask why Brok wake up other side of cave with blue marks on back and Woman-belong-Brok say maybe a bear came in the black time and moved Brok. Bear also maybe eat Brok's meat. Brok look at her hard but she smile. Brok hold woman. Woman smell like meat! Brok confused.

Brok go for walk. Brok still hot in the head when he think about meat and Woman-belong-Brok. Brok need more meat. No man seen deer for many black times. How Brok get meat?

Brok walk under big trees. Small animals in the sky wave their arms at Brok and say "Caw." Brok know this mean other small animal die somewhere. Maybe Brok find. Brok go under more trees. It get like black time in trees. Brok feel cold inside. This not good.

Then Brok see hole in trees, where sky shows. Not like black time here. Brok see man sitting on ground under trees. Man covered in white earth, like after fire. Man open eyes and look at Brok. Brok feel like many buffalo run at him, very cold inside. Brok shake like cold and Brok feel hair move on head like a big breath from mammoth. Brok hear noise like sticks break in fire. Red water drip from Brok's nose. Ug! Brok confused!

Man say "Hello Brok." Man know Brok? Brok say "Hello, who you?" Man say "I am good for you. That my name." Brok say "Why you good for me?" Man say "I give you meat." Brok say "Where meat?" All this talking make Brok tired. Brok sit down with man.

Man say "I make you find many animals. I have all animals. All animals mine. I make animals run to you. Brok must dance, then animals will come." Brok very tired. Brok want to lay down and close eyes. Brok say "How dance?" Man say "I show you."

Brok open eyes. Brok must have gone black time. Man gone. Brok like man. Brok know how to dance. How did man show Brok? Brok see man dance in Brok's head. Brok carry his name in Brok's head – "Good For You" – that his name. Brok go home to cave and dance. Many animals will come. Woman-belong-Brok will get big! "

Or maybe it didn't happen that way! But Brok's experiences, the auditory hallucinations, the feeling of being "jacked", of having electricity in the body, the revelatory dream, are well documented. Nose bleeds are a traditional shamanic sign of trance or possession. Rock art all over the world shows shamans with nose bleeds. It's a blessing, a sign of encouragement and validation. I'm fortunate in that nosebleeds seem to have passed me by. But all of the above are shamanic symptoms. We'll be taking a closer look at such "ecstatic" states later.

Scientific researchers at the University of California, in San Diego, have apparently been able to isolate what they've called "The God Spot", a part of the human brain that programmes us to perceive and interpret external events and sensory hallucinations as sacred, religious events. In other words, this little gland, or whatever it is, is the root of religion. Ok, let's think about this for a moment. This implies two things, apart from the rather banal interpretation that there's no God, nothing spiritual, nothing beyond the material and that we're all just victims of a glandular imbalance or neurological programming. Not that this banality renders the interpretation invalid. However, two things - firstly, if there is such an organ, it's there for a reason. Until relatively recently, scientists and medical researchers believed that the appendix was an evolutionary dead end. Even its name sounds derogatory, an added on bit, a bit left over. It was felt that modern man had no need of this shrivelled little addition. Now however, it's discovered that the appendix has an important, if not actually crucial, role as part of a support for the immune and lymph systems. That doesn't sound like an evolutionary dead end to me. Perhaps in another fifty years, someone will manage to find out what else "The God Spot" does! Secondly, if the God Spot does what it says on the tin, induces in us a certainty that all sensations are divine or spiritual in origin, then we're actually biologically programmed to be religious, in the same way that we're biologically programmed to eat, sleep and have sex. Cool! I'm not going to fight that kind of momentum! Religion is truly in my DNA? Fine by me. That means that my way of looking at the world has greater human worth for my body/mind complex than that of a materialist.

It's obvious that nature is quite smart – for example, fish that dwell in the stygian depths of the world's oceans, where no sunlight ever penetrates, never develop eyes. They don't need them. When we study natural history it seems that limbs and organs, or the ability to fly or swim, can develop or disappear, quite purposefully. The God Spot is unlikely to be an evolutionary cul-de-sac. We believe in something greater than the material world because we're equipped to!

And it's long been a mystery hasn't it? That after countless thousands of years, after wave after wave of technological advances and scientific discoveries, after materialism and consumerism, and despite all "common sense", the majority of people still choose to believe in the supernatural, something over and above the material world. Maybe it's a longing for meaning that just can't be satisfied by any other means.

And let's not forget – "meaning" is not something that necessarily has to be measured against so-called external reality – mainly because there's no such thing as external reality. Literally everything we perceive, from neutrons to nebulae, is filtered through the human brain. External reality is a consensus perception. And sometimes it changes (unless you still believe the world is flat). There's actually no such animal as love, justice or freedom, yet millions of us try to behave as though these things exist and are important.

Of course, another paradigm, and one that I subscribe to (surprise, surprise!), is that all this mystical, magical, shamanical, tantrical stuff - is real! Deities are real. These kinds of visions and experiences are real. Enlightenment is real. But then I'm a religious being – that's my conditioning. That's how I elect to perceive the world.

So, religion comes from within us, either from part of the human brain or from a long history of attempting to connect cause and effect within human behaviour and within the workings of the natural world. Perhaps both. Either way, religion began in the caves of Neanderthal man, who buried, returned, his dead into the earth and covered the deceased bodies with red ochre, signifying blood. The Neanderthals also left grave gifts of flowers, animal bones and stone tools. Religion developed further with our distant, distant Palaeolithic ancestors, who yearned for plentiful food and a pain free existence, and began to seek such things by means of dance, prayer, dream and trance. Religion began with the hunter-gatherers of old. And one of the oldest Gods of the hunter-gatherers is the Horned One, the God of Animals.

Shiva, the Auspicious One – "Good For You" – has long been associated with other pagan/shamanic deities. One of Shiva's early epithets was Pashupati, Lord of Animals. This is also the title by which many other deities are known, most notably "Kernunnos", the antlered male figure, sitting in a "half lotus" position, surrounded by deer, boar and hounds – and holding a snake – featured on the Gundestrup cauldron from the second century BCE. This wonderful artefact was found in a peat bog in Denmark and gives us an insight into the religion of the Celts/Indo-Europeans. Kernunnos is actually a Roman descriptive term meaning "Horned God". Kernunnos is held to be a God of Animals and the consort of a Mother Goddess. Shiva's evolution ran parallel to this, but which came first I don't know. The Aryan invaders that settled in the Indus Valley in ancient India originally came from that whole Russia/East European area. Shiva Shankara tells me (as I understand it) that His name in an ancient Indo-European tongue is Grithanam, which apparently means The Anointed One. It also holds the connotation of deliberately making something holy, special, set aside from the norm, that which is named as holy. Perhaps you linguistic experts out there can enlighten me a bit more on this one!

The classical yogic types of posture, one of which is depicted on the Gundestrup cauldron, have never been confined to the Indus valley area. Several Native American figurines have been discovered, some dating from a thousand years ago, showing men seated in the classic "half lotus".

Mother Goddess symbols have been discovered all over the ancient world, from The Venus of Willendorf, a very plump, huge breasted babe, to cup, labyrinth and vagina shaped marks on standing stones. The cult of the Goddess is old, old. It probably stems from communities that were leaving behind their hunter-gatherer activities and settling into agriculture and cattle breeding. Fertility and the cycles of nature would have been all-important.

Modern Paganism reveres both a Horned God and a Mother Goddess. In many instances, as in the worship of Shakti, the Mother Goddess is accorded the higher position and the God acts as Her protector, lover and, in some sects, offers Himself in sacrifice at regular intervals, so that the Goddess can be renewed. The holy Feminine, variously called Diana, Athena, Danu,

Morrigan, Isis, Nepthys, Astarte, Hecate, Parvati etc, is associated with nature, fertility, intuition, ecology and wisdom. She can be represented as threefold – maiden, mother, crone, and is held by some to be the spirit of the earth itself. The cult of the Virgin Mary within Christianity is undoubtedly pagan in origin, if not in spirit.

Various Wiccan ("witchcraft" – the craft of the wise) and Pagan groups are everywhere in the modern world, in enormous numbers. They try to keep their social calendar close to nature's rhythms, and divide their year into an eight spoked wheel of celebration, holding meetings at the winter and summer solstices, the vernal and autumnal equinoxes, and the midpoints between – Feb 1st, May 1st, August 1st and of course Halloween, the evening before November 1st. All of these last four ancient dates were eventually taken over by Christianity or by modern western culture. Imbolc (Feb 1st), a ritual of light after the winter solstice, became Candlemass, Beltane (Bright Fire), a celebration of new birth and coming summer, featuring the hanging of may blossom around doorways and windows and an early form of maypole dancing, simply became May Day. Lughnasad, a solar festival for Lugh, God of Light, became Lammas. Samhain (Hallowed Eve - held to be a time when the world of spirits draws very close to ours), and originally a time for slaughtering cattle and inviting ancestors to the feast, became All Saints Day. As camp and materialistic as modern Halloween is, you've got to be a bit of a grouch not to feel a quickening of the blood at this time of year!

I've had the privilege of working closely with many Pagan and Wiccan groups in the past. I was once invited to join a Halloween discussion on ITV Anglia with some witches, some Christians and rather bizarrely, ex-Goon Michael Bentine, who turned out to be intelligent and charming. All these various Pagan groups hold their own take on the Palaeolithic/Pagan/Celtic worldview, and their rites and practices vary, according to their particular paradigm. Many are based on moral ecology and lifestyle, some are not. Paganism and Voudon (Voodoo), originally an African religion, both have strong shamanistic roots, as do the beliefs of the Australian Aborigines and the Balinese. Tibetan Buddhism is permeated throughout by Bon, the pre-Buddhist shamanic tradition of the Himalayas. The animal headed deities of Tantric Buddhism and Hinduism are found in Stone Age sites, in carvings and wall paintings, showing that ancient people fused the essence of animal and human together in a spiritual context way, way back. Both shamans and deities have been depicted this way throughout human history. It's just that, in Buddhism, the symbology got rarefied, the meanings of the symbols became more abstract. But Tantric symbology is very old, as old as the religious impulse itself. Tantra has Stone Age roots.

There are many decent books on Paganism and/or Wicca. It's not relevant to this book's purpose to delve deeper into the subject, so we'll leave it there. Actually, if you walk into your local book store, you'll find loads of books on witchcraft and spells! Not that the majority of these are any good, or even remotely connected with the Pagan movement "proper", but it does show that Christianity, Islam, Buddhism, Sikhism and Hinduism have a serious rival for people's affection. And that people want a "hands on" approach to problem solving. Good job too, as far as I'm concerned. All this variety creates evolution. Variety IS evolution. This is as true for religion as it is for biology.

But why am I banging on about Shamanism? What does it have to do with Tantra? Read on...

CHAPTER TEN - HERBAL HIGHS AND THE SHIVA SHAKES.

How does Shiva make me feel sometimes? I wrote this poem a while ago to try and convey the ecstasy of "possession" and the joy of spiritual companionship, shared spiritual experiences.

"Psalm and sing horses in the blood!
And pound and pulp with mustang pump
And feathered hooves and heartbeats thundering
To churn the earth, the long juice grasses
Down to the water's edge

And gape and shine under the plumed, sun illumined trees
Where sticks and stones and leather drums and ash daubed limbs are stretched
And antique root smoke blows and billows to the wide, swallowing sky
And in the trembling heat, burning herbs boom white serpents to coil and catch
Borders break, bridges open and boundaries crack

We dissolve and swim as footskin smacks the earth
Like ancient water deities in swirling salt sting of ecstasy's surge
Everything is crowned now and rattles tightly for release
From our drum-taut visions fetched
Dipped in sweat of the fevered brow to sing of shapes that bend and bow
Emptied, we are strewn open and shot through with belief afresh"

Tantra is often described as the path of ecstasy. Sounds great doesn't it? And having a sexual element, which is usually promoted at the expense of the rest of the system, Tantra attracts a lot of attention. But actually the ecstasy is a religious one, love of a Buddha, God or Goddess, a dissolving in the deity, not a 24 hour orgasm! And if you spent all day every day in convulsive bliss, how would you function? There's a well known medical condition which causes some women to experience spontaneous orgasms every few minutes. And before you say "lucky cows!" it doesn't sound like much fun. Imagine trying to drive a car or close a business deal on the phone while you're crossing your legs and biting your bottom lip. It would get tired real quick! And if you had orgasms every five minutes, what would you do for fun? Embroidery? Sodoku? You certainly wouldn't want to do anything that involved power tools!

Like you, like the overwhelming majority of mankind, I like to feel good! Much of what I do in my daily life connects with nature. I practice and teach qigong, usually outside. I practice and teach tai chi, usually outside. I sit and meditate, do puja every morning, usually outside. Don't get me wrong, I'm not a big grizzly man of the woods, it's just that all these activities are better when accompanied by fresh air, birdsong, trees and whatever the elements decide to throw at me. I enjoy all my daily routines enormously and I know they do me a lot of good, both mentally and emotionally. So of course I want to help my students feel the same way. I want to empower them and enable them to look after their physical and mental health and be able to heal minor ailments without recourse to drugs or surgery. I want to enhance the quality of their lives. Some want to deepen their intellectual understanding of the art by studying Chinese medical theory, acupuncture points and meridians. Many don't, they just enjoy the practice. Some want to introduce a spiritual element into their daily lives. They take up a study of Buddhism or Daoism, even Ryu Jia (teachings of Confucius). Some don't. A few have even followed my spiritual path, making it their own. Their commitment and trust is touching and inspiring. A few become qigong or tai chi teachers in their own right.

Qigong began by watching animals. The ancient Chinese noticed that if they stretched up their arms and imitated a tree growing or a deer's antlers, it stimulated and toned the liver and gallbladder. They also noticed that some liver complaints tinged the skin a light shade of green. So the element of wood, the deer, the colour green and the spring season all became connected in their minds.

They noticed that if they imitated a bird by waving their arms to the side like a bird in flight, it soothed and balanced the heart (the heart meridian runs down the inside of the arm). They noticed that people who had heart problems had a ruddy complexion and were susceptible to heat. So fire, the colour red, the heart organ and the bird all became connected in their mind.

They noticed that people with stomach complaints often had a brown complexion and their stomachs made a rumbling noise like an earthquake! Patting and stroking the tummy, as you see monkeys do or as you'd pat the ground when planting a shrub or making a sandcastle, seemed to soothe the stomach. So, you guessed it – the colour brown or yellow, the element earth, the stomach and digestive system, the monkey – all got connected!

They noticed that the noise a tiger makes is similar to the noise a person with a sore throat or a breathing problem makes and that bad breathing gives one a pale (white) complexion. The sound is also similar to a metallic rasp. So any move that involves pushing the arms out in front and making a growling or quick exhalation (the martial arts "Hah!") benefits the lungs. And of course, the tiger, the colour white, the metal element, the lungs, all became connected in the mind of the ancients.

Lastly, they noticed that if they imitated the hunched forward, rolling gait of a bear, it seemed to ease the lower back and stimulate the kidneys. People with kidney problems often have a dark complexion and are very susceptible to cold. So of course, winter, kidneys, the bear, the colour black – yep! You guessed!

Thus was born the Chinese Five Element theory. Sounds primitive and simplistic doesn't it? And yet this simple pattern of connections, together with the yin/yang theory, underpins all of Chinese Traditional Medicine (TCM). And as we're beginning to discover, there's no system so sophisticated, so efficient at curing just about every ailment known to mankind. From observing animals and connecting with nature, the complex TCM system evolved over thousands of years. Humble beginnings, a basic human urge to make connections, the same basic urge that arranges stars into named constellations, and we end up with something that benefits millions of suffering people every day.

We'll examine in a later chapter, this theme of observing natural phenomena and building up a library of information based on the observations...

(It's a shame that most people don't learn to draw lines, join the dots, between their actions and the consequences!)

So - every qigong form I learn, practice and teach is based on animals and the elements. And of course the Chinese martial arts are famous for their Tiger styles, their Crane styles, even their Dragon styles. Animal movements permeate virtually all of Chinese kung fu. It's all based on nature. That's why it's good for you and though sometimes dismissed as "flowery" by advocates of harder styles, the fact is that the world is full of seventy and eighty year old kung fu and tai chi players. Rather more of those than OAP karate and taekwando practitioners. Now, before you think I'm being partisan here, there's nothing wrong with any style of martial art. You practice whatever style you like for whatever reason. Just make sure it's one that's not going to damage your health later. If you can do at sixty what you were doing at thirty (in martial arts that is!), something's working. If not, better examine your practice!

I spoke in my last book (buy it, it's cool) about Spontaneous Qigong, where we let the body heal itself through natural movements. Watching people do this in class sometimes reminds me of tribal dancing, shamanic movements, animal shapes. There's great wisdom in the body if we let it express itself. Our physical body is still part of nature, subject to the same laws and appetites as wolves, eagles and stags. We have to connect with nature regularly to stay healthy in body and mind. Artificial light, recycled air, junk food, none of this is good for us.

Sometimes we just need to let the body free. I saw a fascinating documentary on TV recently. David Kramer, a South African musician, was touring the old townships of the Karoo area, looking for musicians that still played traditional music on their cigar box guitars and fiddles. Of course, these old players were wonderful, and the programme resulted in a triumphant concert finale. But what I found just as interesting was the dancing. When these musicians were playing, men and women would break into spontaneous dance, the women performing a strange mutation of colonial ballroom dancing and the men crouching in what looked like ancient tribal animal postures. It was great to watch so I just had to have a go! Later that night, lights out, clothes off, stereo slammin' some heavy tribal and me throwing some weird creature shapes. It was very enjoyable. I'm not as young as I used to be so I couldn't keep it up for too long (ooh matron!) and I probably looked a total dickhead but it was fun and I recommend it!

And nature is a great teacher. Any gardener can identify with impermanence, the Buddhist theme of death and renewal, and the notion that nothing stays the same. And that what affects one part of the garden will affect the overall look of the whole area. And that if you don't prune or feed plants they'll either die or crowd out everything else. That's karma! Nowhere is the link between deed and consequence so clearly perceived than in the world of gardening!

There's great wisdom to be cultivated from within our minds too, buried deep in the collective unconscious, expressed in ancient symbols, in dreams, meditation visions, even trance. Being able to access this wisdom often involves an altered state of consciousness. This altered state can either be entered spontaneously, naturally, or be precipitated by drugs, drumming, dancing, chanting, sense deprivation etc. It's often a whole body/mind experience.

The word ecstasy means "to stand outside oneself" and describes perfectly that expanded awareness feeling, the feeling that any boundaries between one's narrow sense of identity, between one's narrow sense of perception and the rest of the living universe, are dissolving.

Ecstatic states, shamanic trances, meditative experiences, these all belong to the sambhogakaya, the shared bliss realm. But "shared bliss" is a bit misleading. The pathways within the sambhogakaya can go up and down. There are hell states as well as paradise realms. Beyond the sambhogakaya is the dharmakaya, the formless, the void. And of course, our "normal" material, rational world, that's the nirmanakaya, the illusion realm, maya. It's not my intention here to further promote the idea of ecstatic states as the be-all and end-all, the main purpose of Tantric practice. But they do occur. Any activity, be it gardening, bungee-jumping, playing the guitar or religious devotion, will bring you transcendent moments, peak experiences once in a while.

For example, I was teaching qigong at a monthly seminar in Cambridge. It was early autumn and very warm so we were all out in a park by a cricket field. We were gathered in a circle, only about half a dozen of us, performing some simple exercises that, by dint of familiarity, didn't require much concentration on my part. I was free to just enjoy the sensations within my body.

There was a really strong wind blowing, but hot, really hot, like the heat you get from an open oven. It was gusting, blowing round and round, changing direction all the time. It was picking up dry, golden leaves from the grass and swirling them around our feet, in our faces. There was a gorgeous, burnt toffee smell from the surrounding poplar trees, gently baking in the hot wind and sunshine. Overhead, giant clouds banged around like drunken albino mammoths in a glaring blue sky. It was a wonderful setting and I was feeling good being there, breathing, moving my body gently.

But the intensity of feeling grew and grew. It seemed I was growing, expanding, getting higher, thirty feet tall, yet the trees around me grew too, so although everything looked the same, it felt very different. Then it began to look different too. I felt myself dissolve. The people I was with became tall columns of gold and green energy, like whirlwinds. We were giants! The toffee smell filled my head and I could hear the wind roaring and crackling. I felt out of my body, part of the enormous vortex of warm, scented, humming energy gusting round and round. There seemed to be no boundaries between me, the other people, the trees, the wind, everything. It was wonderful!

The whole experience, brought on, no doubt, by deep relaxation, breathing, collective energy and the environment, lasted only about half a minute but it was very intense, and will stay with me as long as I live. It was like a glimpse of heaven!

In a way you could describe this as a spiritual experience. It certainly took me out of the normal perceptual framework. But though the whole thing was very pleasant and certainly encouraged me to continue with my practice, these kinds of experiences are not the goal of qigong.

My burgeoning relationship with Shiva has led me into some interesting places. And I want to emphasise that I'm definitely not the "trance and ecstasy" type. I took Buddhist precepts (even kept a few!) so I don't take drugs, I don't drink, I like to be in control of my faculties. So of course Shiva loves to loosen me up a little. It amuses Him and it does me good not to be so anally retentive about things! And despite the enormous efficacy and lure of psychedelic drugs, (some people actually need to take them but I'm not one of them, and you didn't hear this endorsement from me!), they're not the only gateway to other realms.

Here's an experience I had a couple of weeks ago...

"Early morning. Training over. Time to relax. Normally I meditate first and then say my prayers afterwards, kow tow to the Buddha, the deities, all my teachers, the martial arts ancestors. But today, on a whim, I decide to do it the other way round. Nothing like a change of routine to keep things fresh. So I squat in the garden, make puja, touching the earth, touching my forehead. Some mud sticks to my fingers, to my face. I don't think about wiping it off. Bowing to Shiva and offering incense, I say my prayers, make my confessions. Then I sit down in meditation and still my mind.

I create a space within me, a space that Shiva can fill if He so desires. Then I wait. Just wait. It's an easy way to meditate! After a while, I feel Him near. He stands in front of me, grinning. He's naked and covered in mud and ash, his hair a terrible knot of swinging tangles. A real jungle man. He starts to sway back and forth, starts to weave, starts a dance. It doesn't seem very elegant, more primitive, more tribal than classical Indian, but on the other hand, it gets so powerful and His movements so quick that I can't really see what He's doing. He stamps and turns, digs His feet into the ground. He kicks up great clouds of dust. Soon, I'm as covered in a filthy grey film, just as He is! He looks down at me, as if inspecting His work. Then He squats down, gets right in my face. "Now you're the Destroyer too!" He whispers and grins as He says it.

I lick my dry, dust-encrusted lips. I'm a bit nervous, ok? I say "Lord." He moves towards me, chest to chest, skin to skin. I can feel His heat. I'm not sure if it feels confrontational, threatening or reassuring. It's certainly intimate. He moves into me, through me. My whole body shakes. It's weird. Then He's standing in front of me again. "Lord." I repeat. He moves into me, through me. I shake. Three times in all this happens.

"What should I be doing?" I ask. He bares His teeth again, amused. "Destroy!" "But what should I destroy?" I start to ask, then realise the obvious answer is to start with myself, my ego, my doubt, my fear, my arrogance. I look up. Shiva is retreating into the distance.

I sit in meditation. The shaking subsides. Just my legs twitch. Eventually I get up and stretch. I dust myself off, wipe the mud from my forehead. I feel energised by my experience. My chest feels bigger. My legs ache. I feel very warm. Time for a coffee!"

Shiva, and indeed any Tantric deity, brings ecstasy, encourages abandonment of the ego control. The whole point of Tantra is to be able to dissolve one's narrow consciousness into that of the deity. It's the same as realising one's Buddha nature. The methods are slightly different though. Instead of meditation, introspective reflection, Tantrists use highly charged emotional devotion, absorption into mantras, yantras and mandalas, sex yoga, ecstatic dancing and yes – drugs.

I'm not going to advocate the use of cannabis, the holy sacrament that Shiva loves (as do many millions of His adherents and many millions more who couldn't give a toss about Him!) but I'm not going to condemn it either. I don't think it's any worse than alcohol, in fact I think alcohol's more injurious in the long run. So I leave it up to you. If you really, really want to use "artificial" stimulants, you might be better off buying a magazine like the weird and wonderful Fortean Times, a collection of UFO and similar X Files phenomena from around the world. As well as an amusing read, whether you believe in such stuff or not, the magazine contains lots of ads for legal "herbal highs", lawful substitutes for the wacky weed. You can buy online too. But these concoctions are more likely to give you a mellow buzz than full blown hallucinatory states. You can buy what are advertised as legal hallucinogens online but how safe they are, how effective they are, how helpful they'll prove in the long run, I can't say, I leave it all up to you. If you're lucky enough to live near a field where "magic mushrooms" are found, good for you but if you don't know what they look like, and you haven't tried them before, you'd better be very sure of what you're ingesting.

One of the links between Tantra and Shamanism, Stone Age religion, is that in some ways, the Tantrist has to become his or her own shaman. They have to be able to take long journeys into their inner landscape. They have to map out their spiritual terrain, the contours and geography of which are revealed in dream, vision and meditation. And like any landscape, some parts are pleasant, some are ugly, even hazardous. They have to seek out, encounter, engage, assimilate and transform all the monsters of the psyche, just as the shaman would seek and experience spiritual encounters with wild animals. All the classic Tantric techniques such as mantra, yantra and mandala, bring about these shamanic experiences. And many shamans, those Tantrists that practice Kundalini Yoga, and some practitioners of esoteric Daoist Qigong too – they all hold a belief that energy must be cultivated, led up the spine to the head, where it manifests as spiritual power. Sometimes in meditation I feel as if my hair is three feet long and blowing straight upwards, as if jumping from a building. It's the energy coming up the spine. In reality my hair is so short (not much left of it either!) that it wouldn't look any different if you hung me upside down!

Shamans often talk about travelling, being pulled by "ropes", either up into the sky, or deep underground to caves and rivers, where they undergo intense, sometimes painful, spiritual encounters. These shining ropes are everywhere. And sometimes one can see them between living beings too – connecting everything with thin, shimmering ribbons of light. These innumerable strands connect and bind all life forms together. They also lead to what I can only rather crassly term "other dimensions".

Tantra means "that which is woven".

There's one more comparison to be drawn between the Shaman and the Tantrist. The shaman still carries out many traditional activities for his or her community – finding lost objects, affecting the weather, curing sickness, acting as officiator at rituals – but modern advances in medicine, technology and psychology have rendered most of these activities redundant for would-be shamans, especially in the west. So modern-day urban shamans perforce have to reorientate towards another goal, realign their energies. Like the Tantrist they now seek inner change, not external influence on other people, or on the environment. The altering of consciousness becomes an end in itself. The aim is now to use the energies of the sambhogakaya, dreamtime, the world of spirits and ancestors, the world of myth, of Gods and Goddesses, to achieve the dharmakaya, a dwelling in non-dualistic consciousness, spiritual unity, enlightenment.

So I guess that's the main difference between the Tantrist and the traditional shaman, and this is a bit of a generalisation, so apologies in advance. The former has his or her sights set on a religious goal, union with the deity or realisation of Buddha-nature. Any sambhogakaya activity – trance, visions, psychic ability, other-worldly powers (siddhi) – are incidental. They may well be employed in the spiritual pursuit, they may well prove helpful to others, but they are not ends in themselves. The shaman, on the other hand, deliberately seeks knowledge, power and practical application. Any spiritual insight is incidental to the shaman's role. So the symbology, the language used, the methodology, the techniques employed, may well be very similar – it's all consciousness engineering – but the goal of the shaman and the goal of the Tantrist are not the same.

And without a parallel moral training, the danger for the Tantrist beginning to develop siddhi is not just that he or she may get lost in the excitement of psychic experiences, as addictive and as double-edged as any drug, but that he or she may suffer a karmic kickback from unskilful actions, a selfish attitude and self aggrandizement. Shiva sometimes makes me pay for experiences and initiations with a real come-down. And that teaches me to stay humble and keep in mind what the goal is – Shiva Tattva, not Shiva Siddhi. Awesome powers are incidental, even irrelevant, to the main aim, a conscious one-ness with all life everywhere.

For example...

It was a grey and misty autumn morning. Incense smoke curled lazily in the still air, smearing shrubs and the low hanging branches of trees as it ascended. I sat, quite lazily too, in meditation. I was tired, stiff and aching from training, but very relaxed. Suddenly I felt the presence of a female sitting close by, in front of me, with her back to me. She was meditating too. Embarrassingly I was filled with lust, but not the hot, burning kind. This was cooler, and I hate to use the word, more spiritual. It somehow fitted in with the meditation, felt relevant. By an act of will I turned her body round and she sat astride me. We were both naked. We united in yab/yum, Tantric unity. My cock felt cool in her, slightly tingling. The "erection" wasn't throbbing, and it didn't need any thought or involvement from me. It just felt solid and extended, almost electric, but just faintly pulsing. It didn't manifest as a physical erection.

I hope this doesn't sound like psychic rape. It didn't feel that way.

I felt my body change. I became an emanation of Shiva I hadn't seen before. My skin was black and I could feel heavy snakes coiled around my neck. I could feel countless arms coming from my body, waving beside me. We were in a place of darkness. My back felt very straight. There was hardly any sound, just a low noise like the wind under a door. The closest I'd seen to this form of Shiva was images of Hevajra (see earlier chapter, High Voltage Deities), but I could feel the wet smear of three horizontal stripes across my forehead. This was definitely Shiva! I sat there for a few minutes, glorying in the feel of energy pouring through my body and the effortless, almost non-sexual connection with the female. She'd turned very dark in colour too and had her face turned towards me. I didn't have to do anything except enjoy it all.

Gradually the feeling and the visuals ebbed away. Just as suddenly as my experience had given me ecstasy, I was filled with a terrible sense of anti-climax and all my old doubts and fears came flooding in. As soon as Shiva left, my ego gave me a real hammering. "Who do you think you are?" "What do you really think you've accomplished?" "Look at you. All these years and you haven't improved yourself at all!" "Your practice has left all your hindrances intact!" You've done nothing!"

I sat on the damp shingle feeling utterly wretched.

Of course, both inner states could be dismissed as ephemeral, transient. Or I can pick one as being more "real" than the other. Or I can simply believe that you can't have a "high" without a "low", like a hangover the morning after a wonderful party. Or I can just get up and have breakfast. Another day in the life of a council house mystic!

What it amounts to is that I can hold a little bit of Shiva more or less constantly during the day but a bigger charge, enough to trigger off these experiences, being put into my body, opens me up too much, and when He departs, my body can't retain the charge, it all leaks away, leaving me flatter than normal. I'm very sorry, this is my failing and obviously something I need to work on.

And incidentally I now deliberately "feel", psychically draw, those three white lines across my forehead when I'm doing any kind of spiritual work. It protects me, brands me as one of Shiva's creatures as a warning to other-worldly predators (I'll explain that in a mo) and it acts as a mental focus, stops me getting too lost in the experience.

I'm reluctant to say too much about the dangers of spiritual work because I've always been well protected, so my experience of psychic peril is limited. But any sambhogakaya activity can be potentially dangerous or harmful, even if it just results in a false impression of one's ability. There are predators and deceivers in all realms of existence. And some of them may be of your creation! Even the Buddha had to deal with Mara the Tempter on many occasions. I think an ongoing moral training and a prayer before any kind of meditation, shadow work, visualisation, ritual etc helps enormously to keep psychic sharks and leeches at bay. Somehow it cleans up the surrounding area, like putting shark deterrent in the water before you jump in, but there's no defence against plain old human stupidity, so be warned! Stay humble, say your prayers, always be grateful for any insights and you won't go far wrong. In fact, that's how you know if the experience is genuine, as opposed to self-deceiving or orchestrated by some entity who may not have your best interests at heart – there should be an insight, you should understand some thing a bit more clearly than before, you might even have information or abilities you didn't have before. But if it was just a nice (or nasty) experience, take note. If that's all you're getting, it's time to try something else. Don't get big headed, don't think you're special. The world is full of people that can do stuff that you can't. And just because your path is a spiritual one, it doesn't make you "special".

I don't want to finish this chapter on a negative note so let me add this. I respect and applaud anyone who's making an effort to improve themselves, transcend this mean ol' world and move closer to divinity. Sometimes the path is very rewarding, even fun. Sometimes it's hard, lonely and disillusioning. But just persevere. If you have a spiritual calling – follow it!

CHAPTER ELEVEN - SHINING WEBS OF LIGHT.

In which we pick up the stick of speculative imagination and poke around at the seemingly unrelated subjects of dark matter, DNA and the serpent power known as Kundalini Yoga.

Get into the countryside, away from the glare of the street lights one night, if you can, and take a look up into the night sky. Isn't it mind blowing? All those stars. All those possible planets, some maybe even playing host to other life forms. And the distances – we can't even comprehend something that's a million light years away – that's a million years of travelling at the speed of light. That's beyond a long way away! And this incredibly strange, inconceivably enormous universe of ours, beyond distance, beyond imagination, spreads itself over our heads like a vast shining web of light.
How much is there still to be discovered about this incredible web? We know next to nothing...

Scientists can't account for 95 per cent of the known universe. They know it's all out there somewhere, all the unfound mass, the residue of their "big bang". But their instruments can't find it. They call this unaccounted for material "dark matter". Let's think about that for a moment. That's 95 per cent of the KNOWN universe that science knows NOTHING about! So how big is the unknown universe, the bits they don't even know they're ignorant of?

From one extreme to the other - from the inconceivably vast, to something so tiny that each individual human cell carries over TWO METRES of it. I'm talking about DNA, the genetic Rubik's Cube inside us. Scientists can't unravel 95 per cent of DNA's code. So they arrogantly call this 95 per cent "junk DNA"! So it's our evolutionary "dark matter", is it? They think maybe it's an evolutionary left over, a redundant carrier of the DNA material. What? Ninety five per cent redundant material? Doesn't sound likely, does it? It's far more likely that this overwhelming majority of DNA material (which scientists admit IS a code) carries the blueprint for all life everywhere, from every time. And that it's the five per cent code that makes us men, monkeys or marigolds.

So let's think about that as well, for a moment. It's possible that we carry inside, together with all life forms everywhere, the entire history of all life! It seems even more likely that DNA itself is actually the primal life form, which accretes around itself a variety of physical vehicles. And, from the ancients' and the mystics' point of view, it's consciousness that accretes DNA around itself in order to achieve concrete form. The soul, spirit or consciousness of all life forms has an infinite variety of choice – it's only karma or some special kind of spiritual power that "selects" the body-to-be.

In other words, it's pure consciousness, impelled by karma, that selects its DNA "hard wiring" for an incarnation as a leopard, a lizard or a Londoner.

What's even more exciting is that this implies that all life, everywhere, carries all life everywhere. We all carry the entire history of dinosaurs, fish, cave men, crocodiles, the Masai, birds, big cats, Vikings, pandas and all shamans everywhere, deep inside us. We're indeed a microcosm of the whole history of the universe.

And this in turn implies that all this knowledge within us is maybe accessible to those that can unlock the code. And it's not likely to be the scientists, at least for a while. It's far more likely that the shamans and the mystics are the code breakers – and that they've been doing it for countless centuries!

Many religious, shamanic and magical traditions from many different cultures, from many different time periods, talk of the serpent (shudder!) as a holder and guardian of wisdom. And our DNA, the double helix, is often compared to twin serpents. The esoteric Hindu yoga called Kundalini also uses serpentine symbology. It may well be that Kundalini Yoga is an analogy for accessing the DNA coded knowledge within us.

And that's another reason to be careful – serpents, dragons, "aliens" – not one of these creatures, or any system that employs such symbology, or is connected with such powerful and unsettling guardians, is likely to be without its pitfalls, is it? The consciousness of such creatures is closer to our reptilian brain than any other part of us, which, if allowed to resonate within us too strongly, makes us susceptible to negative forces such as selfish abuse of power, racism, territoralism and sexual predation. This applies even to Kundalini, in fact even more so, as it's usually presented as a highly spiritual practice. It is. But it's not without its dangers. Serpents and dragons indeed guard great insights, but can also threaten to devour the unwary, or pull them off their path, destroy their orientation.

Another way to describe Kundalini Yoga is bringing an awareness to various parts of our psyche so that we can work with the energies and obstacles we find there. Each successful integration will enable us to move on to other psychic stations, other inner knots.

So what is Kundalini Yoga? Baldly put, it's causing our internal energy, call it qi, prana, what you will, to ascend an inner channel that runs up the spine. As the energy rises, it encounters energy vortices called chakras (wheels), which store and process various elements of our emotional and spiritual being. A successful ascension (and this process can take years) results in the energy flooding up into our head and bringing about spiritual illumination.

Another way to look at the chakras is as knots, neural clots that slow down the energy rushing around the body and hold various aspects of our psyche in relative stillness. They level energy out, keep things on an even keel most of the time. A bit like locks in a canal network.

There are many chakras throughout the human body but for the purpose of spiritual awakening through Kundalini Yoga there are seven major vortices which are employed. These will be described individually as we reach them in this chapter. To the inner eye, the chakras look like shining, spinning webs of light. Long tradition has assigned many attributes to each chakra - colour, guardian deities, sacred sounds etc, but actually they mostly just look like lightwheels, similar to each other, at various points along the spine. Various sources will cite different colours for each chakra. Remember that, contrary to traditional depictions, chakras don't actually look like coloured lotus flowers. And that their appearance is affected by the other energies of the body. However, the attributes are useful in visualisation, so I'll stick to the colourings generally employed by the majority of texts.

(Someone asked me why, if the chakras have no colour, do they see colours when they look at people's inner bodies? Good question. Well, the best way I can answer that is to say that the colour red, for example, is the closest vibration to the pulse of the base chakra. The colour orange is the closest vibration to the pulse of the sex chakra. But the chakras themselves are not coloured little lotus flowers inside us. Their rate of vibration is interpreted by some people as various colours, by others as various sounds. I'm sure really advanced masters can attribute various smells to them as well! Also the human aura, which can display as various colours, can shade or tint the chakras, especially the "higher" ones. And if you look at a lot of modern chakra charts, you'll notice that the colours just follow the rainbow sequence, from red through to violet. Sorry, but it's not that simplistic.)

Another way to look at this question of colour is to think of a metal rod. Its natural colour is grey. When it's heated however, the metal glows and changes colour. But we always describe this new state as red hot, never just "red", because we know that red isn't its natural, "proper" colour. Same with the chakras – they may appear to have different colours when given the "heat" of our attention, but in fact they're all roughly the same colour – white(ish) light.

Kundalini means "coiled up" and it's held to be the name of the Goddess Kali Herself, in the form of a snake. So it's believed by Tantrists and Yogis that we all have this deity dwelling within us, like a coiled up serpent at the base of the spine, waiting to be roused and then coaxed up through the body, awakening our spirituality as She ascends. Kali means the Dark One, and She represents the devouring nature of time itself. She also holds all knowledge, past present and future, just as our serpentine DNA contains the code of all life. Most of all the time Kali slumbers, undisturbed by our worldly activities. We have to first awaken Her before our psycho-spiritual Indian rope trick can begin.

A reader of my last book (buy it, it's cool!) asked why I made the whole Kundalini Yoga thing sound so unpleasant. "I thought it was supposed to be a spiritual experience!" Well, it is a spiritual experience, or at least a spiritual undertaking, and the word "spiritual" means "of the spirit", "pertaining to the spirit". It doesn't mean "lovely", "pleasant". Not all spiritual work is heavenly or blissful. In fact a lot of it isn't. Just as it's nice to be able to play the guitar or perform Taiji adequately, it's impossible to learn to do those things without patient persistence, sore fingers or legs and a little bit of suffering. And it's not that the whole of the Kundalini Yoga process needs to be horrendous, just that there are pitfalls to be aware of. A lot of those writing about Kundalini, and I'm not making any claims about my own achievements, are either deluded, have never undergone any real work, or have forgotten how difficult some of it was.

Anyway, back to work...

The way to encourage the Goddess to wake up is to begin work on the first chakra, which lies between the genitals and the anus, right at the bottom of the spine. I've given all this stuff a lot more space in The Real Rasa book but I guess it's worth going over again – it's a fundamental practice.

So let's begin with the base chakra. It's called muladhara, which means "holding (or supporting) root". Sit in meditation, say a prayer to your favourite God, Goddess or Buddha and allow the mind to settle. Hear the sound of the seed syllable "larng" in your mind. Now try to feel the chakra, like a small electric fan wheel, red in colour, spinning inside you, about an inch above the anus, two inches inside the body. This is your floor, your ground level. Try to put energy into this location. This sacrifice of energy is like spilling blood on the floor of a hut. The Kali serpent will smell this and eventually begin to uncoil Herself, probing upwards until she unwinds her head into your root chakra.

Low level devotees of the Dark Mother (and most producers of movies!) never get beyond this point. They simply believe that Kali wants real blood sacrifice, and in their folly they're eager to oblige. This is of course bad karma, and binds "mother" and "child" together in an unhealthy relationship. Ultimately Kali will look after Her own and each devotee will achieve union with Her – but not until they've burned off all the bad karma incurred by their ignorant and violent misunderstanding.

To cause Kali to wake up is the beginning of an epic process, a journey that can take years and include various, sometimes quite severe, physical and emotional afflictions on the way. So it's not something to undertake lightly. The speed at which Kali ascends and the amount of suffering (or lack of it) caused by Her tearing and biting Her way through your psychic nerve network depends entirely on how much work you've done on yourself. I wrote in the last book about the correlation between chakra work and shadow work, and nothing has happened to change my opinion – the more readily one accepts, assimilates and transcends "unworthy" or "negative" elements and energies within one's psyche, the easier the whole process will prove.

And how do we do that? Well, the best way is to wait for a reaction – you shouldn't have to wait too long – life is very obliging that way! Sooner or later, someone or something will upset you. The stronger the reaction, the better, it gives you more to work with. So let's take an extreme example. Let's say you read about a rapist in the daily newspaper. This person has subjected an innocent woman to a long, degrading and painful ordeal. The newspaper, whilst making all the right sanctimonious noises, will print as much unsavoury detail as they can prise or surmise from the police and other sources. An extremely unflattering, possibly doctored, photograph will fuel your indignation more. After all, it's the ability to make you tut and cluck that sells newspapers...

Ok. A quick aside here, which I shouldn't have to make, but feel obliged to. Rape isn't pretty. It's not sexy. It's an event which, even if over quite quickly, leaves a horrible legacy of self loathing, guilt, anger and lack of confidence. And that's without the physical pain, the humiliation of being raped, reporting it, being questioned, perhaps appearing in court, being further humiliated by media coverage. It's damaging, it's a violent intrusion – and actually, there's never an excuse for it. I can understand any man feeling angry and used if he's led on and then rejected. I can understand, though not condone, a man expressing himself negatively, violently. But rape is another animal. With violence, it's possible to hit someone and then feel remorse. In a rape situation, a man has the opportunity to stop at any point – but usually doesn't. Rape is deliberate. That's why it's obscene. That's why it carries such a heavy legal penalty and such a moral charge. That's also why it's obscene to "cry rape" when no rape has occurred.

That said, let's get back to the subject of shadow work - recognising, accepting, assimilating and transcending any negative elements and energies within the psyche. When we've finished reading the rape report in the newspaper, finished tutting and clucking and feeling morally superior to this lecherous animal, let's turn that white hot attention back onto ourselves. Firstly, when you read the whole article, and came to the part that dealt specifically with the actual attack, you read that twice – slowly. I watched you, so don't deny it! Did you know you did that? I think it turned you on. If not sexually, then it gave you an emotional charge, made you feel like you'd like to smash this bloke's face in – or his testicles. Don't give me that look! Yes, I know you're a decent person, and you'd never do anything like this horrific assault, but you read that part of the report twice – and enjoyed it. You were disappointed there was no photograph of the victim. You wanted to see what she looked like. Why? To see if you'd "give her one"? To see if she looked like she deserved it?

Of course, it's natural to feel outraged to read about such an upsetting incident, but the measure of your loathing and indignation is probably in direct proportion to your propensity for rape. Didn't like that, did you? Don't pretend you wouldn't like to have read more about it – in much greater salacious detail. Most people enjoy reading something saucy. Don't pretend you've never had a fantasy about forcing yourself on a woman. Or maybe it's the thought of punishing the offender that gets you excited. You'd show that bastard! Which makes you as violent, as mindlessly savage, as him. Forcing a woman into an unwanted dry hump, for whatever reason, is wrong. Savagely attacking a man, kicking his groin, stamping on his head, for whatever reason, is wrong. I understand why you'd want to – but it's wrong. Just wrong. So your fantasy is no different. It's just another nasty sexual assault.

Suddenly you and the rapist are brothers in darkness. Not a nice thought eh?

Rather than run the risk of pissing you off further, I'll cut to the chase. I'm sure you'd never want to hurt a woman in real life but actually it's ok to have the fantasy. We all have dark thoughts, whether fuelled by the rape or the imagined revenge, but we don't have to act on them. Those that do act on them deserve legal redress, but the only thing that separates the rapist and those that read about his actions is that the rapist allows the dark thoughts to manifest as physical action. The rest of us are content with the fantasy – or we masturbate, or we find a consenting adult to play a little rape game with us.

But the same dark forces that drove that rapist to attack his victim, live in us too. Something in us is horribly titillated by the report, is stirred. Our moral outrage isn't pure, it's coloured by our own propensity for lust and violence.

So we have to look at these dark stirrings, admit we could possibly get turned on by the thought of violent, non-consensual sex, by the humiliation of women, by the torture of a man we've never met. Then we can start to bring these dark thoughts into the light of day. The more we think about our base nature consciously, the less influence it can exert on our unconscious mind. So the next time we read about a rape, we may actually think, "Oh, the poor girl! And what on earth drove that poor man to do such a stupid thing?" without the awful, hateful unspoken subtext.

And this scenario works just as well if it's a woman reading the newspaper report. Subconscious propensities for violent sex and for hateful, mindless condemnation of those who offend us, are not restricted to the male of the species.

So what I'm saying is that anything or anyone that provokes a strong reaction within you, is showing you your shadow side. And the more utterly ridiculous and obscene it seems that you could share any of this person's characteristics – the more likely it is to be true! So one needs to nurture a special kind of awareness to be constantly on the lookout for shadow material. And often, it's enough to acknowledge our imperfections, our ignoble attributes, for them to start to lose their power over us.

Ok, back to Kundalini Yoga. I'm very aware that this chapter has dealt exclusively, so far, with the more negative elements of Kundalini Yoga practice. I'll try to address that balance at the end.

And it's worth noting that spiritual illumination, enlightenment, doesn't depend on Kundalini Yoga – which is just another sadhana (method). Having said that, personal liberation is very bound up with shadow work in its many variations – of which Kundalini Yoga is one.

So let's assume you're sitting in meditation regularly, focusing on your root chakra, flooding that area with awareness and energy. Sooner or later Kali will sniff blood and spill out from Her dark hiding place onto the floor of the hut – your ground level. Congrats! You've got Her moving. Now what have you got to look forward to? A hut full of mud, blood and muck and a mad bitch Goddess in the form of a snake boiling on your floor, sniffing around in your psyche! And the root chakra, the aspect of your inner self that she's going to start snapping at and trying to gnaw through is your material world and your most basic, animal fears. Oh whoopee! Remember too that Kali is the Goddess of time - She knows everything you've ever done, every little trick that's guaranteed to give you a tic! Any impurity, any resistance in your root chakra, in other words anything you haven't dealt with pertaining to your material world, your physical being, your fears and the things that cause you to lose reason and lash out at others – that's Her food, the Dark Devourer's pickings. Depending on the inner work you've undertaken, there'll either be an unholy feast and various afflictions ranging from self destructive tendencies, insecurity, depression, leg, bowel and back problems, emotional paralysis and nightmares, OR.. the serpent will move onward and upward, looking for richer pickings.

Yep, I know. Don't I make it sound like fun? It's not usually that bad though, but I can't emphasise enough how greatly your preparatory work will influence your experiences in this kind of yoga.

The root chakra is our animal nature and it's not negative at all, we need most of its energy and wisdom. But Kali will attack your sense of fight or flight, your sense of material worth, your decision making abilities, the things that most make you feel grounded. The base chakra is also related to long term memories, childhood events, traumas. Any weaknesses or problem areas give Her more to sink Her teeth into. The thicker the knots

She has to bite through to ascend further, the more food for Her, the more pain for you!

So what can you do as preparatory work? Well, before flooding the various chakras with energy in a concerted effort to awaken the Goddess, it's a good idea to launch a twofold pre-emptive defence. Firstly, keep a journal. Note down in this journal the various attributes of the chakras, the aspects of your life that they're related to. That way you won't be so surprised when these areas of your world start to get a bit shaky. Become familiar with the likely effect of energising and untying each chakra knot. And you can start to look at these areas of your life right now, engage in a little shadow work. If you can overcome some of your unconscious aversions and addictions now, there's going to be less of a hymen for Kali to tear Herself through. Every little helps. And with shadow work, it builds up its own momentum, becomes more habitual, even addictive (oops!). And if you do enough shadow work, you might not have to, or even want to, undertake Kundalini Yoga at all.

Secondly, you can perform preparatory cleansings of each chakra. Spend a little time a couple of times a week just gently "feeling" the various chakras, getting to know where they are and mentally bathing them in white light. Contrary to the information you may find on various websites, I always advocate starting with the root chakra, not the heart or the crown centre. Some schools believe that beginning with the heart chakra will balance those above and below it. It won't. It'll just distort your heart chakra! The clue here is in the name of the base chakra – muladhara – the supporting root. Trees, plants, buildings etc all begin with a root or a foundation, then they grow upwards. This is nature's way – so follow it...

Bathing your chakras in white lights sounds a bit new agey I know, but it helps as a gentle preamble to Kundalini Yoga and it also empowers the chakras to send their own messages to you, offer up clues as to which issues need addressing in your life. You can try putting your attention into various chakras (and do this in the right order, please) and wait to see if any thoughts, insights, ideas come up. You can even ask questions of your chakras – ie of that part of your psyche. For example, a question regarding your career or a relationship may receive different answers from different chakras. Then you can obtain a balanced view from your "chakra committee". This is a whole new chakra yoga I haven't seen in any other books, so that's my free gift to you.

Talking to one's chakras! For fucksake! But it does work.

When things get a bit too much during the period of time you're practicing Kundalini Yoga, there are two ways to facilitate a smoother, more positive progression. Firstly, be humble - if you're causing other people problems, or if others are causing you problems, remember that you're the instigator of all this by undertaking what is basically a process of possession by Kali. Keep respect for others as a priority. This makes better karma and may also enable you to see where your resistance is, what you need to address in order to successfully move forward in your spiritual endeavours. Secondly, cut back on the intensity of your practice a little – take your time. Especially if you're experiencing physical ailments, you need to give your body time to adjust and recover. Remember too that the symptoms won't go away until you've done the necessary work. You can't stop half way. And if nothing at all happens, despite your most fervent efforts – don't be despondent. This doesn't mean you're not spiritual or that the Gods and Goddess don't love you. It just means that Kundalini Yoga is not going to be the sadhana that works for you. It's no big deal. Find another way, such as mantra or yantra work.

And another thing – it's going to sometimes sound, in the next few paragraphs, that it's Kali's fault that certain negative experiences and processes are occurring. Nothing could be further from the truth. If we've already undertaken moral training, worked hard to eliminate a lot of our shadow qualities, then Kali won't have much to sink Her needle teeth into, when we try to arouse Her through Kundalini Yoga techniques. She's just trying to ascend through our inner body- it's us that have caused the knots, clots, tears and blockages in our chakras. It's us, and no one else, that creates the resistance.

But let's assume you've survived the undoing of the muladhara knot, the tearing of the root veil, the penetration of the neural clot, whatever you want to call it, and you're ready to move up to the next centre, which is the sex chakra. This lightwheel is called svadhisthana ("one's own place") and is situated just behind the sex organs, halfway in between the genitals and the spine. Visualise it as a spinning wheel, orange in colour. The associated sound is "varng". This lightwheel is all to do with your sense of self, anything which reinforces your identity. And Kali is swimming in this orange disc, like a little sea monster in a bowl of tomato soup! From this moment on, anything that feeds your sense of self is going to be poisoned by Kali's presence. Your relationships, the way you interact with others, the way you perceive others, the way you wish to be perceived by them – it all gets polluted. Every sip of "me" soup, every mouthful of "this is me" broth, is either going to taste bitter, full of snake bile, or you're going to feel choked as Kali's body prevents you from drinking your fill and getting nourished by the ego.

Both the sex chakra and the wheel above it, the navel chakra, are about the dehumanisation of others, using others as an instrument of your will. Kali will either slip in between you and others and prevent this from happening, which means you'll have to find other ways of functioning, relating to those around you, or She'll poison the way you and other people see each other. There'll be an outbreak of either exploitation or mutual suspicion. Not nice.

Physical and emotional ailments associated with svadhisthana are impotence, menstrual irregularity, thrush, sado-masochistic tendencies, lack of identity, an inability to sustain sincere communications, irrational likes or dislikes of certain types of people.

The third centre is the navel chakra, situated halfway inside the body, level with the belly button. It often vibrates in sympathy with a minor chakra at the solar plexus. The sound of the navel chakra that you should concentrate on is "rarng". This centre is called manipura, "the jewelled city". Imagine it as a whirling disc, yellow in colour. Manipura is often dubbed the seat of will and is associated with fire. This relates to our worldly interactions, business, competition, status, a clash of wills. To have a fire in the belly can be a good thing – but not if it brings you into conflict with every other person on the planet!

Another way to look at this "jewelled city" is to think of the "bright lights" syndrome, which pulls many people into the big cities to seek their fame and fortune, to make a name for themselves. And the yellow wheel of the manipura chakra also calls to mind the solar disc, with everyone looking for their "place in the sun", their happy-ever-after, the contentment and fulfilment they'll achieve after half killing themselves (and others) in the office for thirty years. In fact, everyone driven by the negative energies of manipura is looking for the big kill, in one form or another, and is willing to ride rough-shod over all obstacles to achieve it. But whether it's the bright lights of the big city, the showbiz spotlight, or the rays of the sun in an early retirement, Kali will slip in between you and your star of dreams and cast a long, writhing and menacing shadow over everything you do. You'll never be able to relax, never feel settled.

This principle holds true for the spiritual quest as well. If you spend your time looking for the light, ignoring the darkness within, trying to be holier than your neighbour, or if you seek identity through a "superior" religious faith, then the serpent Goddess will wriggle Her way into your gut and start to gnaw at all your hypocrisy, your high morals and ideals, your spiritual aspirations. And the brighter the light, the darker, the denser the shadow. More food for Kali.

The other side of manipura's energy is exactly the opposite of the religious, commercial or social predator, it's the individual with no self esteem at all, the doormat, the worrier, the blame-taker, the wallflower, the sheep.

Physical and emotional ailments associated with manipura are ulcers, digestive problems, over-eating, bulimia, obsessive anxiety, an inability to absorb information, an inability to nurture self or others, treating people as cogs in a machine - and of course, being treated that way by others.

Which brings us to the heart chakra. And this is where real change can start to happen. This is where you know you're getting somewhere. Hear the sound "yarng" and try to feel the heart centre as a jade green disc spinning behind the breast bone. This chakra is known as anahata, the unsounded, the "unstruck" note. It implies that, until we awaken the heart, develop empathy with other human beings, and with all forms of life everywhere, we stay in the realm of function, perceiving others as an extension of our own needs, projections and identity. When we learn to blur the distinction between ourselves and others a little, we move into the realm of feeling, also the world of "sensing". Empathy and intuition strengthen each other. We start to feel connected to life.

Imagine lying on the ground, staring up through the branches of a great tree. The leafy boughs form a perfect circle over your head. You have a choice now - to try and catch glimpses of the bright blue sky through the foliage, to watch the birds and butterflies flitting in and out of the tree, or to feel the dampness or the hardness of the ground under your spine, your shoulder blades. It's up to you. And if you elect to watch the wildlife, you might be a little startled and afraid to suddenly notice the unmistakeable dark shape of a serpent in the branches. Suddenly, this radiating network of greenery, reaching out to the world from a strong central core, becomes the abode of something sinister, deadly. And that's where we are when Kali meets the human heart. We can descend again, into selfishness, encountering other people with an attitude of arrogance or anxiety, we can try to develop a sense of common humanity and kinship, or we can strive ever harder for transcendence, with the attendant possible risk of misinterpreting our hubris, our spiritual superiority, for elevation and spiritual achievement. The human heart is our common middle ground, whatever our race, colour or religion. We have to learn to resonate in harmony with others, like the sympathetic strings of a sitar, which vibrate and hum when a note is struck on one of the main playing strings. Or like a tuning fork that can make a whole table hum with its vibration. If we don't feel a kinship with all life forms, something is usually wrong. Buddhist detachment is one thing, coldness is another!

The presence of Kali can poison this centre by infusing us with naive trust, blind faith in others, or with suspicion and paranoia. We can also suffer from infatuation or a delusion that it's our task to teach the world to love! Associated physical problems would be palpitations, shortness of breath, middle back problems (like being stabbed in the back!).

In certain esoteric Shaivite schools, and in many shamanic accounts, the Guru (teacher) or animal spirit is said to insert a magical crystal into the neophyte's body, usually the heart or head. Nine times out of ten, this crystal is symbolically, not literally implanted! This is believed to impart an indestructible consciousness, an awareness, a link between the human world and the realm of spirits, or we could say between the nirmanakaya and the sambhogakaya. Both the shaman/devotee and the spirits/deities can enter each other's world through the light in the crystal. Fuck! Will you listen to me? I sound like something from a new age magazine -"Angels and Haloes in the Home"!

This has obvious correlations with the development of vajra (diamond or thunderbolt) consciousness, that highly desirable blend of personal power and the ability to transcend, to flow. I've heard this crystal called Manaratni. Mana (masculine) means dwelling place and Ratni (feminine) is a jewel-like reception to light and wisdom.

The point is that the heart chakra is, or can be, the great balancer, the spiritual fulcrum between the energies of the upper and lower chakras, or further, between all "higher" and "lower" energies.

Moving up, with the sound "harng", we visualise the throat chakra, visuddha, "the pure". Feel it as a blue disc humming and spinning behind that throat hollow that lies between the collar bones. This centre is all about expression and communication. Imagine you're sitting at a table, with a paintbrush, a big, blank sheet of paper and a burning desire to paint the brightest, bluest, most radiant and beautiful sky anyone has ever seen. You wet your brush, dip it into a jar of gorgeous blue paint, give it a little stir, then apply your brush to the paper. But... disaster! Your brush must have been dirty! There's the start of a blue sky all right, but there's also some horrible dark streaks as well. These dirty smears look almost serpentine...

So what you thought was going to be a meaningful and attractive communication has turned into a distorted and confused mess. And of course, this is what happens when our communications aren't as clear, as honest or as meaningful as we think they are – Kali slithers in to highlight our impurities! We can become arrogant, patronising, divisive, hypocritical, or maybe just unable to communicate the simplest message without causing more confusion or negative reactions. Related physical ailments might include stuttering, loss of voice, a sore throat, involuntary shouting, inappropriate language, constantly interrupting other people's sentences, a frozen neck etc.

Assuming that we can clear our throats (Groan! Bad pun!), we can move on and up, or rather, Kali can. To the sound of the primal mother vibe "aum", She ascends to the white or pale lilac disc of the ajna (command) chakra in the middle of the forehead. Here we begin to evolve spiritual autonomy. We develop a stronger intuition, our will becomes stronger, we can begin to advise others on matters spiritual. But we can also become dictatorial, a religious fascist! With control must come responsibility.

Imagine the archetypal control centre. You're seated at a round table, coloured white, surrounded by computers, monitors, telephones. Snake-like wires and electrical leads coil everywhere, forming the veins and arteries of your world. Through these black coils and loops you receive and transmit information and commands. You're at the centre of a web of command!

But we all know only too well what can happen here! It only takes a faulty lead, a loose connection and all hell breaks loose. And don't pretend to me that you've never lost patience with your pc, never shouted at it, threatened it with extreme violence! We think we can impose our will by shouting louder, by employing force. And that's what happens if Kali finds imperfections in our ability to relate to others, to lead and take responsibility, to make decisions, for ourselves and for others. We lapse into coercion, bullying or violence.

Possible physical ailments associated with an overloaded or unprepared ajna chakra are severe headaches, intolerance and eye problems. The ajna chakra is also related to any kind of unrestrained or irresponsible psychic ability, invading other people's thoughts, psychic abilities without a spiritual background, commercial fortune telling etc.

From the ajna chakra it's now possible to marshal all one's resources for the final push, up into the rainbow-hued crown centre just above the top of the head. This is called sahasrara, which means "one thousand" (usually referring to lotus petals). This centre represents one-ness, a unity with the divine (whether that's a deity or a Buddha for you, it doesn't matter) and a feeling of kinship with all forms of life. This is also the centre of absorption, deep meditation. You have to be careful here that you don't get so blessed out that you sacrifice individual, positive action for blessed-out torpor. If Kali reaches this chakra prematurely, ie – before you're stable enough as an individual, before you're grounded, then severe depression, mental instability, hearing voices, paranoia and lots of other shitty stuff can occur.

So how long does all this stuff take? Well, it varies enormously, from individual to individual, depending on their innate abilities, the quality of their teacher(s) and how much material needs to be processed in each chakra, at each level of the individual's psyche. Some people are very spiritual, work in an ethical job but are crap at relationships. Others may be very well equipped for psychic work but can hardly tie their own shoelaces without help. Everyone's different. When you perform chakra cleansing, chakra conversations, you can spend just a few days on each centre. More serious work requires months, even years on each chakra. The whole process can take as little as three to five years intensive practice (with accompanying pitfalls) or a whole lifetime...

I've deliberately painted a worst case scenario concerning Kundalini Yoga in both books. It won't be nearly that bad, except in very rare cases, honest! But you need to know the signs. If you, and the people around you that care for your evolution, can recognise any of the symptoms I've listed, then you can do something about it that much quicker, and minimise possible damage and suffering. The golden rule is to take it slowly, make a sincere effort to put things right in the concrete, outside world as well as within yourself when you notice a problem. Keep a diary. Ask friends to keep an eye on you. It'll be ok, so don't let me put you off. Just play safe, ok?

If, however hard you try, you get no feedback, no sensations, no information, from your chakras, there could be several reasons why. The first is that you're simply going about it all wrong. The second is that you're getting feedback but don't know how to interpret it, you don't know how to speak that particular language. The third is that the attention of your energy simply isn't strong enough to flush anything out of your chakras. (The fourth is that you're already enlightened – or at least you think you are!) If any of this is true – please don't panic. Kundalini Yoga is just another method. Don't waste your time. Find another sadhana. You might be able to come back to Kundalini Yoga at some later date. You might not need to.

It's also a well circulated myth that one has to give up sex in order to build up a lot of energy to perform Kundalini Yoga – or to be "spiritual". To be honest, it does help in Kundalini Yoga though – the available energy is that much greater and one has a bigger reservoir of energy to assist self healing and recuperation after chakra "breakthroughs". But. We live in the Dark Age, the age of Kali and She's easier to reach than ever before. The sacrifices needed are of a much lower standard than in earlier, more spiritually evolved times.

So what are the benefits of Kundalini Yoga, or of some kind of chakra work? Well, firstly a vastly increased self knowledge – and remember – self knowledge is spiritual currency. Secondly, a cleaner inner network, which makes for smoother flows and exchanges of energy throughout the entire energetic body. In other words, better functioning internal organs, clearer thoughts, cleaner emotions and a stronger intuition, psychic ability.

And it's that very faculty, psychic ability, that we discuss in the next chapter. Turn the page, dear reader...

CHAPTER TWELVE - DIVINING THE DIVINE.

I was on the train to London the other day, looking forward to a Taiji seminar with a visiting Grand Master. I was seated with my back to the engine, watching the fields and telegraph poles appear from behind my left shoulder and then recede into the distance. Opposite me was a quiet elderly man, immersed in reading his classical music magazine. Occasionally he'd look up and then bury himself in Haydn and Mozart again. I suddenly realised that if a tunnel was coming up, he'd see it before me and wouldn't be surprised when everything went dark. I, on the other hand, would need a minute to realise what was happening when the fields and telegraph poles suddenly disappeared!

So actually, this guy could see my future. He could foresee an event that could affect me, way before I experienced it. On the other hand, I could see his past. If someone in a field noticed the train but only waved once my carriage had gone past, I would see the wave but the guy sitting opposite me wouldn't. The man waving in the field would have already receded into his immediate past.

So time is very subjective. My past, present or future may not be yours!

We call this glorious, mysterious lightwheel we live in, "the universe", meaning "entire as one". This implies that everything in the universe is also one. That everything in the universe is one with everything else. That every seemingly individual "thing" is actually just another way of looking at all the other "things". Magpies, lollipop sticks, electrical fuses and the colour purple are all aspects of each other. So the way a bird flies across your path at the bus stop may tell you how your cousin is doing in their new job. The number of times the telephone rings may give a clue to tomorrow's weather!

Okay, okay! This way lies madness! Or does it? Actually, to those who can train themselves to read the signs, the universe can reveal hidden patterns, unsuspected connections. Several of my students read tarot cards or the Yi-Jing (I Ching, the Chinese Oracle of Change). Now what sane person would think they could predict the future by looking at coloured pictures or tossing some coins? Yet it works. It works. Economists and meteorologists are capable of making very long term predictions, many years in advance. I don't know how they do it. Country people can tell how the weather will change by observing natural phenomena, such as wind direction, the flight of birds, the sound of a rooster fart. I couldn't do it.

But I can often predict, as soon as someone starts a Taiji form, where they'll have problems with certain movements. Nothing supernatural about this.

I've just been trained to observe the way people move and to predict which kinds of movements may prove difficult for them. I can also sense their energy, read their emotions, get a feel for their character. Again, not supernatural, just the result of good training and experience. But I can also tell how friends and loved ones are doing by observing natural events. It may sound crazy to you but if a pigeon flies in a certain direction I know to expect news or a communication from certain people. A seagull doing the same thing often brings more sombre tidings. Don't worry, I shan't write a whole list of weird stuff that I believe in. I just want to make you think about the nature of reality.

You've probably heard of the butterfly effect – if a butterfly flaps its wings in China, then there could be a rainstorm in Panama. In other words, there are no unconnected events. No event occurs in isolation. It cannot help but have an effect on something, somewhere. Certainly we can see, in the natural world, how climate changes affect the growth of vegetation, which affects some local animals, which will affect the predators that feed upon them. And we know that the destruction of the rain forests and the ever increasing output of industrial pollution are going to have dire consequences. In nature, nothing happens in isolation. And we live in nature. We're not separate from natural laws, even in our climate controlled cars and houses. In fact the very way we built the cars and houses affects the natural world.

Some people are sensitive to changes in the environment. Some aren't. Some can observe these changes and predict a consequence. Some can't. Some people can do that freaky loop thing with their tongue. Some can't. No big deal. We all experience "reality" according to our conditioning and our abilities. My "reality" may be very different from yours. Not better, not inferior, just different.

And in my reality – deep breath – the Gods and Goddesses are real, living beings. Time is not linear. There are other, parallel worlds. Everything has significance, meaning. Karma arches over everything. All life is sacred. All life forms are born many times. Animals have "spiritual intelligence". One can predict the "future" by observing the world around us – all the clues, all the necessary information is already here. Most importantly, especially in this Dark Age, I believe we can have a direct, visceral, intimate relationship with the Gods and Goddesses. This doesn't stop us being Buddhists, if that's how we like to think of ourselves. The Buddhas, or rather, those that achieve Buddhahood, are exalted in all realms. The deities will help us evolve, develop spiritually, if we ask Them. Tantrists, shamans, pagans and Gnostics are closer to the truth than many scientists. This is my reality. To a lot of people I'm sure it sounds a bit "out there".

And yet I function somehow! I earn enough money to eat and pay the rent (usually). I have friends. I'm healthy. I haven't fallen prey yet, on a personal level, to the social and political naivety and short-sightedness that caused extremely religious, spiritually driven ancient cultures such as the Tibetans and the Aztecs to stagnate, crumble and fall. I've managed to avoid becoming a bigot, a sexist, a chauvinist, a hater. I don't think of myself as any kind of messiah, or even anything remotely special. I'm a regular, middle-aged man. I just love Shiva, love having Him around.

The reality I chose to inhabit, at some point, nurtures me. And many of those around me.

A reader of my last book, and a very good student of mine, writes with a different view...

"I love to talk about - or at least hear about - these kinds of themes. But I feel very out of place as I am not a Buddhist and don't practise any of the rituals or meditation. Prayer is not my thing - I am too self-conscious. I feel that most the things that get talked about go straight over my head and I feel embarrassed and uncomfortable. I feel like I need a beginner's course in meditation or something so I can ease into it gently. Something is definitely missing, but my hectic lifestyle does not lend itself to a gentle, leisurely spiritual practice. I spend 8 hours a day trying to make my eyes and mind focus on something I don't want to focus on, trying to get through the day so I can focus my body and mind on doing the physical activities I enjoy. I feel like I'm on the outside knocking on the window to get in, but I can't find a way in. My mind will not get over this problem I have with seeing spirituality as internal and self-centred, and consequently self-serving, potentially pretentious and consequently hypocritical. I see no difference between spirituality and psychology, which is reinforced when I hear of you studying psychologists such as Jung. Usually at lunchtime I drag myself round the city shops, spending money. Today I went and sat in the car with a book on Taijiquan to try and get some background knowledge into my fried brain. It was peaceful and quiet (until someone sat in the car in front of me with the radio on full blast) and it was the closest I've felt to being at peace for as long as I can remember. Usually I am too impatient to get to "the next thing" or feeling guilty at not "doing" something. I spend my life with actual or mental lists of things that I can tick off as "done". Sorry, I'm jumping - back to the feeling of "knocking on the window". I can happily read tarot cards and I believe in the intuitive response I get from my mind; I am comfortable with trusting my instincts about the "feel" of places; I can look at a statue of Buddha or Ganesh, or even of Mary and Jesus, and feel drawn to them and sense a kind of spiritual warmth coming from them. I can desire to maintain an altar or shrine in my house, or to devise my own rituals - but I still feel embarrassed and uncomfortable with actually doing it."

A voice of worldly reason, and probably a typical story. I found the above very honest, and very touching. And of course, this student is correct, Jung saw no conflict between spirituality and psychology. They are both introvert activities, they're both about self knowledge and they're both about self healing. That needn't make them pretentious or hypocritical, though heaven knows there are enough religious hypocrites in the world. And enough pretentious wankers too! Having a relationship with the divine is a personal business, and religion needn't be about joining a church or worshipping en masse. I think a beginners' course in meditation is a good idea for anyone – the problem is that these courses sometimes come with a hidden agenda, or they're organised by particular religious groups with their own spiritual hardwiring. Having a group of like-minded people around is very useful – but no one has to bend to peer pressure, especially spiritual peer pressure. And such groups should be encouraging each individual's practice, not moulding people into an anonymous homogenous whole.

There will always be those who, instead of empowering people, encouraging them to find their own way, will try to impose their own particular worldview on others. They'll simply transfer all their natural selfishness or arrogance into the spiritual sphere. There are many religious/spiritual teachers like this, some of them are even devotees of Shiva. But some of them are so holier-than-thou, or smarter-than-thou, more special-than-thou, that they drive people AWAY from the divine, not towards it! They may not be deliberately self-serving but they may not be serving God. Shiva Shankara says (as I understand it), "These people may be full of knowledge, but they're not full of me." They don't, or can't, convey that Shiva vibe to their flock. Having said that, there's a Shiva for every occasion. He has so many aspects, so many faces, so many flavours. No one could possibly convey all of them.

To be able to find time for any of this spiritual stuff is the first challenge. The hardest part. Often it's only some kind of breakdown or trauma, such as illness or redundancy, that forces us into change. Until the suffering becomes too great, we lurch from crisis to crisis, driven by needs and energies we don't even like. That's no way to live. I know from personal experience how much we can do without when we have to. But taking the plunge to make positive changes in our lives isn't easy. If sitting in one's car, reading about tai chi, or anything for that matter, reduces the stress, then keep doing it!

As for feeling embarrassed about maintaining an altar in one's house, devising one's own prayers etc, well, a lot of people would be embarrassed to talk about masturbation – but the overwhelming majority of people do it! That's hypocritical! No one's going to be watching you (I'm talking about praying again now, by the way!) so just go ahead and do it. I think the one fundamental message of The Real Rasa book is to GIVE YOURSELF PERMISSION to open up to this stuff. Healing ourselves through some kind of spiritual activity or practice will eventually benefit all those around us. This student (who is bright, capable and very (too) self effacing as well as honest) is correct – something is missing from her life. I can feel her yearning. So if you're drawn to any kind of spiritual activity, then follow your heart. Please.

I know that yearning. And often we're most resistant to help when we most need it. Especially in matters spiritual. It feels like we're giving up the last of our rapidly crumbling autonomy. It can feel like failure. But that yearning can be stronger than our pride. Good job too.

TO GOD/DESS

"Come by snowfall and foxtrack, beloved one!
By fall of final curtain
By neglected, overgrown trails and weed-wild alleyways
Come by moon-crusted fills
By deep ruts of silence
In winter's cold burning

And through summer's yawning open windows
Through glimmering evening blossom drills
Shimmering in the heat, as if still asleep, dreaming
Find me standing at the edge of some field
Ankle deep in my many lost causes
Quiet in the imminence of something greater than I know
So, beloved one!
Steal upon me slow...

But oh! Come especially in the angry slap of tilting sleet
Tossed iron grey skies
Where ships rear in fear in threatened harbours
And the sea flares in feathered fury
Whistle in through locked doors and tight lips
Open pinched and torn love notes
Barge in through my chest
When I turn my back
When I need you most

As you know, as you know
I tend to disintegrate if left alone
As you said, as you said
I'm a stranger to myself
But here you are at last, beloved one!
Pulling rust from my harpooned head..."

That says it nicely. Come especially when I turn my back, when I need you most... So many people I talk to, and whether the subject is meditation, martial arts, music, or even gardening or reading, I hear the same lament again and again, "I just don't have the time." Everyone is so busy. It's sad. It takes a powerful will or some kind of upheaval to kick the "busy" syndrome. And no one, no one, likes to be told that they could find time if they really wanted to. They just come up with a long list of reasons why they can't meditate, paint, do pottery, read a book, visit their parents. And usually all these proffered reasons are entirely logical and acceptable. Except that these people are yearning for something – something they unconsciously refuse to allow into their lives! Constant busyness is like constant laziness, it numbs us, stops us thinking, feeling. Stops us looking at ourselves. So it can be quite comfortable!

I speak from experience. I've been there. I spent nearly a quarter of a century in a job where I wasn't appreciated and where my achievements were overlooked, where every month there was a new golden boy or girl, or a scapegoat to hang every negativity on. It took a row with the boss and a spontaneous resignation (which was what my boss wanted anyway) to free me from my institutionalisation. And I was very institutionalised – I couldn't envisage myself doing anything different, couldn't see how I could possibly manage on less money. I was wrong, so totally, utterly wrong. I really started to live again as soon as I walked out of that job. It was scary at first, but exhilarating too. I'd never go back to that kind of existence. There isn't enough money in the world to entice me!

My student is very perceptive when she considers that spiritual practice can be self serving, therefore hypocritical. We have to be very careful we're not creating more problems for ourselves by becoming arrogant, pretentious, pompous or self-centred. It's easily done. I've met a lot of religious people, Buddhists and Hindus included, whose conversations are a thinly disguised "me, me, me!" And we shouldn't use our religious practice as a substitute for having a personality either!

Anyway, back to the plot and the point of this chapter. Divining, predicting. When we learn to read the tarot cards, the runes, the Yi Jing, it's great fun. We can learn how to use them, do readings for friends, ask them a few weeks later if any of it came true. By constantly reassessing the feeling, the information we get from each card, rune, hexagram (the Chinese use the word "gua" – shape or diagram), we begin to build up a library of meaning. We'll begin to intuit which level to interpret a reading on – physical, mental, relationships, spiritual – and we'll begin to create a relationship with the system we employ.

But the magic isn't in the cards or the runes. It's in our minds. Most of the time we're unaware of how much we know, how much information we absorb. We could pass someone in the street and hardly notice them. Yet a hypnotist or a skilled interrogator could put us back there, ask what colour hair they had, how tall they were, what colour jacket they were wearing – and we'd be able to give accurate information! At some level we absorbed all the information, but as it was of no immediate use, it was shunted to the back of the brain to be stored away under "irrelevant". And we were totally unaware that this whole process was even happening!

The pack of tarot cards, the bowl of water, the mirror, whatever we use in our divinations, acts as a focus for our minds, allowing subconscious knowledge to be accessed and interpreted. It's possible to expand upon this process and do without the cards or the mirror, just use whatever spontaneous natural events occur. My Taiji and Qigong Sifu can make Yi Jing predictions from clouds, birds in flight, passing trains. He doesn't need coins or yarrow stalks. His charming wife, my Simo, has also learned to do this astonishingly well. We all have this latent ability. It's just a matter of practice.

If you're used to the tarot or the Yi Jing, then look for clouds or anything that reminds you of a card or a gua. Maybe you'll see six birds flying past, vertically stacked – that could be the first gua of the Yi Jing – Qian – heaven. Or maybe you'll see someone who reminds you of the Queen of Pentacles. If you're accustomed to using the runes, look for comparative shapes in the surrounding environment – for instance, a trident, a zig zag, the letter "R". Use the meanings you already know for these shapes - eel sedge, the sun, a journey etc, and see if you can make a prediction based on your observation.

It's bound to be a bit of a hit and miss affair at first, as you flex your psychic muscles, but confidence will grow with practice. Eventually you won't need props – your intuition will be sharp enough to read the world around you like a book.

If you don't already use a system – tea leaves, numerology, astrology etc, then that's fine. Use the people around you. That guy at the bus stop. He's wearing a red tie for the first time since you can remember. He usually wears blue or grey. See if anything different happens at work today – an accident, a row, a celebration. Start to build up a library of meanings. But don't just use that one guy – if he decides to use another bus, you'll have to start all over again!

I know it all sounds a bit silly but, as I said, there's no such thing as an unconnected event. Everything that happens is a clue to something else happening, because it's already part of something else. So, without getting too bogged down in it all, or getting too afraid to cross the road until you see a purple goat (!), have fun using your intuition, connecting events around you with events down the road, later in the day. At least it'll make your journey to work more interesting, and you'll have a back up plan if the batteries in your I Pod give out!

I chose, at some point, to live in a world rich with meaning. I'm not particularly interested in predictions – I don't walk around looking for deeper relevance in dog shit and pedestrian crossings – but I do feel connected to the world around me with a karmic web, threads of er... light. These threads, called them The Force if you like (Apparently there's an awful lot of Jedi Knights out there!), bind us together, connect us. Not just humans, but the trees, the birds, the cars, the buildings – all connected with these threads. When one thread vibrates, they all vibrate. If someone has an accident, if someone pats a dog, if a child is born, if someone buys my book – the rest of the world will feel it somehow - subliminally, unknowingly, maybe (usually), but it will be sensed.

Everything is connected. We have no secrets from each other really. What we are stands at our shoulder and shrieks far more loudly than the little whispers of our ego. And how we act, how we speak, how we think, will affect the whole world.

We're all connected, to all life forms - in our DNA, in our unconscious minds and by a karmic web. We can learn to read these unseen, unsuspected connections. We can also learn to "read", to access, the deities, the Buddhas, the Gods and Goddesses. And that's the whole point of this book – to encourage and empower you to have a direct relationship with the holy, the sacred, the divine.

Psychic ability isn't the same as being spiritual, or leading a deity-orientated life. But it is useful, a beneficial side effect of spiritual development. This skill, innate or cultivated, can be turned to shamanic purposes – which in this day and age is more likely to be spiritual mediumship, talking to the dead, or to "higher" purposes, communing with the Gods and Goddesses.

If you meditate regularly, get visions, insights, images, information – even if you're not sure whether it's just your imagination – you're already flexing your psychic muscles. Just keep doing it. Try to find ways to find out if what you're receiving is valid. Question everything. Keep a journal. Look at last month's entries. How does that all look in the cold light of a new day? And if you don't know how to use your psychic skills to reach, access the deities – well, that's why we use such "external" aids as mantras, yantras and mandalas. They are maps that we can use to help negotiate our inner landscapes. They are all tried, tested and true methods.

In the next chapter we can read what happens when you elect to use such maps...

CHAPTER THIRTEEN - THE DARSHAN DIARIES – PART ONE - THE PAN REPORT.

This is the first of a couple of chapters on darshan – face to face intimacy with the divinities. Kali will feature heavily throughout the next couple of chapters!

The first time I ever encountered Kali was terrifying. Duh! It was all the more unsettling because I wasn't looking for it, wasn't consciously working towards it. This was late in 1973 or 1974, not sure when exactly. I was heavily into Tibetan Buddhism at the time, meditating regularly, doing a lot of inner work. I was living in the country then, also doing a lot of gardening, playing guitar. Very hippyish. It wasn't a bad time. I had a lovely altar upstairs in the bedroom, a low table with a reddish-golden cloth, some flowers. I went upstairs one evening to put an offering (some blackberries) on the altar, which didn't have any rupas (Buddha statues) back then, just various pictures in frames. There was a bowl of wine, representing blood, sacrifice, in the middle of the pictures and the smell of the wine blended very pleasantly with the Tibetan incense I was using. I was kneeling in front of the altar when I realised it was very cold. I felt uneasy for some reason and looked at the bedroom windows to see if they were more open than usual. The curtains were shivering, from top to bottom. It was very weird, and it got real weird at lightning speed when I realised the windows were completely shut!

Somehow, the mingled smell of the wine and incense intensified and the small bowl of blackberries I had in my hand as an offering began to look sinister, quite revolting, like innards. I don't know why I concentrated on one particular picture on the altar. My gaze was drawn to it. It was dark in colour, in a thin gold frame, only about eight by five inches. As I watched, it changed, from a portrayal of a Tibetan Lama to an emaciated crone! She was black in colour, Her skin was similar to that sooty parchment look you see on Egyptian mummies. Her ribs were showing. She was snarling, showing Her long teeth and Her bony hands were like claws, contorting in front of Her withered breasts. I was really, really frightened. I didn't know what to do. I kneeled there for what seemed a long time but was probably only thirty seconds, before everything started to return to normal. I was quite shaken. It wasn't so much the experience, which was spooky enough – it was that I wasn't "in tune" with Hindu deities. I hadn't given Them a thought before (despite all those yantras on the wall in the '60's!). I somehow knew though that this vision was of Kali and that this visit would be the first of many.

I was right. I experienced Her quite a few times over the next ten years, especially when She was the last visitor I would have invited, the last presence I wanted to feel. Whenever I got uptight, angry, frustrated, arrogant, proud, there She was, quivering inside me, ripping into me, demoralising me, jumbling my words, making me look stupid. Even my hands would contort, as Hers had done in the picture. It was fucking embarrassing! It was great training! When at last I began to work harder on my unsuspected, repressed aggression, She began to change in nature, She became softer. It was almost as if She'd become my anima, my secret self, the female principle as expressed by my subconscious mind. As I worked hard to improve myself, She was able to show a different face. She didn't have to torture me quite so much.

But I still don't recommend having Kali as your inner woman.

Things got better. My relationship with Kali mellowed. A few years ago I "met" Her husband, Shiva Shankara and things got even better. We got on really well and now we hang around a lot together. I'm His creature now. But the strange thing is that I never, ever expected any kind of relationship with what I regarded as Hindu deities. I never expected to "work" with Them. I certainly didn't expect Them to come visiting.

As my relationship to the deities has evolved, the way I experience Them has changed. They feel much less Hindu, less Indian in look and feel than They used to. They're less ornate, less "foreign-looking" less "big screen", but more immediate, more visceral, more physical. Does that make sense?

To illustrate how much my relationship with Kali has changed, here's what happened to me this very morning...

I'm sitting in meditation, trying to settle my mind. My body too – it's creaking and groaning from a heavy training session. Though the weather is sharply cold, it's sunny and bright. Steam curls up from my forehead, hands and ankles. The sun is directly in front of me so I close my eyes. There's a lovely red glow behind my eyelids. Suddenly Kali comes walking in diagonally towards me, from my left hand side. She's naked and emaciated, dark and decorated in skulls. But it all seems perfectly natural, matter of fact. She grins at me, knocks her knuckles on my skull in a humorous parody of respectfulness (I think this is good!) and sits down, cross legged in front of me.

She starts drawing something in the dirt with a stick but I'm not really paying attention. This earns me a sharp rebuke so I apologise and look interested – fast. She draws Her yantra, a downward pointing triangle. "This is Shakti's symbol," She says, "From this comes all material. There's no end to its power, to its creativity. All its power is focused down into the material world. It's limitless."

She then draws another pattern in the dirt. This I recognise as Shiva's yantra. It features a six pointed star, like the Star of David, but with the upper pointing triangle solid, to the fore, and the downward pointing triangle subordinate to it, hidden behind, hollow. "This is Shiva's sign," Kali says, "It denotes consciousness, the ascension from physical matter to sentience. But notice how Shiva's upward pointing triangle – the flame, the mountain, the lingam - is held, supported, by Shakti's downward pointing triangle – the yoni, the vulva (She doesn't use these words exactly!). Consciousness for cattle (ordinary Joes like you and me) is contained by physical bodies. It takes a lot of training for consciousness to be both non-physical and autonomous." (She actually uses the terms "formless and free")

"Physical matter is infinite in its variety of forms. And these are all shaped by the consciousness that inhabits them." (I assume She's talking evolution or death and rebirth here) "But consciousness itself needs physical form, physical organs, to experience itself, particularly in relation to other forms of itself." I nod sagely, almost understanding. She head butts me! I mean it! She really head butts me! I'm quite shocked. But She regains my attention real fast.

She points to Shiva's yantra. "Sometimes Shiva has to be held down." Then She traces Her symbol, behind the "up" triangle. "Consciousness needs limits, a framework. And sometimes (She leers) Kali (she said Her own name) needs to be elevated."

Right on cue, Shiva walks in. He looks fantastic, glowing a beautiful blue. I'm really, really happy to see Him. He looks faintly amused by the scene in front of Him, by the sight of Kali teaching me. I bow low, apologise, saying "Please Kali Ma. May I ask a question?" She nods imperiously. "Why do you sometimes need to be elevated... and why triangles? I can understand that they can represent male and female characteristics (I don't use those words exactly!) but er... why triangles?"

"Because," She drawls, "A triangle, as well as representing male or female, also shows where power is being focused. Downwards from pure energy to form dense matter or upwards from sense data towards pure energy, seeking transcendence, understanding." Not wanting another head butt, I try to look pathetic and obviously succeed, because she continues, "From energy to energy – but knowingly. This is why physical form is essential, why Kali (presumably meaning Shakti) has to be elevated." This I can dig so it seems the lesson is over. They depart and I sit for a few more minutes in a kind of psychic afterglow.

The above scene may sound bizarre to you, dear reader, or maybe it seems like just a harmless fantasy from a middle-aged man trying to make himself sound all-wise and important. I don't blame you for thinking that (but fuck you anyway!) – such an episode would have been unthinkable to me at that moment, many years ago, when I first clapped my appalled eyeballs on the black crone Kali Ma.

So let's leave my little adventures in Kali Land to one side and turn now to the experiences of others. In this chapter, and the next, we'll be reading the journals of two courageous spiritual seekers. Suzie and Elaine are two of my finest, long term, most loyal students. They both elected, a couple of years ago, to try out for themselves various ways to achieve direct communion with the sacred. I'm very impressed by their commitment and their achievements. When, a few short months ago, they decided to intensify their efforts, I asked them both to keep a meditation/dream journal for possible public consumption. With typical generosity they both agreed. I think their experiences are astonishing.

There are some Jungian archetypes in their accounts – crones, wise women, half humans etc, and there are some Freudian moments too, that involve aging, acceptance, self esteem etc. But to use these psychological systems frameworks as an interpretative framework would diminish what are obvious authentic religious experiences, so I prefer to let their words speak for themselves. We're dealing with the spiritual realms here, not the psychological.

It's important to note that both Suzie and Elaine have done extensive shadow work, have never been afraid to delve into their inner worlds and work with whatever they encountered there. They also both have a legacy of many years of Buddhist practice, which keeps them balanced and sensible. It also gives them a keen sense of ethics – they'd soon feel if anything unhealthy or harmful, for themselves or others, was developing. You begin to read these journals from a "middle point", so to speak, when Suzie and Elaine have already developed the ability to tell the difference between imagination and revelation.

Both women experience what are classic shamanic experiences, the elevations, the being pulled down or swallowed, the feeling of being initiated, of being validated, the emotional instability that results from being "all shook up!" and of course, the intuitive insights – into self and into the world of the deities.

Their progress has been rapid, and their achievements are amazing. Suzie's journal has a kind of "sequential" authority, an internal, linear unfolding that gives it gravitas and validity. One can feel the tentative beginnings, the development of trust, the growing depth of insight. It's a kind of "ideal" journal. This is how it should be. Elaine's record, on the other hand, has the validity of dream, of trance. One couldn't make this stuff up with the normal, waking, controlling mind. The very incongruity and fluidity, the uncontrolled nature of her imagery somehow makes it more convincing. This stuff is really happening to her.

Sometimes the things that happen to me in meditation would sound silly to a third party. See above! It's either that the material is intensely personal to me, or uses imagery or language that, although perfectly valid in a meditative, dream or dream-like state, would be inappropriate or just plain ludicrous in the narrowed language and symbology of the conscious world. I've had to doctor my last conversation with Kali quite a lot to render it readable. The actual experience is more physical, more dreamlike, not so intellectual. The deities often just use three or four words to explain a great deal, so I have to pad it quite a bit to bring the meaning out.

So I tend not to share those more "out there" moments! Elaine, however, has chosen to share, without censorship or apology - and I applaud her courage and generosity.

For all three of us, myself, Suzie and Elaine, whatever our favourite deities, our favourite practices and preferences, our focus, Kali's presence has loomed large. She seems inescapable...

Elaine's journal – The Pan Report.

** I first came across Pan in a poem written by Julian Wilde. It was subsequently printed in The Real Rasa book.*

From the fur stirs ancient impulses
Wisdom buried in the forest floor
When the neck pricks at the shifting scrape
The hollow knock of wood and horn
The cloven hoof on mossy rock
The crouch, the muscles tight knot, the antler knock
The goat eye blinks
Sounds are swallowed by your attention
By skin wind chills
And the groin pulled tight

Half brother to thunder
From mountain cave to marble column
And back again to the darkness
Neglected and disgraced
Packed into nightfall, tree shadow and dream
Buried in shame
So shamed too are we by that burial
When the thunder inside our skin rages
And the tempest destroys the temple
And the guts roil and the bowels twitch
And a void opens between the legs
Between the horns
Between the worlds
And the goat eye blinks
And through that invisible root
A terrible communion

Of course I had heard of Pan before. I knew He was an ancient god or something! But I had never given the gods much thought. The way He was described in the poem touched some part of me - there was a resonance in my soul. This was several years ago but the image stayed and every now and then I would remember it. There came a time when I had been exploring my more creative side and realised I would like to do something with clay again. It has been a passion of mine since my school days. I decided I wanted to give the mental image I had of Pan physical form, so I researched on the net to find some references. I wanted to see how others perceived Him, and came across some more poetry and a passage taken from "Wind in the Willows" where Rat and Mole are out looking for a lost baby otter. It tells how Mole felt a great awe fall upon him, a peaceful feeling that although it prevented from moving, instilled no terror in him. Rat was shaking too, and they looked up into the sudden silence to see the swept back horns, the hooked nose, the bearded mouth and the smiling eyes of Pan. Rat and mole were afraid and yet... not afraid, full of love. This passage, together with Julian Wilde's poem resonated with something deep inside me, spoke to me of the numinous, allowed me to feel the nearness of a God I could relate to. So I set to work to give the image I had in my head a shape and form. I was like a woman possessed - for two days every spare minute I had was used on this project. It was in part rediscovering my love of clay, but more than that, it was making a connection with an energy I had been aware of but unable to express before. In a way it brought Him to life for me. The figure I made then still stands on my mantelpiece today.

It was a year or so later when I finally met Him. Sifu Jules, Suzie and myself were on an instructors course, staying at an agricultural college. We met for meditation, as is our custom on these occasions, early in the morning. We like to meditate outside if at all possible. It was a fine summer's morning with clear blue skies and birdsong all around as we settled into meditation. It felt no different from any other meditation. I was just sitting there trying to quieten the mind, when all of a sudden there He was, Pan - huge and awesome, but not terrifying. I didn't know what to do, I was mesmerised. He looked around for a moment, sniffed the air and it felt as if He had given His approval, then He was gone. He's appeared in meditation regularly since then, though I never know when it will be. Sometimes I can feel Him when I'm outside, He's very much a god of Nature.

** "The Tattoo Dream – I'm in a kind of ward, with other women, though I don't notice them at first. There's a tube in my nose. The first thing I remember is looking down at my left leg. On the inside of the calf is a large, ornate tattoo in pastel shades of pink and yellow. I see my ex-husband off to one side, shaking his head in disapproval. I think "Fuck him!" I see my friend Suzie and ask her when the tube in my nose is coming out. She doesn't know but says she'll try to find out. It's then that I realize there are* *lots of other women around and that it was them who gave me the tattoo. I also realize that I didn't choose the design of the tattoo, nor was I aware of having it done. Somehow I know these women are witches. I have to arrange flowers and I try putting different sizes into various pots and vases. It all feels like some kind of initiation."*

* *"Sitting in meditation, I become aware of a couple of crow's feet next to me. I look up. This isn't a crow – it's a very large vulture! Then I see a big brown bear coming towards me from the right hand side. It looms over me and opens its jaws. They gape wider and wider until it's just a big black hole over me. Then the bear vomits! It's an unpleasant situation and I want to pull away but I realize that, although it's unpleasant, it's not actually hurting me. It soon stops. I'm covered in chunks of goo! But then it starts to change and becomes almost crystalline, diamond-like. I feel I'm absorbing it through my skin. It's a kind of transmission from the bear to me. I'm wearing long robes and I'm about to be led away by some women when I hear the phone ringing – end of meditation!"*

* *"I sit down for meditation as usual. After a while of quietening down, I look inside, sort of an internal scan, and become aware of my internal workings. This is different from normal – usually it's just sensations or patterns of light – this is so much more vivid. I can see/feel my guts, all the tubes and organs, all the secretions, fluids - sticky, slimy, messy. And blood pumping through my heart. When I move my attention around the body I see muscles, tendons, bones, all from the inside.*

I become aware of an old crone nearby. As I look down at myself, my body is emaciated, with black, leathery skin, taut over the ribs. I have sagging, shrivelled breasts. I realise that I too could be an old crone. Images come of being in a coffin with maggots and insects eating my rotting flesh. Needless to say, this brings up a resistance on my part. It's hard to see yourself as a bag of pus and sinews, or as a shrivelled, mummified old crone. But the images keep repeating, then the old hag I'd first been aware of appears again, and she's dancing around me, almost like a tribal dance. Her skin is black and drawn tight over her bones – a dancing skeleton with a few wisps of black hair and wild, wild eyes. As she's dancing she keeps poking me with a long bony finger and repeating "This is you! This is you!" The feeling I get from all this is not to be so attached to physical form. Appearance means nothing. I must face the reality of what this human body really is. It's easy, when one spends so much time and effort on staying fit and healthy to be proud of one's physical appearance and abilities. It's also a trap!"

* *"I sit down to meditate. I don't chant, I just want to sit. After a few minutes of settling, I become aware of a huge snake, closing in on me – again from the right hand side. It has huge jaws and teeth. It opens its jaws wider and wider. This all feels familiar. I feel a connection deep in my*

gut – I wonder if it's Kundalini, but perhaps not... I wonder if this is a personification of my anger – it's hovering over me now. I decide to put it to one side, just sit with it, and see what happens. It snaps around in front of me again – jaws wide open, showing lots of fang! I hear it say, "You dare to ignore me!" "I don't want to ignore you!" I reply, "But I don't know what to do with you." The jaws open even wider, like an invitation into this vast, scaly tunnel, descending into – I don't know what. It's getting scary now. I call for Pan, ask if He'll watch over me. I feel His presence, huge and awe-inspiring, and I see Him catch the snake by the tail and pull on it. "Nature can be rough!" He says. I feel calmer in His presence. I feel protected. I sit at His feet for a while and ask, "What should I do?" He picks me up and hugs me, as you would a child and replies, "There, there, little one. Sit. Meditate." So I do.

The images of the snake begin to fade, to be replaced by everyday ephemera. But then the snake comes back. I feel stronger this time. Pan is around and it feels important to go back and face whatever this is. The snake opens its jaws again and I'm drawn down this dark, scaly tunnel, towards something hot and furious, ranting, tearing, rending. My guts throb in resonance. It feels like Kali on a rampage, stamping the ground so hard that it shakes, tearing flesh, pulling limbs apart in a real bloodlust. She/I, we, are covered in blood, we're tearing at flesh with our nails and teeth. This goes on, I don't know for how long. At some point I feel like sobbing "I can't go on!" but it's not done – yet another wave of hot bloodlust and rending. As this second wave hits me I can see/feel Kali and somehow I know that the only way to end this is by placing my feet on Shiva. I can see Him on the ground looking up at me, with a half smile on His lips. His body is a wonderful clear blue, like the deep translucent blue you see in icebergs. I can feel the cool, calming effect it has. There's also a recognition in both Him and Her that this is the way it should be, that He should lie down at Her feet willingly, as a service to Her, as She serves Him. There's no hint of shame, from either party. I go through all the bloodlust but feel strongly that with all this there's a kind of ecstasy – a rapture. Eventually it all subsides and goes quiet. I finish the meditation and thank Pan for being there to look after me. When I get up I'm astonished to find nearly three quarters of an hour have gone by – it only felt like ten minutes!"

** "Later, much later – I remember to thank Kali too. I flash back to a time not long ago – I'd sat down to meditate. There was a feeling of something about to well up, but I didn't want it, didn't feel I was ready. Out of the corner of my eye I saw a flash of red. There was Kali, all dressed up to the nines in a scarlet sari. I asked if I could just sit – I thought to myself, "No, not now!" Remembering that incident I smile. I can't help wondering if my Kali experience would have been so intense if I had accepted it at that time, rather than making the Goddess wait! I guess I should think myself lucky She decided to come back!"*

* *"I settle down to meditate, just try to quieten the mind. Pan appears. He's in his awesome aspect, huge and scary and He has a goat head with massive horns that curl around and down beside His head. I'm surprised, I've never seen Him this way. It obviously shows – and Pan explains He can take many forms. He changes into His normal form – half man, half goat – but younger and more athletic looking than usual. As I'm sitting with Him, I feel myself being gently "pushed" towards something, not sure what – Pan speaks in images and feelings, few words – I'm shown some people in what I would call a "safe Buddhist practice" – that is, they follow the teachings, meditate regularly, try to lead good, useful lives. Nothing wrong with that, but they never really turn and look inwards in any real depth – well, not what I would call real depth. My whole being is screaming, resisting being pushed into this kind of practice. The strength of my resistance surprises me. The image fades and I'm shown the Buddha-to-be as a prince, leaving home, leaving family and comfort and security (in the material sense), searching for truth and reality, The Way It Is, lifting the veil of ignorance and delusion we all live under, and finally achieving for Himself the enlightened state, Buddhahood. I'm in awe of what I see and it makes me realise just what He accomplished. I also realise I want to get some flavour of that in my own practice. I'm not after enlightenment or nibbana as a goal, but I do want to work hard towards breaking down my own ignorance and conditioning. I want to work towards seeing things as they really are. It's not to belittle enlightenment just that, at the moment, working on my own ignorance seems more important and will hopefully lead to a better understanding. The whole experience leaves me with a greater resolve to bring my practice into every area of my life – to live it more."*

* *"Sitting in meditation in the Amaravati group. Pan is sitting nearby, just relaxing. He's often very laid back! I see huge jaws and sharp teeth coming towards me (seems to be a recurring theme). They belong to a big cat of some kind. As I watch I can see the rest of the animal, it's a beautiful tiger, with a golden coat and black striped markings. (I'm reminded later that the tiger is the preferred mount of Durga) Pan goes over to it and strokes it, I can feel the sensation of the fur under my hand too. I wonder how He tames such a wild and magnificent animal and He shows me – He sees the tiger as a cub, fully grown and as an aging and dying animal all at once. There's something about being able to see the whole creature in all its aspects – and the tiger senses this, knows it is seen and accepted in its totality. This seems an important lesson. Pan walks off into the forest, tiger by His side. It feels as if I should follow but I can't keep up with Him, though I try.*

The image fades. I focus on a body sweep and watch the breath. My body feels very light. As I mentally watch the sensations of the body I feel like I have another set of arms behind my own. It's a weird sensation when they move. As I look to my left I can see a shape. Closer inspection reveals that it's peacock feathers! On my right is the peacock's head, so I'm sitting sideways on a peacock for God's sake! And I can feel a breeze as we fly through the air. This starts to fade – I have no idea what it means or where the images are coming from.

Pan seems to be with me a lot of the time now and when I sit to meditate He's there again. We're on the edge of a forest, standing in the undergrowth. I realise that it's night time and there's a full moon in a clear sky. I look across the undergrowth and see a beach curving away from where we stand. I don't know how I know but it's a lake side beach, not the seashore. It's very calm, with moonlight shimmering on the water. On the beach there are four or five men squatting around a campfire. They're dark skinned, with black wiry hair, like Aborigines. They have white paint daubed on their faces and chests. I feel very drawn to them, that natural life style, living in harmony with nature. I ask if I can go and sit with them. Pan says it's fine. As I'm walking over to them, Pan says "Talk to the medicine man instead." I can see another figure standing just beyond the group, sitting down, so I walk over to him. He takes my right forearm and presses what looks like the head and fangs of a snake into the inside of my arm. It hurts! But this seems to be the way he makes a connection to "read" me. After a few minutes he says I'm on the right path but I have a long journey ahead of me. Thanks! I'm shown the forest again. It's thick but not impenetrable, full of mystery and the unknown."

**"The thing I've started to notice more and more when I'm outside, especially when I'm training, is a very sharp sense of joy and connection to the natural world. Even on a bleak, grey day there's a real sense of wonder and excitement. It thrills me! Weird I know – I also feel like the buildings are in the way, an intrusion. And everything has more meaning, if only I could read it. As I get into meditation Pan is there again. He's in His awesome aspect. He's huge and I'm glad to see Him. He comes down in size and sits nearby. I don't touch Him but it's as if I can feel the coarse hair on His legs – weird! Then I realise He's smoking a pipe! It's small, rough, white clay, unglazed. I'm surprised to say the least – not something I'd expect Him to do. He says it's ganja!!! He finds it relaxing! His image blurs as if I'm seeing double and another figure separates from Him – it's Shiva! He sits next to Pan. Pan is still the one with the ganja – not Shiva!*

I go back to the feelings I've had recently, the joyfulness of nature. As I've said before, the communication is not through words, more through images and feelings, but what I get is a sense a how everything comes from this joy or love. Sounds so bloody new-agey. But the constructs of man get in the way – on the outside it's the buildings, roads and all the material paraphernalia we surround ourselves with. These are like a metaphor for what happens on the inside. On the inside it's the mental constructs we put up to make ourselves feel safe and real – all the ego stuff and self protection. But it gets in the way, stops us from seeing the true nature of being, and that means "being" anything, from a blade of grass, an animal, a human or a God. We can be all of these things. So the task is to start deconstructing all this clutter. Some mental constructs have to stay and are useful – but so many are not."

**"I settle into meditation. Pan's there in the background. As I'm sitting I become aware of someone else sitting nearby. I can see blue legs and a leopard skin loin cloth. It's Shiva again. I'm alarmed. I look at Pan and ask if He's leaving. I don't want Him to go. He says no, He'll be around in the background. He also "says" something like "You're beginning to understand, little one." Shiva comes up to me and presses His thumb, first into my sternum, near the heart, and then into my forehead, at "sky eye". He says, "These two are connected, like citta - heart/mind, and both have to be opened." I'm thinking about this when I realise He's walking away. "You're leaving?" I ask. He turns and says "I'll come back." Then He's gone. I guess I've been shown what I need to work on but I'm not sure how!"*

**"This is the first time in days when I can just sit and not worry about time. Before I settle into meditation I fiddle around a lot with the incense, trying to get it to stand upright so the ash won't fall all over the cloth on my altar- I even have a bit of Blue Tack to hold it in place. Then I close my eyes- almost immediately I can see a circle of fire. I try to ignore it and settle into quietness but it won't go away. It looks like the circle round the Nataraja and I can "feel" the invitation to step through it. Somewhat reluctantly I do. I find myself standing high on a mountain top, with panoramic views over lush green valley, all under a clear blue sky. I'm standing on the edge of a vertical drop. Shiva and Pan are both there and the unspoken invitation is to jump!!*

I'm afraid and I look to Pan on my left for reassurance, He says it's ok, so I lean forward as if to fall but find I'm sort of flying, I can feel the air rushing past me, but I don't understand what it means. Shiva tells me I should ask more questions, not just wait to be shown things (fair enough) Then we're back where we started. I think I asked something along the lines of "what is the spiritual quest for?" Duh. I look for Pan and am reassured to see Him sitting on His haunches behind me, quite happy with the proceedings. Shiva says" Why are you looking at Him? Look at me, look me in the face" I try, but no matter how hard I try to focus all I can see are lots of different images flashing in front of me, all sorts of things from demons to flowers. It's weird. I can't put a face on the head in front of me. Then it dawns on me, I am looking Him in the face, He is everywhere, in everything, wherever I look I will see Him and I will also see Shakti. The two are inseparable, aspects of the Absolute, the Void, the Dao, whatever you want to call it. Shiva/Shakti are the first, the primary source of all things, They come from the Void, that formless, nameless, nothingness that contains everything, every possibility in every universe. It has no beginning and no end. It is beyond my comprehension yet I sense it is there.

I stay with these thoughts for a while, and then I find myself back at the fire circle, going through and stepping off that edge again. This time I fall and it's a weird sensation, almost as if I'm on fire, it's not hot but the image is of something being burned off. And I understand that we have to do this over and over again - stepping into emptiness, trusting the process, maybe burning off karma (I don't know) again and again every day, every year, life after life! Just keep letting go over and over, again and again. I open my eyes and burst out laughing - the first thing I see is the incense stick I had so carefully made to stand upright is now virtually horizontal and there's a long line of ash on the cloth. Ok I get the message - let go, stop trying to control!"

How cool is all this? My thanks to Elaine for sharing her meditation journal. It takes a lot of courage to open oneself like this, but I know that Elaine, and Suzie too in the next chapter, has a sincere wish to help and inspire others. Some of the above material may seem fantastical and trippy, but then dreams are like that, aren't they? And once the ego stops trying to interfere with meditation material, then that can get a bit weird too. The weirder the better I say – information from the unconscious mind is usually surreal and ambiguous - it's the task of the meditator to then sift through the material and try and make sense of it all.

CHAPTER FOURTEEN - THE DARSHAN DIARIES – PART TWO - THE KALI KHRONICLES.

Suzie's record of her experiences differs from that of Elaine's. Her practice is quite structured through yantra work, so her journal is very structured too, and her progress very thoughtful. Her experiences are no less vivid than Elaine's but the chakra work she undertook some time ago – which apparently had slipped from her mind! – makes her a very lucid and disciplined meditator. Her decision to use the Kali Yantra as her sadhana also helped to give focus and a framework to her efforts. Her journal reads like the ideal diary of a determined yogini!

Suzie's journal.

* *"I feel as if the Goddess Kali has been around somewhere, nudging me, pushing me to pay attention to her. I have had Lord Shiva and Ganesh in my life for some time, but Kali (unbeknown to me) has been with me for two years at least. And I never realized!*

Julian Wilde was kind enough to share some of the draft chapters of this book with myself and another couple of his trusted students. It was the preliminary chapter 'Designs on Divinity' in this book that started the whole thing. There she was! It was like an invitation, open and full-on. Scary or what! All I knew about her really was the lolling tongue, the severed heads, the skull necklaces - Kali."

* *"With some advice from Sifu Jules, I chose a yantra to study. I practiced visualizing the Kali yantra, until I could duplicate it quite easily in my mind's eye. There are a few, slightly differing, designs to choose from, I chose one that appeared to be blood red on the screen of my pc, but my printer coughed out deep pinks and blues, quite beautiful actually, and of course as I looked 'into' the yantra I felt the power of it, drawing me into the five layered triangle and into the tunnel. It opened up to me, came out to meet me, pulling me in like a magnet. It felt familiar somehow, warm, reddish, like I imagine it was in the womb, floating in amniotic fluid, surrounding me, holding me. The anticipation was that of the unknown, strong yet spelling "caution". At the same time, or was it much later? I don't know, I got the feeling I was being deliberately held back. I understood, and yet I didn't! and I pulled out quickly the first time. I put the Yantra beside my bed, but I had to move it, it was such a force, such a distraction, like a clock that ticked too loudly.*

.

I tried again the next night. It felt less 'full on', the colours were dark red, deep plum. Again there was a cautionary yet inviting vibe. There was a point when I pulled out again.

The next couple of days felt as if I was waiting around, just to see what may happen, rather than trying to force anything.

I looked at the Yantra and still felt the pull, I closed my eyes feeling and seeing it in different colours, then it's over."

* *"Yesterday morning I felt Her presence in that space between sleep and awakening, I could sense a putrid smell, burning kind of smell, I asked Her what I had to learn from Her. The dark side of the beautiful Shakti, wife of Lord Shiva, the Mother Goddess, She turned slightly and gave me a guttural snarl. The sound was fluid!*

I feel I should be really scared, but I'm not. The feeling does remain that of caution though, that I may be getting myself into dangerous unknown territory, which I may not have the skill to handle."

* *"Today has been a 'mindful Kali' day. I have decided to draw it tomorrow, Her yantra, I wonder if it might help me understand this shadow self. I feel quite excited by the possibility of getting to know Her.*

Well, with all the best intentions, I was about to sit down to draw the yantra when I got called away!

It's ten past midnight, I'm going to settle my mind now. She is almost palpable - and I'm sorry I've been unable to give Her the time She deserves.

I kneel before Buddha to say my prayers and pay homage to the Triple Gem. I also bow to Lord Shiva and Ganesh, as has been my practice for some time. I guess this is a strange practice, but even the Gods revere Buddha. I'm no different."

* *"I speak to Kali. Her hands appear long and thin, very dark, her nails are long and pale, like the dead. She is a calm presence, but alert. Is She waiting for me to do, say, something? Did she call Jules, because he came, and bowed before her, then stood at my shoulder, as encouraging me to 'know' what I am supposed to know ... looking into her, into her real nature...into me?*

* *I went to Amaravati Buddhist Monastery today. I felt my heart was open, my qi was strong, I felt tingly and alive. As I sat in front of the golden Buddha rupa, I asked for blessings to be bestowed on my teacher and his family, friends and relatives. I was also embracing Kali and the Gods and deities.*

* *I've just traced Kali's Yantra. I suddenly remembered a dream I had a year or two ago, it went like this: I was walking through a forest where I came across a young man. He was wounded, hungry and in need of*

nurture. I nursed him like an infant. Kali is sometimes shown as nursing Shiva. I didn't know that then.

Another time (this happened more than once), an old hag appeared, looking down on me. She was green and ancient, deeply lined. When she appeared again, she smiled, a kindly smile - behind that ugly mask was a tender heart. As if she understood the suffering of the world.

I now believe this was Kali. And She was approving my caring for the young man – which of course was me!"

** "Kali in my head. She has become very much part of my day to day life, venturing into her Yantra is like moving across into another dimension... I am in another mind set, I can feel the change psychologically, this as yet unknown place, a deep pulsating cavernous space. For a moment I imagine all the stories about the bloody devouring of humans or demons, but then She's there, leading, following, waiting, watching, trusting me to carry on. I feel depressed and paranoid, wondering if I am way out of my depth. But there is a clarity that I have a choice, always, I don't have to stay here, or I can carry on. What's the worst that can happen? No, somehow I don't think I'll be annihilated!*

It's just a visit into Kali's world. She has a kindness about her. A mutual respect is growing. (That statement feels like tempting fate!)

I came upon this story of Kali - after she had destroyed all the demons in battle she began to dance, a frenzied, joyful victorious dance. All the worlds trembled and swayed with the impact of her swirling rhythmic movement. The Gods asked Shiva to intervene and stop this wild behavior, but it is said that she was too intoxicated to listen. (Wilful child!) The Lord Shiva lay like a corpse among the slain demons to absorb the shock of the dance into Himself. When Kali eventually stepped on her husband she realized her mistake, and bit her tongue in shame.

Only Shiva could tame her. As only He could match her wildness. It is also written that He challenged her to the wild Tandava dance .... outdoing Her! The two of them danced together, driving each other into such an uncontrollable state that the world came close to unraveling.

So, what's this got to do with my growing relationship with The Mother Goddess? She is showing me aspects of myself that I need to attend to. She reflects back to me (like finding the demon story) that I can be "carelessly careless", thoughtlessly uncaring of myself in certain situations. Right now I would be fearful of treading (symbolically) on anyone close to me, as a powerlessness overcomes me at the thought! She is showing me how to...what? I shall do the work, just how I am not yet sure but there is a trust in Her that is difficult to ignore."

* *"I and a friend set off happily on the journey to Amaravati Monastery again, to attend a much anticipated weekend retreat. We arrived safely after fighting our way through rain, wind and hail, reveling in the blissful peace and tranquility. In time, fortunately, for lunch! Always a pleasure here, the warm spices and aromatic dishes of our once-a-day meal beckon us. Desire arises!*

I was wondering eagerly when or if at all I would encounter Kali. I'm even feeling a little disloyal, being here in this place for a Buddhist retreat (I have a long way to go, don't I!).

When the meal was finished we joined a few people to pay our respects to Lung Por (Grandfather) Sumedho. As one of the people turned to go - there She was! Kali, in the form of Durga sitting on the back of a tiger, blazoned across the front of this beautiful black woman's T shirt.

HOORAY!!

I manage to contain myself...... just.

The problem is mine of course. When it comes to Buddha and/or God/dess, there's me thinking I'm not prejudiced in any shape or form. Generally speaking I'm not, but as you see there is something needing attention in me - where was all that expansion, and embracing of all beliefs that I truly feel? I'll have the opportunity to explore all that this weekend.

But here She is, meeting me here in a Buddhist Monastery, in the presence of our beloved Lung Por. No one is fazed by Gods and deities around here. Way cool. Well it's new to me but I should have known better. Our retreat leader spoke freely of deities, in relation to Buddhism."

* *"Why Kali? I was introduced to Lord Shiva earlier this year, and Ganesh, the elephant-headed son from the union of Lord Shiva and Shakti. I knew Kali as Shakti's dark side. As I work with Her yantra, I can feel the pull, a bit scary at first. But actually, feeling Kali's presence is powerful but not that threatening. She's snarled at me once but only, I think, because I felt unsure of myself in Her company. That time there was a putrid "bloodlust" smell too. I thought of her as a blood-thirsty demon type but actually She feels much softer, although there is a strong willfulness about Her, and if I don't "get" what She's trying to show me, She stops wasting her time and goes! She just goes! I don't like it much, and that of course is why She does it. I'm catching on. She mostly feels within reach, She's teasing me out of my scaredy-cat low esteem. When I don't shift from it, it's like She's saying .... Ok, it's your choice - just stay there then!*

And maybe I have to let go a little, of this desire of waiting, wanting for something to happen. And if something does happen it may not be the 5th of

November firework display I'd like. So it's back to basics then. If I sound flippant it's not intentional - it's the excitement and fear (of missing the point) and the expectation of being right in there but unable to comprehend. Ah well, it's not as if I have anything to prove to anyone.

So here at Amaravati we're sitting to meditate as well as practicing our walking meditation. On a whim I choose to do my qigong after a 45 minute sit. I hardly notice the others around me – and they're lost in their own mindfulness. It's lovely.

The next time we walk we're advised to do a free will meditation. A rather wonderful thing happens! I see the Kali Yantra everywhere - in every blazing autumn tree, in an evergreen I had never seen before that looks as fresh as spring - in the grass where, in the tread of a tractor wheel, is the five line deep triangle of the yantra. I see it in a deserted rooks' nest at the top of a small birch. I see it on the 'spire' of the temple and in the vapour trail of a plane flying off somewhere warm on our cold and frosty morning. Kali has enriched my life in unexpected, inspiring, ways - and She seems to be saying quite clearly that She loves the Amaravati environment as much as I do.

My body feels loose and supple, moving easily - the mind is trouble free, holding those I love with tenderness."

** "The Chakra Experience. As you will read, or have read, the author has written in depth concerning the chakras relating to Kundalini Yoga. This really brought up some old stuff for me, and set me off on a hunt for an ancient chakra chart I had made many years ago, when I was attempting to arouse the Kundalini. There it was! And there was the awaited 5th of November firework display too! I realise that Kali and I have met before. I remember stopping the process then because of the overwhelming feeling of fear...of the unknown. How could I have forgotten? I knew even back then that something I was only "playing around" with was real! I know now it was my ignorance and lack of understanding - worse still, I didn't really believe in what I was doing. But now my awareness is beginning to grow, working with a group of close friends, beginning to study the yantra, picking up and staying open to the signs, dreams, Kali is part of my life. Looking at my ancient hand drawn chakra chart from many years ago, I remember the story of Kali in the form of Maha Devi, the Great Shining One...*

A bull-headed demon was threatening heaven so all the Gods gathered together. There was Indra, Agni the Fire God, Suraya the Sun God, Chandra the Moon God, Yama the God of Death, and many others. Their indignant energy created a great luminosity and from this glow a deity was born, partaking of all the power of the collected Gods. Each God gave various parts of Her body different powers – Her many hands held different weapons and a conch to call warriors to battle. When She arose, complete in Her perfection, the Gods shouted "Jaya!" – "Vanquish!" And She did vanquish – She slew the demon army. I can feel Her now – fearless, exuberant, terrifyingly wonderful!

I feel Her energy stir within me, holding me in a place of joyful anticipation of things to come."

** "There is a noticeable change in the atmosphere as Kali comes. One could argue that "going into Her yantra" predisposes me to the experiences I have when She is present, and I can't prove to others what happens. I know what I experience though.*

I enter the movement, and colour. It feels like a living organism, pulsing, dense yet flowing. Maybe I'm dreaming, maybe this is what it felt like in the womb. It feels easier here, there is no outside, or inside - there is just "being here" - wherever "here" is.

There were no more questions in my head - I wasn't wondering what to do, or what was going to happen. There She is, in full view. My heart quickens. Now She's sitting in a half lotus. I raise my hands in anjali, She returns the gesture. My body is alive, buzzing with energy. I don't have to tell Her this, I know She knows how it is. I know she has the patience (as long as I stay alert) to wait for me to understand what She has to say, which is not always in words. She has been known to make me feel I'm wasting her time! But this is what She's showing me - to look at my fearfulness of "exposure", which becomes so much a part of how I am. If I don't respond She will turn and go - quite angrily!

I'm unsure of the significance of what she shows me next. In one of her hands she held a silver, I think they are called pomanders, a sphere-shaped, open-worked object that could be filled with sweet smelling herbs, rose petals, that sort of thing. In another hand was a vessel, shaped like an Aladdin's lamp, but open, no lid, scooped out. It looks like finely carved wood, which is black, very rich looking. A third hand holds a piece of cloth. Could it be to cover the head? Or maybe it's to sit on whilst meditating. I thank Her for the image, and ask what I may need these objects for? She looks into me with smouldering, beautiful eyes. She speaks, saying that these things were my past and would be my destiny.

I can't hold these gifts in my hands but gifts they are, and it's up to me to discover their purpose. At this moment I just feel bewildered.

A warning now as She's going, to be careful of someone who envies me. Me! Envied? Nah!

When She's gone, wisps of her energy remain. I smell her smell, feel her fire, her oh so absolutely pure "Goddessness". Is there such a word? I feel

Her inside me.

One last thing, for now. I keep Kali's yantra by my bed. I took some pictures to class the other day and when I opened the book I had put them in for safe keeping, the yantra had come too! It's back by my bed now."

** "After offending Kali yesterday with my stupidity (don't ask!), I humbly pay my respects, asking for forgiveness. I am so honoured by Her presence in my life, and could so easily sully that by my ignorant behaviour. And that was it for today - She didn't come. I don't blame Her.*

I sit to meditate again in the evening. And now, again, in the morning. I ask Her for guidance.

And then it's "Hello Mother Goddess, welcome!" We sit quietly, no words pass between us. And that is how we stay 'til She withdraws, 15-20 minutes later.

The rest of the day I had a singing heart thinking about sitting with Her, feeling so grateful that She had returned - especially after being less than respectful to Her a couple of day's previous... Having felt her wrath, Her displeasure, I am eager to please Her now!

When I sit to meditate in the evening I ask Her for more guidance. I learn about her yantra. She says the very centre point, the bindu, is She, Her very essence, that of divine love. I remember my Sifu telling me that's how to approach a yantra, sit before it with eyes open taking it in from the centre. One of my faults is I get a bit big for my boots sometimes and try things my way - of course this is very childlike isn't it, and invariably I set myself up to fail. Sometimes though I have got things amazingly right!

This time I listen and practice, internalising every corner, circle, the five triangles - the colours envelop me. It feels wonderfully different from before, partly because I have settled into a less emotionally charged way of being with Her, I don't feel so conscious of how to behave (I've learnt a lesson, I've been forgiven. Just think, I might have ended up on Her necklace of skulls!!) No offence, honest. I sense her smile at this.

The bindu/atman (self)/divine love/Kali is, I'm told, the eternal link with the Absolute. That's like WOW, isn't it?

I've found some info as I felt I needed to be a bit proactive, just so when Kali comes again, hopefully whilst I'm meditating, it would be good to share this stuff.

Kali the Goddess of Regeneration, Transformation. She reminds me I am only human. I suppose this is suggesting that I may well mess up again!

"Kali Gifts" I think she does give me gifts, when I am not expecting anything. Her yantra appeared on the back of a van a couple of mornings ago, just after I happened to see a dear friend - a one in several thousand chance at that time of day - sending me of to work with a little song in my heart.

I talk to Her a lot, and hear Her/ sense Her answers or reactions. She uses words I don't understand at times, and then I stumble across them later. I read somewhere about one of Her meditation chant and couldn't figure out how on earth you can chant the sound "so" whilst breathing in. Then I heard a rather mirthful Kali said "Chant in your mind!"

** "Look What's Happening Now. Kali is dwelling in me. Her presence is forceful, She is pushing me to look at aspects of my life that need to be looked at, but would actually be a great loss if I were to follow her direction. I know that doesn't sound right. I'll explain in a minute.*

The main thread of my practice is Buddhism, that is unquestionable. I may have said before that I feel I was born a Buddhist - in the centre of my Catholic upbringing lay the Buddhist teachings waiting to be discovered. My life took one of those changes that happen periodically, if allowed to do so.

Lord Shiva and Ganesh became part of my life a while ago. I've asked far more of Them than I have given. Shiva will show up, mostly when I am meditating. I am greatly honored by His presence. Ganesh has a playful, make everyone happy, feel about Him. He has brought a good feel to my home.

Kali though - She dwells in me, taking me to uncharted territory - fearful anger, was that really me on Saturday, so angry towards one of my friends? Kali told me I behaved like a floor cloth, I was allowing myself to be used like one!!

Unwillingly I am being "forced", although I am free to walk away - or am I? Who knows? But here it is, I find myself beginning to look at my life anew. If changes were made, the kind I'm considering, it would cause great loss to me. I feel the urge to travel, to leave everyone behind. I'm not sure if I could manage another change just yet, and yet it is coming to me that I should. She is not about to let it rest. This is why at this time Kali has come to me. I can feel her pleasure at me arriving at this place!

I have to get ready for work now but I'll be back, something's happening and I want to be around for it!!"

** "Changing Foot - I noticed earlier, as I was struggling in the company of someone I once knew well, and had not seen for sometime, that as they were pouring out the usual (for them) ailments and dissatisfactions about* *almost everything - the rhythm in the Kali/Suzie relationship changed - the feeling was that of 'changing foot' when riding, or watching the tide turn. The reins were being gently tugged to suit the situation - the growing frustration within me simply changed to that of acceptance, tempered with compassion. I felt within me the deep joy of Kali's smile. She had made her point and sensed my realization.*

A step nearer to the ending of attachments. I breathed one of Her meditation chants "So Ham", feeling my feet a little more firmly planted on the earth (for now anyway). The heart opened in acceptance of, to use a Buddhist phrase, "The way things are."

Sharing my recent experience of feeling a strong urge to "up sticks" and follow my desire to go off to India and lose myself in a journey of discovery, before it's too late – well, thanks to the counsel of a close friend and confidant, I am able to hold that wish, to wait for my Goddess. To truly make Her "my" Goddess. He rightly pointed out that She is not Indian - or English. I didn't HAVE to go anywhere, She is right here where I am. I know this is true.

Am I dreaming though? When I feel the swish of silk around my ankles, and the smell of heat/spices in my nose, I see the huge yellow sun through a sand saturated atmosphere...There stands my Kali, as straight as a Chun Yuen Master (Kung Fu), nostrils flaring, smouldering eyes, inviting me to stay here.

'Here I am, I am everywhere and anywhere I choose to be'.

As the relation ship between the Mother Goddess Kali and me grows, I have a deeper understanding of letting attachments to anything go. Well almost anything, this is always the obstacle, isn't it - to let go of certain things feels like tearing your heart out, however sincere the aspiration is to do so.

I get the sense that attachment merely restricts the possibilities within a relationship, as one 'expects' or 'wants' certain things from the relationship. Once the contact is made, the attraction to another sealed, it is all together possible, in fact it's very likely, to develop and grow. Hopefully, meeting in a companionable, spiritual or a more intimate place can become entirely a non-selfish union on all levels. Kali seems to be saying 'ownership is out', although that contradicts the making Kali "mine" statement. This is not meant as "attachment".

She, Kali, makes herself available to me whenever...

I pay homage to Her, I breathe Her mantra in meditation. To me she is a tangible presence, I always get a response. She makes it very clear if she is not pleased! Scary!!

What is really something is that whenever I have approached Kali, Shiva or Ganesh, there is a response. (Think I'm making this up? Try it! With reverence though - if you ain't serious, you may not get the response you think you want.)

The energy of that feels... well, dare I say it? FEARLESS! Yep that feels ok.

Kali is Fearless, strong headed, willful - and She dwells willingly in my heart."

**"Breaking Old Habits. As this New Year (2007) gets underway for me, as usual and I guess for many of us, reflections of the past come to the fore, our behaviour and how others perceive and treat us.*

I am feeling the urgency of Kali's direction. She is quite motherly at first, but it seems I am quite stuck. Am I stubborn or is it laziness? I hadn't realized I was 'lazy' and felt quite offended when my Qigong, and Taiji Sifu said I was. But he's right, so it helped me when Kali clearly felt the same. Laziness in my case comes from resistance - 'Can't do this bit, so I'll fluff it and move on to the bit I am sure about", but like everything else there is a method, a 'form' to follow. If you mess up along the way it's back to basics, learn, understand, then move on.

In my youth I was a freedom fighter - in my own way of course. I banned the bomb at Sizewell, hung around Greenham Common, marched with millions on London. Great huh? BUT I never freed myself!!

Kali comes.

Kali is here, a strong soothing mother sense of her. I don't always see Her but I can speak and She hears me. I must be doing something right to deserve this. I feel her behind me. I rest in Her. One of my most blissful moments is melting back into a lover's arms. I sink into Kali Ma. She wants me to remember.

Lord Shiva comes.

Another gift from Shiva. He appears as a vision wearing only a snake around his neck, leaving me with no doubt of his manliness!! Turned his back on me (equally as beautiful) then went! Thanx ... So. What is that about?

As the year wears on I'm reminded of past situations that have been repeated over and over, a repetitious pattern is emerging, (oh lets just ignore it , it'll go away) But it wont! I keep feeling as if Kali is coming, the atmosphere changes, becomes charged with anticipation, my mind clicks into alertness. I hate to make Her angry by seeming not to pay attention. God(dess) how could I not!

It's all coming together. I can see a trail of past habits that forms a familiar way of being. At that point I felt a palpable release, a clearing, a block unblocked. There She is then, like Yes!

So there's the thing, the pattern, my pattern of committing. Once committed I stick with it even if it's potentially harmful or useless. Why do I do this? Now there's the question. Let's see if I can push through the 'lazy' me on this one to find an answer!"

**"How it is". My very good friend and mentor asked me how the practice is going, "Quiet," I said," It's quiet." I should have added only as far as Kali Ma is leaving me to it, so to speak. She has a way of quietly being present. I feel she is enjoying my interpretation of Her yantra. Of course I have researched the geometrical pattern, observed the breathtaking beauty and power of it. The colour of the yantra is apparently red, blue and black, mine printed out as a rich deep pink, light blue, dark blue, and soft pink .*

Starting from the bindu, the centre - this represents the soul 'Atman' the internal link with the Absolute. This is the entrance if you like. There seemed no choice - if this is the intention, to study this yantra, then the power of it draws you in. This was my first encounter with my Mother Goddess if you remember. I could never forget, snarling guttural noises came from Her then, looking at me sideways on, head down, testing, daring me to continue. Well, I took the challenge!

But: the point of recording this part of the process is to say Kali is here. When I sit to meditate She is with me, I am honoring Her by studying her yantra. I only have my experience of that, I know what I feel, and see. It's complicated and unfamiliar, yet I know it! Somehow the blueprint is filed away in my psyche. No worries about deviating either, I would soon know if I was outa line!

It seems important, as it was my intention from the beginning to do just this, that the yantra was to be (and is) investigated in meditation. It was Kali who caused the diversion (how cool is that?).

So, it's quiet at the moment, yes, but humming and vibrant, alive with the beauty of Shakti, and the horror of my scary Goddess - skulls, blood, severed heads and all."

Phew! This is all great stuff. My heartfelt thanks to Elaine and Suzie. Both women have found that a real connection with the divinities is self regulatory. That is, a relationship where the communications and the resulting insights are genuinely from the deity, or at least from the non-ego based unconscious mind, rather than from the "imagination", from the ego-self, tends to prevent the devotee from slipping into delusion, self aggrandizement, superiority or, on the other hand, into self abasement and depression. The Gods and Goddesses, if approached correctly, actually seem to care!

I get the feeling sometimes, and Suzie and Elaine may have had the same intuition, that the deities, particularly the more extreme or marginalized ones like Pan, Shiva Bhairav (wrathful form of Shankara) and Kali, are very wary of over-institutionalisation, of "cold" rituals, where the devotee isn't really emotionally involved. They like you to pay attention! I know from long experience how easy it is for prayers, for morning puja, to become automatic, routine. The God/desses' presence and their teachings, come and go spontaneously, with little rhyme or reason. They can be "called", but with varying degrees of success. They exhibit very human characteristics – impatience, unexpected humour, tenderness etc. Their teachings may not make sense at the time, or may even be uncomfortable. However, enough seems to happen, both "in contact" and in daily life, to maintain the devotee on a generally even emotional keel. This isn't to say that there won't be periods of depression, self loathing, bursts of self congratulatory pride, what psychologists call "elevation", or even just great clouds of confusion. There will be all these elements, at different times, but generally the trend should be towards greater self sufficiency and a healthy, if still critical, self regard.

The divinities also seem suspicious of "anti-life" systems, spiritual paths that either repress or ignore unattractive or base aspects of ourselves or our lives. They seem to prefer an "authentic mess" to a polished illusion, an honest muddle to a pretended perfection. This may be because They're not perfect either – They're still conditioned beings, though compared to our habitual states of being and awareness, They're transcendent, omniscient and omnipotent!

One thing is for sure – just as in ancient times, the one thing that is sure to bring heaven's fire scorching into your underpants is hubris – arrogant pride. So be careful, if you have any reason to believe that your imagination or your ego is taking over your spiritual practice, your relationship to the Gods or Goddesses, do some basic meditation for a while, no visualization, just sitting in emptiness, reflecting on your conduct. Give things time to settle down before carrying with on your usual practice. Do it before the divinities have to do it for you!

Buddhas, on the other hand, are huge, limitless repositories of wisdom and compassion. It's very unlikely a Buddha would zap your ass! But the Buddhas are more remote. Their very liberation has released them from conditioning, from much of the human world, from interaction. They tend to act more like beacons, like moral compasses, like inspirational examples, whereas a relationship with, for example, Shiva or Kali, feels more like an interactive computer game! You soon know when you've screwed up!

You also know when the presence of a deity is authentic, when you're not just day dreaming or imagining...

"Ash paste on skin, wood smoke stings in hair and eyes

Fire in fingers and inside ribs
The heart crashes
Thin wires sing within the skin
Red mud like clotted blood on knuckles, ankles, shins
Snap back, crack back, the head is slapped back
Ecstasy's surge brings numbing limbs
The shape of other worlds sensed
Through palms tensed, pressed up and in
Body hair floats in the liquid, swelling, darkening air
And visions come when the world goes numb"

Way cool! And all without drugs!

Even as you're reading this book, I'm sure new entries are being made in the Darshan Diaries. Both Suzie and Elaine have come a long way and their journey continues to unfold. It's a delight and a privilege to be able to share my inner life with them both – we each understand what the others are experiencing, where we're coming from. If I couldn't communicate this stuff I'd go mad, or be afraid I was going mad! Spiritual companionship, mutual support, is very precious. The Buddha Himself said it was the whole of the holy life – not part, not half – the whole.

CHAPTER FIFTEEN - BUDDHA, BHAIRAV AND THE BOGEY MAN

The commercial world wants to sell us dreams – all Christmases are picturesque and snow covered - delightful days, where happy families play board games together and eat mince pies and turkey, perfectly prepared in a happy, stress-free kitchen. All summer holidays are endless golden interludes of sun and sea, where white-jacketed waiters bring you exotic cocktails on silver trays. All relationships can be salvaged with a diamond or a box of chocolates. All men laugh together and cheer, with their adoring sons, at football matches. Electric razors really can shave as close a blade. Pine scented tampons (you couldn't make this up, could you?) enrich every woman's life. The only physical symptom of thrush in TV land is a slightly perplexed wrinkle of the brow. Every new album by any artiste you've never heard of is "stunning" and magically already features ten hit singles! All cars are driven at seventy miles an hour on totally empty mountain roads...

Buy the product, live the dream. That's the message, isn't it?

Now, in our heart of hearts, we know this is, what's the term...ABSOLUTE BOLLOCKS! don't we? But it's so insidious, so intrusive. And this pushing of fantasy extends into the spiritual life. I was heartened to see, in a local bookstore, so many, many books on Shamanism, Paganism and Wicca, complete with a community notice board for such individuals and groups to meet, practice and trade stuff. Mucho brillyfab. But how many of these books are just pushing a variation on the commercial message? Buy this product, live the dream. How many Shamans could kill a weasel and inspect the guts to tell the future? How many would know how to get a weasel without a credit card? How many "witches" wouldn't dream of holding moots (meetings) outside their cosy, centrally-heated houses? And certainly not when The X Factor is on! How many pagans just like to dress up in hessian robes and call themselves Thor Bloodbollocks or Lorelei Frigfinger because it compensates for their sad, impotent little life in the stationery supplies department of a local insurance company?

Ok, ok, I'll calm down. And I know most of you out there are sincere in what you believe and efficient in your practice. And I'm aware that people could think the same about me, that I'm just a sad little middle-aged man trying to make himself sound special, more important. And it's good that there's so much information available now about "alternative" religious practices. But we have to be careful that we're not unconsciously buying into the conditioning, that we're not just trying to live the dream by adopting a new pagan name and buying a new athame (that's a Wiccan ceremonial knife) every friggin' Halloween. I suppose what I'm saying (apart from "sorry") is "keep it real."

And Buddhists can be just as bad. They think they can "think away" their darker side, their hindrances, the poisons of ill will, ignorance and attachment. They think if they sit and meditate long enough, they'll somehow whitewash themselves into enlightenment. They're forgetting something, something important...

Long, long ago, the Buddha started to teach those around Him, or at least those that would listen. He did this WHY? Not so He could claim to be a religious founder, not to score with chicks (It's a scientifically proven fact that chicks dig bald men in orange robes. Honest!), not to make people his slaves. No, He did it to enlighten people – TO MAKE THEM BUDDHAS TOO. And the implication, in those early days, was that it was attainable, achievable within a few years. It seemed to be taken for granted, back then, that if you followed the Enlightened One around, adopted His lifestyle, His moral code, practiced what He told you – then before too long, you'd get good results, win liberation.

So what happened? Are people so dumb, so busy, so distracted, so lazy these days, that no one can enlighten themselves? (And many that do think that they're enlightened are either charlatans or complete nutters) Have we fallen that far?

Many would say yes, we probably have, but basic human nature doesn't change much, even over centuries. There are saints and bastards in every age. If anything, people are perhaps more tolerant now than they were a thousand years ago. (That's a debatable point I know – argue amongst yourselves) So why have we elevated the Buddha's achievements out of all reach? Why have we placed His accomplishment, which was admittedly pretty cool, on a high pedestal and now content ourselves with walking round it, saluting it and wistfully hoping that one day, if we just meditate enough, read enough literature, refrain from lust and anger or at least have the good grace to feel guilty about our lust and anger, we'll float off into the white light and feel, well... good about ourselves.

Of course, the Buddha removed Himself by His very accomplishment. We can't really understand what it's like to be a Buddha, how it feels. We can't ask Him. If He could answer, would we understand? He left a vast, vast, I mean vast, literature behind Him. There are rules and teachings and sub-teachings and widely different interpretations of everything He said, did, failed to say or do. You could spend many lifetimes becoming a better Buddhist. But that's not what He wanted for you. He said so many times – question the teachings, use what works. He wanted us to be awake.

But of course, unless we're very smart, we don't know what works unless we try it first. So there's an awful lot of stumbling around, disillusionment with various schools, methods or teachers, until we find something that appears to work. And just because something feels good doesn't mean it's working.

The religious life can get extremely challenging, extremely uncomfortable at times. Sometimes we have to face stuff within us, stuff that's very unpleasant, in order to evolve.

I'd like to share a nightmare I had many, many years ago. It was a bad time for me. I was suffering from lack of confidence, work wasn't going well, my relationship with my family was shaky, I was permanently tired and stressed out. I'm sure you can empathise! I felt somehow frozen, trapped, like a fly in amber. I went through a period when I was experiencing really horrible, vivid, shit-ya-pants nightmares two or three times a week. But this one was somehow the worst, but also pivotal, the turning point for me.

Picture the scene. It's late autumn, a real Halloween kind of night. It's dark and windy. I'm in an old house, which I assume is my family home. It's very large, at least three floors, Victorian in style. The furniture is dark and cumbersome. The lighting is bad, the lamps give out a sickly, sallow glow that somehow manages to conceal more than it reveals, and is actually scarier than darkness would be. I stand in the middle of the hall looking up the stairs, which go up to a landing and then veer off to the left to go further up. I can hear something, I'm not sure what. I strain my ears. I can hear bare branches scraping against the windows, but that's not it. I can hear the low moan of the wind under the door – that's not it either. There! A sound from upstairs. It sounds like a door is banging somewhere at the top of the house. I know I'm going to have to go up there to take a look, and I know I don't want to. Whoop de freakin' doo.

I call out to my wife but I know she can't hear me. I sigh and start up the stairs. As soon as I start to ascend, the feeling of isolation and some kind of impending doom intensifies. I'm not a happy bunny. I climb as far as the landing then turn to look up the next flight. It seems dimmer, the light a dark mustard colour. The whole feeling is very Victorian, like Jack the Ripper is waiting up there. I can hear the banging door louder. I sigh again like a brave little soldier and continue to climb. I'm actually very frightened by now. I get up as far as another landing and there are two or three doors off to the left. One of them is slightly ajar, just a couple of inches. This door, I know, is the culprit, but now there's no sound except the wind and the mad banging of my heart. I go into a kind of paralysis. Something awful is waiting, I know it, beyond any doubt.

I move to the door, so reluctantly, and try to push it slightly. It slams shut! I nearly die right there and then. I turn the handle and try to open it again. There's a resistance, as if someone, or something, is on the other side of the door. It feels as if the very air pressure inside the room is higher than on my side. I can actually feel my heart hammering right up in my throat. I think my testicles are trying to climb up there too. I gulp, put my shoulder to the door and PUSH! The door bursts open – and the room literally S-C-R-E-A-M-S at me, like a great wind. It knocks me backwards. Then it all goes quiet. But this isn't the end. I know that...

I have to go into the room. But somehow I know it's an L shape. This means I have to actually go into the room and shut the door behind me in order to go further. Do I want to? What do you think! But I have to. There's something in there, waiting to be uncovered. The room is lit, or rather, not lit, with the same unholy, sallow light as the rest of the house. There's a small mirror on the wall, a single bed with an old army blanket and further in... a dressing table. There's a window but it's closed. The room waits...

I walk further into the room. In the gloom I notice something moving on the dressing table. No, it's a mirror. I have to look into the mirror. Sweet God, no! I walk closer. I can see a shape. I have to see. I lean into the mirror. I scream.

A face is screaming back at me! It's like a mask made of wax which has melted. All the lines of the mouth, the eyes, turn downwards. It's grotesque. Oh no. With a cold sinking in my guts I realise it's me. I can feel the hardening of my face. I'm screaming, the face is screaming. I realise somehow I'm about to wake up from the nightmare. Part of me welcomes this, wants it. But another part of me has been trained better than that. I force myself to stay in the horror, I force myself to concentrate on the feeling of my hardened waxen skin. I accept it. I stand there and scream and scream. Then I start to feel the wax softening slightly, my face becoming more mobile. I can't take any more. I wake up, sweating, clammy, still afraid...

The bald retelling of this nightmare can't convey the horror, suspense and disgust I experienced. I've had other, more obviously scary nightmares, I 'm sure we all have. But this was so much more intense than anything I'd ever experienced before. I was really there.

And of course the point of all this is that as soon as I was willing to look at, and accept, the frozen monster I'd become, the locked-in horror, the petrified creature wearing a mask, then it started to change. Paying attention to it began the thaw. Denial would have prolonged the horror, the suffering, perhaps for many years. I started to build bridges with those around me again. I was prepared to leave my job, though thankfully I didn't have to because, somehow, things improved. I found a workable level of self acceptance and carried on with my life.

Before this awful dream, I'd become petrified inside my own suffering. I'd become everything I hated – cold, unfeeling, ineffectual, spiritually disfigured, a creature of the shadows. I'd become destructive to those around me. I felt dirty, contaminated by some kind of inner filth, which was actually my own coldness, my inability to take any kind of positive action. I'd become a destroyer of warmth and communication. I was haunting myself. Until that moment, when I'd been able to do the work within the dream, I'd become... the bogey man!

The term bogey man is very old, and probably stems from ancient North European words for ghost or frightening spirit. We can picture him in many ways – masked or of hideous countenance, dressed in rags or as a clown, an undertaker, tall and gaunt, or small enough to fit under a child's bed or inside the wardrobe! Everyone you could talk to would give you a different description.

The bogeyman haunts dark places – cellars, the corners of bedrooms, deserted country roads, moors, anywhere we feel we have to keep checking for his presence, looking over our shoulder. But it's in the dark, deserted areas of our own minds that the bogey man is most likely to be found. It's in our own unsuspected, repressed and denied cruelty, pain and emotional distortion that he lurks, waiting for opportunities to pounce and... feed!

Given half the chance he'll rob us of warmth, empathy, compassion, humanity. He grows stronger on a diet of paranoia, fear, hatred, mistrust, indifference, cruelty. None of like to think that we have enough of these horrible elements within us to nurture the bogey man but the sad truth is that we probably do. We're all capable of being indifferent to the suffering of others, we're all capable of being a bit of a bully, a bit of a coward, a bit two-faced – we're only human after all. But it's the unconscious emotional material that's the strongest, potentially the most damaging, and of course, being unconscious, it's almost impossible to access and work with. It's only when something provokes us into a strong emotional reaction that we have a chance to sense what's happing, and then we're usually too caught up in our own processes to have any awareness. You have to get into the habit of making a little time each day to review what has happened to you internally over the past few hours. If there was any kind of inner conflict or any strong emotions, it's worth reflecting on these feelings, especially with a view to trying to uncover shadow material, the presence of the bogey man.

And the reason the bogey man is so horrible, so enraged, so conniving, so bent out of shape, is that you've kept him in a cage for so many years. You don't have to let him do what he likes, you don't have to like him, but you have to acknowledge him. How would you feel if you went to a family occasion two or three times a year and one person refused to speak to you, claimed you "weren't family"? You wouldn't like it would you? Well, that's what you do to your shadow self, at regular intervals. It's worth thinking about this stuff – I feel it's essential to spiritual progress or I wouldn't keep banging on about it!

The Buddhas are beings that have totally processed, assimilated and freed themselves from their shadow side. Even the historical Buddha had a bogey man, known by the name Mara. Mara means The Killer. He's the Buddhist version of the devil! The fascinating account of the historical Buddha's enlightenment and His (internal?) debate with Mara the Tempter, shows us the kind of problems He was facing when trying to overcome the power of His own ego, the most crucial question being whether to try and teach humanity or not. Mara did His best to present this as a fruitless, thankless task, but luckily for us, the Buddha decided to stick around for a while. He successfully reasoned with Mara (His own bogey man) that some people might be able to understand and travel the path to enlightenment. Mara wanted none of this – He hadn't even wanted the Buddha to take up a spiritual search in the first place, arguing that the Buddha should use worldly means such as education and social reform to achieve a better world for those around Him. As we all know, the Buddha choose the language of religion, and despite several visits from Mara in His lifetime, managed to found the hugely successful and influential system of philosophy and practice we know as Buddhism, the study of enlightenment.

So, if the Buddhas have overcome all negativities such as doubt, confusion, greed, hatred and anger, why are They sometimes depicted in wrathful, demonic form? Why are They red or black, covered in skulls and flames, clutching a female deity close in a sexually charged embrace?

Well, firstly because it looks way cool! Secondly, because these wrathful forms of the divinities represent awesome energies. Remember I described them as high voltage deities? They show us the illusory nature of physical appearance, of conventional thinking. Their energies are of love, compassion and wisdom, masquerading as anger, terror and destruction. They skilfully depict, pretend to be, Their own shadow qualities! Thirdly, because it shows us how even the demons within us, the bogey men and women, our own personal Bhairavs, can become enlightened beings. When we first encounter our own dark energies, they appear angry, demonic, out of control, frightening. Once we work with them, recognise their hidden worth, then they calm down, change appearance, and assume their rightful place in our inner world – they become kings and queens rather than ogres and witches! Or maybe it's just that our perception of them changes. Our anger can become fierce compassion. Our greed can become generosity. Our ignorance can become insight.

"Bhairav" means terrible or fierce, and it's a generic term for any kind of wrathful depiction of a deity. Bhairav is also one of the names of Shiva. And of course, he looks scary – He's meant to! He's black skinned, smeared in dark cremation ashes, decorated with snakes, skulls and severed limbs. He's said to haunt burial grounds, walk by night, be a friend to wolves and jackals and His retinue is comprised of ghouls, monsters and demons. Just what you'd expect from a bogey man par excellence!

As an exercise, it might be worth sitting for a moment and visualising your own personal bogey man, an image of a Bhairav that you can work with in meditation. Try and imagine a figure that really gets to you, affects you at a gut level. I don't want to influence you too much because the image has to be personal, individual to you. I can give you a check list though.

First of all – what aspect of yourself does this figure represent? Your anger, your stupidity, your cowardice, your greed etc? If you're not sure, don't worry, just create the image. You can ask this bogey man or woman yourself later!

Secondly – is it male or female? Human? Monstrous? Half animal? Tall or short? Emaciated, thin, bloated, tiny, distorted? How is this figure dressed? Are they carrying anything? Are there any animals or other creatures accompanying them? What kind of voice do they have? Any particular associated smells or noises? Do they make their surroundings hot, cold, darker? Use your imagination. And don't worry if the image changes at any point, that's only to be expected. New insights bring new images.

Sit in meditation. Say a prayer, ask for protection. Settle down, calm the mind and then see if you can picture this bogey man or woman coming towards you. Let your subconscious mind fill in more details. This can often be very revealing. Notice as much detail as you can. When you're ready, try and talk to them. Ask who they are, what they represent. Ask why they're angry, or sad etc. Ask them what it is you do that contributes to their emotional state. Don't argue with them, or criticise – just listen – they want to be heard, they need to be heard. And you need to listen. They may not be very skilful at explaining their feelings – this might be the first opportunity you've given them! Remember, this is not an "external" event. This is from your own mind. Different aspects of your character talking to each other. If you created a bogey-Bhairav when you were six years old, the Bhairav may have the voice and vocabulary of a six year old – or of a six year old's parent!

When you've had enough of this exercise, or it stops working, or you suspect your ego is beginning to interfere, then thank the Bhairav (this is important), allow them to dissolve, fade away, and then reflect calmly on what you've learned. Sit for a few more minutes before you end the meditation.

This kind of work can be very illuminating. Regular practice will make you better at it, enable you to distinguish between genuine, unconscious knowledge and the machinations of the ego. It can also present you with other avenues to explore, other parts of your psyche to visit and communicate with. More opportunities to turn lead into gold. You just never know what might come up!

CHAPTER SIXTEEN - SATURATED WITH THE SACRED.

HERE'S part of the prayer I offer up to the deities every single morning and evening – and I try to mean it like it's new every time...

"I pray for all the weak, the lonely, the abused, the vulnerable
The hungry, the homeless
The ashamed, the scorned and reviled, the unloved
The bereaved, the abandoned
Those that have to move on
Those that feel unable to move on
The afraid
All those trapped in unhealthy relationships or situations
All those under duress, under threat of violence
All those caught up in some conflict
Or imprisoned through no fault of their own
All those who have to lead or take responsibility for others
All those unhappy in their bodies through illness, injury or defect
All those unhappy in their minds, upset in any way
Anyone in any kind of physical, mental or emotional pain
May You touch their lives and heal them"

Sometimes I fail and it comes out all mechanical, automatic, so I say sorry for that, and try again. Then I move on to my more personal petitions. I try to be honest, say I'm sorry for things I could have done better, words I could have chosen more carefully. I say what's on my mind. I don't whitewash it – I say it like it is.

Back in the old days in India, a Tantric ritual, usually held in a secret location after dark, would involve the forbidden offerings of the five M's. These are Madya – wine, Mamsa – meat, Matsya – fish, Mudra - grain or bread (often with a hallucinogenic fungus) and Maithuna – sexual intercourse (sometimes with a young, low-caste girl). You have to remember that Tantra deliberately flew in the face of all that was conventional in India, especially vegetarianism, abstinence, chastity and the caste system. Why? Because the orthodox religion of that time was perceived by Tantrists as actually keeping the people and the deities apart. Tantrists believed that access to the deities could be, should be, an intensely personal experience, not dependant upon the intercession of priests. Religion had ossified, become stagnant. It needed a shock, a kick start. Or at least, that's what Tantrists believed.

It's said that those of little understanding performed these Tantric rites believing that their forbidden pleasures would lend the ritual a frisson, a spiritual charge, energy that they could then offer up to the deity. These kinds of people were referred to, rather disparagingly, as "pashu" – animals. Those of higher intelligence, or experienced initiates, were content to reenact the ritual symbolically, internally. They were called "vira" – heroes or conquerors.

Actually, as attractive as this sort of orgiastic ritual sounds, there's no need for all that now. The society we live is much more liberal, offers many different opportunities for spiritual practice. You might like the idea of lighting a few incense sticks, getting pissed and inviting your neighbors round for an orgy, especially in the name of religion but I think you'd be kidding yourself if you thought it might bring you any kind of enlightenment! The offering, especially the sex, has to be performed by those are intoxicated, not with wine or bhang (cannabis syrup), but with love of the deity. They have to be saturated with the deity for the ritual to have any meaning.

The so-called pashus of ancient India risked severe punishment if they were discovered flouting society's conventions, so I like to think that they had some kind of fervent faith in Shiva/Shakti, not just a desire to see what they could get away with. Maybe I'm just being naïve!

It's much more relevant these days to offer the deities that which you consider to be your own personal "forbidden" offerings – the parts of yourself you deem unworthy, unspiritual. It's your arrogance, your laziness, your aversion, your greed, your physical body with its secretions, smells and imperfections, that constitutes a real "authentic mess", not the pious, holier-than-thou prayers you offer up like a good little Buddhist or Hindu (or good little anything else for that matter). Be sincere, is what I'm saying.

You think God/dess doesn't know, doesn't see, exactly what you are, where you're coming from? So be honest, and the more you listen to yourself being honest in your prayers, the more comfortable you'll be with it, the more you'll like it.

Not that you're any more likely to have your prayers answered but the nature of your prayers will change. They'll become more an opportunity for sincere self reflection, for "confession" if you like, than your former long list of wants and don't-wants.

Daily prayer gives you a chance to look in the mirror once or twice a day and take a good, long, hard, honest look at what's reflected there. Make the most of that opportunity and make the most of any revelations that come your way.

Real spirituality isn't about being better than anyone else, or going to the temple more than anyone else, or knowing more Sanskrit than anyone else. Of course it's about being the best person you possibly can, but don't pretend - and don't believe your own hype – or anyone else's. Real spirituality means that you never forget God/dess. Never. Not when you're on the toilet, not when you're fucking, not when you're in a fight. Not even when you're doubled up in ecstasy over that first early morning coffee! God/dess is with you at all times, when you're at your best and when you're being a real turd. Don't forget the divinity – not for a minute.

We've seen, from the extracts from The Kali Khronicles that we've been privileged to read, that it's possible to spend a lot of one's day immersed, to some degree, in God/dess. To be SATURATED with the deities. And what a wonderful feeling it is. Sometimes.

And sometimes it's challenging. When I first met Shiva, He was all blue and sparkly, electric, wavering slightly, as if seen through a heat haze. He felt very warm, almost flirtatious. I was very surprised, to say the least, as I hadn't consciously been looking for anything like this. But I quickly grew to love His presence. Looking back, I think I called this aspect of Him "Electric Shiva" or sometimes "Dragonfly Shiva". His teachings were very visual, almost scholarly. I grew comfortable with it all. After a few years, He revealed another face. This one I called "Jungle Shiva". Jungle Shiva was a bit of a handful at first – very physical, bared His teeth a lot, poked me with His fingers. He was always naked, caked in mud and ash, had matted hair, danced around. He had no inhibitions. His teachings were stronger, more visceral. I'd feel things more, the experiences were quite physical. I had my first experiences of "possession" (don't panic!) with Jungle Shiva. I was quite wary of Him initially but after a few months I really, really liked Him. In fact I loved Him. I still do.

Both these manifestations of Shiva are what I call "hot weather" deities. Their presence was warming, uplifting (though still challenging at first). Then Jungle Shiva disappeared, which upset me a lot, left me feeling quite desolate. Another, more disturbing, face was uncovered. This one I call "Halloween Shiva" and again at first I wasn't very comfortable with Him at all, though it's getting better. Halloween Shiva feels "colder", more remote, less friendly. He's covered in pale grey ash, but it gleams wetly and the snake (shudder!) around His neck is very (too) mobile! He feels quite spooky and He often appears surrounded by mist and lightning and green flames and animal headed deities and what I can only describe as demons. It's very Tantric in a cheesy sort of way. There's always some sort of unholy barn dance going on. Sometimes I join in, sometimes I feel I'd rather not. There's a whole underworld out there that I don't really want to get too involved in. As if I have a choice...

"Sky chill shaded grief, the colour of ash
Pale bars of cloud hang suspended
Exactly level under the charcoal branches
Like ghost shadows
I watch the moon climb like a spirit bird
Too fast! Into the tree
And emerge the other side, pale and fevered
Sweating phantoms

With a horrible, unheard fanfare
Something stirs at the base of my spine
And the invisible world swims near

Something felt, un-namable but predatory
Like a dark shark cruising somewhere close
Waiting below in cold black waters
My hair lifts, my fingertips freeze
And the Lord of the Dead lifts His head"

And Kali is strong with Halloween Shiva. She seems to hang around sometimes. I'm not scared of Her. I'm more nervous of Her husband now! Never used to be that way!

So each new manifestation of Shiva has challenged me and made me deal with various aspects of my spirituality. At first, being a Buddhist and trying to keep my practice quite narrow – dealing with my shadow and any kileshas (defilements) I might come across, I found the idea of a 3-D cinematic, technicolour Hindu deity hanging around a bit distracting. It was a challenge. So what denied, repressed, FORBIDDEN aspect of myself did Electric Shiva make me acknowledge, force me to own? It was bhakti, loving devotion. Of course I can be loving, I can be loyal, I can be useful to others, but I'd never been the devotional type. That kind of emotional radiance just wasn't me! Electric Shiva helped me to nurture that quality of selfless giving, that unquestioning devotion. I'm not the kind of guy that uses the "L" word a lot but now I feel much more able to express tenderness to those around me.

Once I learned how to use His gift skillfully, I was presented with another challenge – my unconscious rejection of my own body. Oh, don't get me wrong – I look after my body well and I like my creature comforts as much as the next guy, but subconsciously there was part of me that regarded my all-too-human body, with all its demands, appetites and imperfections, as somehow inferior, somehow subordinate to the spirit. I was a bit of a puritan! It was Jungle Shiva that helped me to feel really at home in my own body, see it as something more than just some kind of vehicle for the spirit. I've always been able to access my own body, learn its wisdom, but I've always been able, indeed too willing, to over ride it. Sometimes this is necessary and sometimes it's better to actually give the body what it wants. Knowing the difference is high level wisdom! With Jungle Shiva I learned to revel in my physicality and in the role of my body as a spiritual being in its own right, a creation of Shakti ...

So, I got over all that, enjoyed the process too - and now there's another challenge in town. I've always been very careful to keep spirituality and psychic stuff apart. The sage Ramakrishna, a famous devotee of Kali, had this to say on the subject...

"I have heard that man can acquire superhuman powers through study, and perform miracles.
I saw a man who had brought a ghost under control.
The ghost used to procure various things for his master.
What shall I do with superhuman powers?
Can one realize God through them?
If God is not realised then everything becomes false."

The twin currents of spirituality and psychic ability often get mistaken for one another – and of course the two currents can overlap, sometimes quite a lot. But this new Hammer Horror Shiva is SO obviously a "psychic", "invisible world", shamanic Shiva that now I have to heal that rift within me, learn to embrace, even enjoy, any small ability I have, any "special" little insights I might get. This is anathema to me – I really don't like people who, when they're talking to you, suddenly cock their head on one side and come out with something like "Forgive me, but why is it, when I'm talking to you, I keep getting an image of a pumpkin?" My unspoken answer is usually along the lines of "Dunno, maybe because I want to carve holes in your fucking skull!"

I don't like people that wear their psychic ability like a badge and now I have to learn to deal with my own "forbidden" talent. And I really don't want to. I don't want to waste time testing myself, asking other people if their great-grandfather was Jack the Ripper, or if their mother was scared of parsnips. In the past, any information I've needed has come of its own accord. I've never had to go and look for it, never had to practice looking for it, and I don't want to start now. And from a "qi" point of view, anything to do with the dead brings on an awful lot of yin energy, which can create an imbalance. For example, it's not healthy to practice Taiji or Qigong in a cemetery, you can open yourself to too much yin qi. I respect the dead enormously. I try to leave them alone and I hope they leave me alone. I really, really don't wanna fuck with the dead.

Ho hum. I'll keep you posted...

The point is that each new face of the Absolute has brought out some repressed, denied, forbidden offering from my unconscious. Each initiation has been like a Tantric ritual, except that my offering was unconscious rather than deliberate. I don't need to offer a leg of lamb, a spliff and a bottle of rum and have sex with the next door neighbor to achieve a greater degree of union with the divinities– I just (just?) need to put myself on the line as it were, offer myself up – in my entirety.

All growth is into uncertainty. I'll repeat that louder. ALL GROWTH IS INTO UNCERTAINTY. I don't know where all this stuff is going – or why. I only know that, after the initial, and justified, wariness and after the initial, and willful, resistance, I learned to love it all - the process, the experiences, the insights. My life is now saturated with the sacred; every aspect of my everyday existence has taken on a new meaning. Again, I want to say that this doesn't make me any better than anyone else, it doesn't make me special. It doesn't make me a nutter either! Or a self-deluder. I'm just yer average council house mystic! And at the moment, I'm happy that way.

I'll finish this chapter with a sweeping statement. I say this in all seriousness. Here goes... (and remember – I don't take drugs, I don't drink and there's no sign yet of a tumour, a chemical imbalance or any kind of brain abnormality!)

There are invisible worlds out there – lots of them. The world of the dead is just one of these realms. As is the world of the Gods. The shamanic world of animal spirits and ancestors (which in the west also includes the Faerie world, vampires, werewolves – and UFOs) is another. And these worlds are deeper, darker, more dangerous, also more radiant, more glorious, more bizarre, more intense, more tangible, closer, than you could ever imagine. And we're like little minnows swimming around in a huge ocean. We have no idea...

CHAPTER SEVENTEEN - TEA TIME IN DREAM TIME.

I'm sitting here with a cup of tea, having just typed the last paragraph of the previous chapter. I don't feel I have to justify it, but it seems a little rude to just leave it sitting there, without any commentary from me. So...

Sometimes it feels as if there's a whole world happening inside me, all the time. In fact, more than one world – many worlds overlapping. And sometimes it feels really important that I just take the time to look at what's happening in these worlds.

And not just in me – it feels as if I could journey down into a green bud on a tree, shrink myself down into that microcosm, and find whole worlds in there too. And in the skull of that pigeon flying overhead. And in my dreams – and in your dreams too. All these worlds interweaving, and evolving simultaneously. And each world has an epicentre, and that epicentre can be – anywhere! In infinity, every point is the centre. Infinity radiates out from every single point. Any point can be the centre of all these other universes.

From each new thought, from each action, whole new worlds radiate out, expanding under the momentum of their own "big bang", the energy created by the thought or action! Phew! What God-like powers we have! How mighty our screw ups can be!

And as every world exists side by side with every other world, and as every point is the exact centre of every world – this means that every single event is meaningful. Every occurrence is charged with significance. Most of the time we don't know how to read these happenings, don't know how to recognise their significance. But again – sometimes it feels important to sometimes stop and try to intuit what's going on.

There are archetypes in this world and in these other worlds – the trickster, the witch, the wise crone, the hero, the evil sorcerer, the tragic king – all these and more. And hybrid creatures, part human, part animal, and huge luminous serpents (shudder!) and dragonflies and birds of every hue - and darker beasts, the psychic equivalent of sharks and jackals. Spirits of the dead, aliens, all kinds of creatures – all have their worlds, all co-existing, though usually oblivious to one another's presence. Sometimes, however, these worlds overlap, either through drugs, mental breakdown or "magical" ritual, and then other realities intrude, interact, disrupt, even threaten.

And all these other worlds operate under their own set of laws and rules, some of which would appear bizarre or even impossible to us. It's not my mission to describe these other worlds to you, or to convince you of their reality. Most of the time, it's pretty bloody irrelevant to you and I both what's happening in these other worlds. And whether they even exist. It's just not pertinent to our spiritual unfolding.

I suppose I can use the analogy of light or sound. Though we can't see them, we know there are X rays, ultraviolet light and infrared light rays all around us. We also know there are ultra high and very low frequencies of sound too, beyond the threshold of our hearing. And though we don't usually pay attention to them, we know there are other "wavelengths" of consciousness too, dream states, drug states, states of extreme concentration. And all this light, all these sounds, all these other states of consciousness, are probably happening all around us, all the time, but filtered out by the normal, everyday mind. Good thing too, or we'd never catch the bus, pay the bills or feed the cat. Different light waves, different sound frequencies, and different states of consciousness, all horses for courses, all with their own particular function. Choose the right one for the job at hand!

I suppose, all this, it's a bit like the Aboriginal "dreamtime", the world of ancestors, spirits and magical entities. A lot of the time this realm (or realms) ticks along quite nicely without us, doesn't need us, and we don't need it.

So let's look at the other extreme. Maybe all this is just fantasy – a dream, a waking vision caused by small chemical reactions in the physical brain, or subliminal environmental factors. Or maybe it's wish fulfilment – not just for me but for all mankind. Maybe there's nothing except this material realm. Maybe we're all just frightened wolves, howling down the long night of the centuries, trying to distract ourselves from the unsuccessfully buried feeling that we're alone in a soulless universe - and we make up all these heavens, hells and afterlives to impart some small spark of meaning to our fleeting and insignificant little stretch of existence. Maybe from the very beginning, when we gazed out of our caves, fearful of the darkness, fearful of what it might conceal, fearful of the emotions of vulnerability it stirred in us, maybe it was then we started to people the night with spirits, mythical beasts, with invisible beings.

That howling darkness, the feeling of being alone – or the feeling that perhaps there's something out there in the darkness, is probably mankind's oldest, original enemy.

"The beast wind roars and rattles
Rockets through the rolling darkness
Shadows ripen blackly, swell and drop from the witch-clutch branches
The overhanging, pregnant trees tremble from the terrible weight

I stoop my shoulder to memory's gate
The iron and wood

And grate and squeeze
Creaking on reluctant hinges
Fate comes loping over the vision-fringed fields
My eyes are open wide

I choose, I choose
I choose the disused path

And softly, imperceptibly, stirring
Shapes in mist and memory blurring
Blood-cousins, pelts ruffled, pads murmuring
The Were-clan gathering, drawing near

Through the wild lands of the north
Rucked with rocks, rippled by ridge and hollow
Through cold, owl-echoed forests
We run – and call
And thicken the night with our breath

Taste the free air around the world
Chase the rim of rebirth's wheel
Rule the night under moon and starfrost
Reclaiming heaven under our hearts
Earth beneath our heels

And in the morning, when the night is set to mist and stillness – men will awake
They will blink and stir
Call to each other hesitantly
They will bring lanterns to the deep breathing pre-dawn calm
Stare and say
"I never thought that light could take up so little space!
But look!
How bravely our small lamps drive away the darkness!"

Gold tipped spears against the original adversary
The night born
And these men will walk the earth
And in waiting and walking and talking
They sketch heaven anew this coming dawn"

All creatures sketch their own heaven anew. All create their own fears in the darkness too. Many things are born of the night – hunger, fear, isolation, perhaps the need to bond, the need to create monsters, the need for friendly or antagonistic spirits, for ancestral spirits, for Gods. And the word "Were-clan" used in the verse actually means man-clan, we-clan, the clan of us! So you can make up your own interpretation of the meaning of the poem!

Great things can blossom from that swelling darkness out there, beyond the mouth of the cave. Kali was born of rage and frustration. Shiva was born of the terrible storms that rolled through, and shook, the ancient forests. Pan was born, according to which story you believe, of either thunder and proud arrogance, or of implacable fate, "the inescapable". The Buddha was born of emotional turbulence and disenchantment. They can all still be found in the modern world, in the neon lights, in the suburban avenues, in the mind of every devotee. All born of darkness and commotion – all bringers of light.

Very clever of mankind don't you think? To take the very things that occupied us way back when, the very things that scared us – the darkness, things that walked in darkness and maybe preyed on us, the mysteries of birth and death, the violence of the elements, the need to find food, all these preoccupations – and turn them into religion, into that which gives our lives meaning and comfort. To turn lead into gold that way was a very skilful thing for ancient man to do.

And whether you believe or not - wherever your reality lies along that spectrum from one world to many worlds, from atheism to polytheism, from materialism to hyper-spirituality, one thing is common to all – all we really have is right now. Right now if we just let go, forget who or what we are, what the rest of the world is doing, that short space can be the hub of our life, the still point around which the rest of our life revolves. Right now is that sacred, safe moment, the one time when we're still alive, still conscious. That one special second without thought, without a name, an identity, friends, a job, anything. That one moment when we come home. That one moment when we're pure, free. And that's it – gone again.

But we can catch that moment again if we want to. In meditation or just by practicing the art of letting go, falling back on that shining consciousness that no one owns yet no one can take away from you once you've experienced it. That radiant "knowing" is called Buddho and it's the goal of Buddhism. You can keep it for a few seconds at a time or you can try and stretch it out to last longer, it's up to you. And whatever your beliefs, whatever realities you may wish to inhabit, or find yourself in, if you have Buddho within, then every one of those realms that I spoke of – has a Buddha living there. If you have Buddho, even for a second, or from a memory from long ago, or as a future aspiration – then wherever you go, there'll be a Buddha there.

Or if for just one moment you've dwelled in Shiva Tattva, Kali Konsciousness, or within any other deity, then that deity is with you wherever – a connection has been made that can't be broken, and can be carried anywhere, under any circumstances.

You can carry your own small "gold tipped spear" – a light in the darkness. Or even if you can't grasp that kind of consciousness right now, can't even quieten the mind (and God knows I have enough trouble some days), you can orientate yourself towards that path. It takes commitment though. Everyone I know is busy, busy, oh so busy these days, and it takes an enormous effort of will to shoehorn another few minutes into an already stuffed-to-brimming day, especially for something as tenuous as a spiritual practice.

So why bother? That's a good question, and it's not my appointed task to coerce you into meditating or praying. If you weren't already interested, you wouldn't be reading this book. So you must already kinda agree that to be a complete being one needs emotional fulfilment, physical fulfilment, mental fulfilment – and spiritual fulfilment too. As much as I enjoy my creature comforts and all the luxury that science and technology can offer, to merely have one's physical needs attended to – is not enough, is it? I don't want to sound greedy, but I want more! I can do without non-stick frying pans (with me, there's no such thing as non-stick!), coffee-makers, even TV and central heating if I have to, but I can't manage without my God, or talking about religious matters to my friends. Spiritual companionship, the sharing of private thoughts and experiences, is like fresh air for me, it's essential. I'm a religious being. My religion gives my life meaning.

And I like to keep working at it, working my way back, through all the various cultural accretions, superstitions, rites and rituals, do's and don'ts, not to some imagined primal purity, because there probably isn't one, but at least to something that's directly connected back to antiquity.

Remember the shaman in the cave of the stags a few chapters back? The guy with the scars, the gelled-up hair and the erection? (I call him !skian, that's a tongue click (against the front of the palate – for some reason that's important) and gee-arn, dunno why) I've been thinking about him a lot lately! I empathise with him. Maybe 40,000 years ago, he was trying to keep his clan together, feed them, give them a feeling of solidarity, probably trying to maintain his own position too, as an intermediary between the clan and the spirit world. Perhaps still trying to perfect his craft, his own abilities, his own rapport with the creatures and beings that would come to visit him in trance or dreams.

And if it was 40,000 years ago and we count say thirty years as a generation, that means there's perhaps only 1,400 men, or women, between !skian and me. Fourteen hundred people in a line, with him at one end and me at the other. That's not so many. Manchester United's football stadium, Old Trafford, holds easily that number forty times over! You could take forty Stone Age shamans and all their linear descendants and still only fill one football stadium. !skian feels a lot closer now, doesn't he? At the end of that long line, we can't shout to each other, but maybe we can wave...

Or maybe we can pass messages back and forth, bearing in mind the inevitable distortion of "Chinese whispers"...

Perhaps that's what's happened to religion. Each culture has created its own "Chinese whispers", distorting the original religious impulse, the hard-wired urge to find supernatural answers to the world around us. And science is just another of those ongoing, self-revising, religious quests. It changes, just as Paganism, Tantra and Shamanism change and develop. Sometimes, probably, the distorted version of the programme becomes better, more beneficial, more suited to the times, than the original. And that's fine. Though we still have Stone Age bodies and Stone Age instincts, we don't actually live in the Stone Age anymore. But I still have that impulse to journey back, to find points where Shamanic practices, Pagan worship and Tantra overlap each other. To find something that's outside my little English culture, with its mix of Saxon, Norse, Celtic, Roman and now American influences, something that transcends all that, and yet is entirely relevant to my life here and now.

Tantra, as I now understand and practice it, isn't some exotic offshoot of an eastern religion. Though that's how it started – the exotic aspect was part of the appeal. It now comprises a lot of what most would recognise as shamanistic practices and techniques - and especially a shamanistic worldview - but with a view to working inner change, inner development, rather than locating lost door keys and herds of reindeer. My aim is still a Buddhistic one, enlightenment and liberation. My path, my sadhana, my method, is working with Shiva. Not the Hindu Shiva with the bling and the bhang (deep sigh!) but the original God of nature, of animals and storms. In this role He has much in common with similarly categorised deities such as Pan and Cernunnos, but maintains, despite many guises, His own identity, His own vibe.

So, to Electric Shiva, Jungle Shiva and Halloween Shiva, I suppose we'd better add a kind of Pan Shiva or Horned Shankara! What a crazy mixed up kid I sound! But actually, it all feels perfectly natural. It all has its own internal logic, it's just God wearing different hats for each visit. Under the hat I can see who's come calling. I know what "my" God "feels" like. And He's not any more "Indian" than He is "English". And He's equally Stone Age and Cyber-Age.

And as enjoyable as all this cosmic musing is, it leaves me with one inescapable, inevitable conclusion – if I get carried away by my own verbosity, my cup of tea goes cold! Ho hum. Now I'll have to go and pray to the God of Putting the Kettle On!

CHAPTER EIGHTEEN – THRESHOLDS AND DECONSTRUCTIONS.

Many Wiccans and Pagans divide their calendar in two – the summer months belong to the Great Mother, in Her many guises, and the winter months to the Horned God, the Mother Goddess's consort. The deities step over the threshold of the year, probably nodding to each other as They pass, at Beltane (May 1st) and Samhaim (Halloween, October 31st). Tantrists tend, in theory, not to divide the male and female energies in this way. As Kali Ma explained to me (as I understand it), Shiva is the pure consciousness of pure being. He is the consciousness of being conscious. It's not the "empty" consciousness of the early morning, not-quite-awake mind, or the "have no future, have no past" mindset of a goldfish (allegedly), but more like the "feeling one with everything" expansive mind one can experience sometimes in meditation. The difference is that Shiva KNOWS He's one with everything – all the time.

And Shiva is pure being. Again, not the pure quiescent being of a potato or a member of a boy band, but a knowing, a sentient state of being. And this state of being and consciousness, this aware one-ness, is called Shiva Tattva. This glorious energy of awareness flows through all life, like liquid fire. Some life forms can't hold much of it, can't know much about it – for example, a cabbage (or the members of a boy band) – and some can, such as many human beings and other higher life forms. Shiva's spark is in all life forms – in fact needs physical form, or at least "shape", to realise itself. Without sense information, consciousness would be an eternal blank page. There would be no evolution.

And without Shiva's spark, Shakti's creation, the material world, would be inert matter, dull and bereft of the potential for self-knowledge. Shiva and Shakti need each other, define each other, and should therefore be honoured jointly most of the time, not have their worship performed in six month shifts! Having said that, in practice many Tantrists will honour either Shiva or Shakti, in Their various forms, almost exclusively, rather than jointly. At least the Wiccans and Pagans strive for a balance.

So Shiva's energy is this outpouring of awareness into all life forms. And it doesn't end. It doesn't end. As Shakti endlessly creates, as life evolves, new life forms appear, old ones disappear, and Shiva is in all of them. Shiva catches fire in every single being. There's never an end. Shiva constantly explores Himself through all life, and explores all life through His own consciousness. It never ends.

New forms of life mean that new states of consciousness can evolve. And new forms of consciousness mean that new life forms can evolve. It never ends. Shiva and Shakti feed each other, fire each other. Their union is an atomic bomb of form and awareness. And it's happening constantly, right now, and for ever.

And it's happening inside us too, at every level. All the time. Any new state of consciousness within us breeds new ways to be, rebirths. New births bring new possibilities for consciousness. Shiva and Shakti are "at it" right now, inside us. It's amazing. In linear time this has been happening forever, in an endless series of big bangs and subsequent implosions, cosmic heartbeats. In "Indra Time", that's non-linear time, it's happening simultaneously, constantly.

I recently read an article by Stephen Hawkin, the world famous astrophysicist and thinker, who was still claiming that, one day, scientists would understand the "Mind of God". He also said however, that in order to do this, their master theory would require more than three dimensions of space and more than one of time. He hoped the theory would be ready in about thirty years. I'm sorry but YAWN! It's hard to be impressed. The more cutting-edge science gets, the more it seems to cross over the threshold into mysticism. More and more it seems to just confirm what the ancients have been saying for millennia – the universe is intelligent, some parts of it (sub-atomic particles for a start) don't obey the laws of physics, in fact they communicate and influence each other simultaneously over vast distances. Space and time are multi-dimensional. All life is intelligent (apart from many scientists, politicians and boy bands) and all life is interconnected. Every occurrence is meaningful. It'll take the boffins a while to work all this out, I think.

I also believe that an enquiring mind is a good thing. But it's the attitude of knowledge-fascists, both scientific and religious, that can ruin it for the rest of us. Arrogance, thinking that you can know it all, is dangerous for everyone. Doctrines come flying thick and fast from laboratories and ashrams and a lot of it is just bollocks – a short sighted glimpse over the threshold of human knowledge, into the mysteries beyond, and then this myopic flash is then presented as a glorious revelation – the truth, the only truth. You know Shiva has the Goddess of the Ganges River sitting in His hair? This prevents Her from overwhelming the world with a deluge. From His matted locks the water falls out in a manageable fashion. This is a metaphor for wisdom too. We can't hold the whole universe consciously. We can't take it all in. To see the entirety of it all would blow our fuses. So we need a dam against the flood. This dam can then allow a little of the waters of wisdom out at a time, so we don't go mad.

And this dam can either be viewed, depending upon your cultural or religious predilections, as a deity, holding all the knowledge of the universe, and apportioning it to those that have the will and the ability to receive it, or as our conscious minds, acting as a filter, screening out all the data we have no immediate use for.

But if, under the influence of drugs or in a dream/meditation state, we creep under the linem, that threshold where the rational mind meets the subconscious mind, we can glimpse the vast totality and unity of creation. We can interact with other worlds, other realms, other states, other ways to be. We can see Mother Ganges flowing down from heaven, silvery, shimmering and unutterably beautiful. Maybe more scientists should take acid or magic mushrooms!

(Lawyer advised addition – of course they shouldn't! What was I thinking! They should stick to slide rules and microscopes. Maybe.)

From cutting-edge science back to the Stone Age. Something Elaine said in her Pan Report (The Darshan Diaries) has been quietly buzzing away at the back of my mind. She was talking about construction – how we build little houses in our inner landscapes, and then live in them. We have different houses for our social selves, our family selves, our work selves etc. She compared this societal conditioning to the way we've built houses on the earth itself, replacing the caves, the round huts and the forests with steel and concrete roads and buildings. Nothing wrong with this of course. Many roads and many buildings are important. Inside us too, some constructions are necessary – we need to learn how to function within a community, how to relate to various situations. We don't live in caves and forests any more and we don't go out hunting for deer or mammoths much either. Most of us don't even have a community any more.

But it interests me, this whole Stone Age thing, this (probably totally imaginary) purity of life, this harmony of religion and the mundane business of food gathering and community –building. Of course, Palaeolithic Man had a sophisticated society, they weren't mindless savages. Just look at their astonishing cave art. That still blows me away every time I see it. So they already had a little bit of construction work going on in their heads, it wasn't virgin forest any more. And I don't want to go and live in a cave or hunt rabbits. I like central heating, TV and cheesecake too much.

But they related directly, viscerally, to their Gods, their spirits. I like that. In fact, I need it. For me, God is very physical, very here and now, not sitting in white light on a cloud or a lotus somewhere. In fact my favourite incarnation of my God, the one I call Jungle Shiva, is almost Stone Age, naked and covered in ash. Very present, very in-your-face. And this incarnation feels very connected to the natural world, to the elements, to a functional religion rather than a speculative one. I'd better expand on that, hadn't I?

His approach to teaching me was to poke me, bare His teeth at me, point at things, draw pictures in the mud. And it was all to do with seeing the material world as meaningful. Not merely a veil beyond which the world of spirits shimmered darkly, but as an expression of His consciousness. Every life form was an expression of His limitless being. So I could use the material world skilfully. I don't mean make more money (long sigh) but I could relate to energies more impersonally. Everyone around me was like different animals, so I treated them that way. Some you avoided, and didn't feel bad about it, some you allowed near, some you didn't, some were friendly, some weren't to be trusted. I know, it sounds obvious – we all do that to a certain extent. But I could see, feel, smell and taste these people's being, their intentions etc. I had a 360% perception. It was very interesting, and it worked. Treating people like animals (and that doesn't mean treating people badly) enabled part of their being to communicate with me in a way that would have been uncomfortable for both of us before. Try it! Talk to the animal you sense inside your partner, your neighbour, your boss! Good luck – and don't sue me if it goes horribly wrong, you accidentally call your boss a warthog and get fired!

In contrast, the form I call Halloween Shiva is very concerned with the invisible world, the various realms of spirits, Gods and Goddesses, demons and t'ing. To this other-worldly incarnation, the material world is merely meat. It's over the threshold of rationality, and into the world of trance, meditation and dreams that Halloween Shiva wants me to explore (and express) more.

I've also seen Shiva as Pashupatinatha, the Lord of Animals. He looked a bit like a cross between Pan and Jungle Shiva. He had horns and He didn't have a single word to say, He was just a presence, and not a very approachable presence at that.

I realise how glibly this all rolls off the keyboard and onto the page and how ridiculous it will sound to some of you. Others of you are nodding, though. And I passed the stage of caring a lot time back. This is my religion now and I have to be sincere about it, not coy, not clever. You deserve that much. If anything I write is of any use to you then I'm happy for both of us.

I want not so much as to deconstruct the houses I've built in my inner plains and forests – they have their uses after all - but I don't to lock myself up in them and I would like to live outside a little bit more. To use Elaine's words – not let them get in the way of pure being. I want to stay mindful of when I'm taking shelter in one of these dwellings in various situations, watch to see if different people tend to want to push me into one of my inner constructions. And then make a conscious choice whether to walk over the threshold or make them stay in the forest with me. That sounds a good sadhana, doesn't it? To be very aware of which dwelling inside us we allow people to back us into. We'll call it Threshold Yoga. Try it for yourself.

Now, I'm as aware as you are that, glorious as the natural world is, it's basically a constant quest for food, for a decent breeding partner, a safe place to breed and rear young, all with the constant stress of killed-or-be-killed. In other words, more or less like our world of humankind. Yet we can be so much more than that, can't we? We can strive to live in a different way. We can strive for more self knowledge, for some kind of spiritual autonomy, for self-evolution. We have the capability to work against our own conditioning. So what is it about the natural world that's so appealing? Well, of course, it's the sheer variety and exuberance of life forms out there, the beauty and the strangeness of it all. The fact that there's always something new waiting to be discovered. Inside us too, there are many forms of life, different "us's", strange and beautiful, waiting to be discovered.

Above all, I think a lot of people secretly admire the "sincerity" of the natural world. Animals don't apologise, don't pretend, don't put on airs and graces, aren't ashamed of their natural functions. Some animals are beautiful partly because we sympathise with them, they're often victims - either of other animals or of man. Creatures such as deer, gorillas and tigers are undoubtedly gorgeous and fascinating. Some animals are beautiful even though they're killers – tigers again, and even sharks have a terrible majesty and grace about them. But sharks don't pretend to be cuddly (could they?) and lions and chimps are actually nasty, cannibalistic bastards. They still have admirable qualities though. All animals are what they are – we can't always say the same about people.

And I've already mentioned that the Gods prefer an authentic mess to a pretentious or non-involved devotee, so don't be afraid to let your true feelings show, to be honest, when performing puja. I sometimes call myself one of Shiva's "creatures" but that's more of a play on the term pashu, which can mean animal or soul. Calling myself that doesn't make me less human, or less autonomous. Sometimes when I'm walking through a large city, I stop and look around and think, "All these souls!" All this busy-ness and striving. All these radiations of God, all blissfully unaware of their own divinity. And I've been frightened sometimes, thinking, "How will Shiva find me in all this?" Sounds a bit silly I know, but I'm just being honest.

And it's good to be honest and sincere on the spiritual path, to speak your heart, to follow your heart. Sometimes however it's hard to know what our true heart is. We may think we know what we want (or don't want) but in talking it through we sometimes discover the truth has eluded us. That's why holding conversations with the deities is so important. They can act as sounding boards – and when no one else is listening, we can be really honest, and not pretend.

And, as soft as our bodies and our minds may be compared to our Stone Age ancestors, we still basically have the same bodies and instincts as Brok and !skian. We still decorate our caves with artefacts and paintings. We still have to hunt or forage for sustenance every day. We may or may not believe in benevolent or hostile spirits "out there", we may or may not believe in a God of Animals or a Great Mother, but we still hope that fate will treat us kindly, we still perform ritual, "lucky" actions, such as "touching wood", walking around rather than under ladders, not breaking mirrors, not speaking ill of the dead. All modern rationality aside, we still talk about "tempting fate" or "talking things up". In many respects Brok and !skian are still alive and with us today.

And so are their Gods. The God of Animals and the Mother of All, the Fertility Goddess - these tribal deities are still around, though often in modern guise, masquerading perhaps as Jehovah or the Virgin Mary, or as Pan and Athena, or Shiva and Kali. As the wise say, in a profound codicil to the Vedas, "By whatever name you call God, by that name will God come." If you call Shiva, He will come, if you call Jehovah, He will come, if you call Baphomet, or Tara (Saviouress), or Astarte, or Parvati, or Ka'atas (a high ranking daemon) or Kernunnos, or Kali – They will come.

Various "tribes" have taken these divine prototypes and grown their own, culture-specific varieties of the original stock.

But whichever "tribe" we may now belong to – we have options. We pays our money and we makes our choice. And we're incredibly blessed, incredibly fortunate, to be able to make such choices, and to pursue our spiritual path, usually without any censure or recrimination. So very, very lucky.

Just across the limen, the threshold of response, the threshold of the door of the everyday mind, and into our sub-liminal minds, awaits a journey into experiences and teachings you can't even imagine right now. Whether you call this realm the invisible world, the spirit world, the dreamtime, the world of myth or the sambhogakaya, it's the same thing – the meeting ground, where you and your God can encounter one another. So just call out...

CHAPTER NINETEEN - ONCE WE WERE WANDERERS...

Way back in the day, we used to roam this earth, searching for food. We'd hunt and trap animals, forage for fruits and nuts that were in season, stay in caves, build dwellings - but communities were small back then. We could move people if and when we had to. We had quite a lot of spare time on our hands, so we'd create artefacts, often with an animal theme – after all, animals were important to us – they represented life, food, renewal. And of course, we'd use the whole animal – nothing was wasted. We learned to make twine from sinews, clothing from fur and leather, weapons and tools from horn. Even our religion was animal-based. God was a hunter like us, and He caused the animals to keep breeding, to keep wandering. We were healthy and strong.

Somehow though, we began to settle down a bit more. We had time enough to formalise our religion, formulate worldviews. Communities interbred, grew bigger, our buildings more elaborate. We learned to domesticate some animals, grow some crops. You'd think that was an improvement, wouldn't you? After all, that's the birth of society. But there was a price to pay. We actually had to spend more time being farmers than we ever did as hunters. Disease became a problem too. And communities weren't so mobile if there were food shortages. We were harder on the environment – and that could cause problems too.

And our religion started to shift. Fertility was vital to us. The Great Mother gradually came to have ascendance over the God of Animals. This was perfectly natural of course. The round of existence – birth, growth, maturity, decay and death – could be seen all around us in the natural world – and came to be included in our art. The phases of the moon, which we utilised in our planting, also became connected with the symbology of our beliefs. Even the symbol of the God (His horns) was replaced by a crescent moon. We began to be obsessed with fertility and its opposite – death. Our practices around death - interments, keeping decorated skulls, grew more elaborate. We became farmers. And actually, our health suffered a little. But competition for food and living space has always brought out the best in human enterprise and initiative. We learned how to cultivate plants and herbs as medicines. We learned how to interbreed animals to create hardier stock. We coped well. And humans have been coping well ever since.

We're very tribal and territorial as a species. We're very violent. But clever. Our religious beliefs and our practices are quite culture-specific and shaped by our received legacy, our history, our customs. At some point the Great Mother was supplanted in our hearts – but not by the God of Animals again. This time it was a tribal God from the Middle East who assumed dominance.

And who's stayed in the top ten ever since, mainly through zealous promotion and violent suppression. Most monotheists manage to believe in a God that is the World Creator, the Father of All, who wants us to love each other and will still nevertheless take our side in any conflict! And this God won't tolerate other Gods, oh no! And this God allegedly condemns men and women who love those of the same gender. And this God quite specifically says - DON'T KILL! But He'll be ok with us if we kill those who worship the same God – BUT BY A DIFFERENT NAME! In fact, it seems almost compulsory.

And you monotheists - stop telling me I should be doing it your way! Do I come knocking on your door? Do I stand and preach in the middle of the city? Do I take to the streets in protest every time someone knocks Shiva? For fuck's sake GROW UP!

I'm sorry to all you Christians, Jews and Muslims out there – I don't mean to put your religion down. I just can't subscribe to it. And Hindus – who have to be born, not made – you can't elect to BE a Hindu, though you can adopt Hindu beliefs and practices – sorry again, but I think you're weaving such a tangled web of culture and custom around divinity you're in danger of losing the plot. Keep it simple!!! Darshan, face to face contact with a deity, can be quite straightforward. Of course you want to show sincerity in your pujas, you want to "get it right" – I can appreciate that, but just bear in mind that just because something has evolved a certain way doesn't mean it's got to stay that way. I'm a bit of a traditionalist myself but even my beloved Taiji has developed and changed to suit the times over the centuries. And Shiva – well, that guy never stays still! There's always new ways to worship Him!

Who else can I piss off? Oh yeah – Buddhists. Sound worldview, borrowed from the Hindus. Sound practices. Nope, you're looking ok, Buddhists.

Pagans – you're ok too – mostly.

And in case you think I'm being a bit one-sided here – firstly, I know a lot of Buddhists and Pagans – and some of them are sanctimonious assholes too. Secondly – like I can hold the moral high ground! I believe in a God who's covered in ash, smokes dope and likes His missus to stamp all over Him! So I'm not going to slag off anyone's beliefs – only their hypocrisy. Thirdly, it's quite possible that it was the Indo-Europeans, the so-called "Aryan Invaders", the ancestors of modern-day Hinduism, who were at least partly to blame for the suppression of the feminine principle in religion and society. So the very guys that brought Rudra-Shiva to the world, also contributed to the gender-mess we're in today.

So – in my jaundiced view – we've evolved from a nomadic culture, where we worshipped a God of Animals (who had many names), begged to remain connected to the world of spirits, some of whom were half animal and half human, through a culture of farmers, where we worshipped the Great Goddess (who had many names), the bringer of fertility and death, arriving at a worship of a transcendent Creator God, known commonly as "God", "Yahweh" (Jehovah) or "Allah". This God we petition, as we probably did the Horned God, for daily bread, for protection against that which would harm us, for instance - natural disasters, famine, plague, people that stayed connected to the world of spirits (who were called witches), and of course co-worshippers of the same God under a different name. Some things have changed, some haven't. Maybe the most interesting development has been the idea of evil. Everything and everyone who threatens us and our lifestyle is evil!

Unmarried mothers, homosexuals, non-believers, the young, the old, non-believers, foreigners, immigrants, non-believers, beggars, non-believers - all evil. But not nearly as evil as our hypocrisy, our egotism, our sanctimoniousness, our paranoia, our coldness, our willingness to look the other way when it suits us... Great evil has been performed in the name of the God of Love. And some great acts of compassion and charity too, of course.

When was evil born? When did this whole concept of evil grow so strong? Certainly the Greek, the Norse (and the Hindu) Gods and Goddess behave in ways that are amoral, unfeeling, even evil sometimes, but these are amoral, unfeeling or evil actions, performed by beings that are also obviously also capable of great love, compassion and empathy. They aren't inherently evil beings. Maybe we externalise evil, make it "out there", give it names like Satan, Beelzebub and Nigel because that somehow reduces our personal responsibility – it's not us, it's the devil's fault! And it's all conditioning anyway – you look at a cave painting of a Horned Animal God and see Satan, I see a powerful and compassionate mentor. It's all in the eye of the beholder.

And all religion is in the eye of the beholder. Someone has a personal revelation. They either keep it to themselves or they manage to persuade others that this revelation is relevant to them, also involves them. And so the commonly held beliefs begin to cluster around the original revelation – which is still just one man's (or woman's) experience.

I want you to have your own religion. It may be nominally Buddhist, Christian, Pagan – it doesn't matter. What matters is that your personal practice of this religion makes you happy, makes you a better person, enriches your life, keeps you evolving, empowers you. That's what I want for you. But that's my problem, not yours! Do your own thing. Just be careful – there are all kinds of charlatans, fools, frauds and sick freaks out there!

So, as I sit here in my cave on this frosty winter's day, gazing out at the field where the metal buffalo pack together, I reflect on all that long history of religion, all those centuries of revelation, structure and dogma, and I wonder why more of us aren't breaking away from the pack, trying to find those original, inspirational revelations for ourselves. And of course, a lot of us are. But many more don't give a shit – they're too busy chasing the illusion of security that a job, a new car, a home and a relationship offer so well. Nothing wrong with earning money, having a partner, a new metal buffalo and your own cave – that's all fine – but isn't there anything above and beyond that for you? It takes a certain kind of person, probably someone like you, given that you've bought this book, to commit to any kind of spiritual practice, let alone one that doesn't come pre-packaged. So congrats for that, dudes and dudesses.

We've become wanderers again, spiritual nomads, spiritual seekers whose shamanic energies are turned inwards, towards revelation and inspiration. Hopefully we're not going to burden ourselves with trying to keep a big clan together, like !skian, but we're his descendants, we inherit his spiritual legacy. And it's up to us, each individual, how we use that legacy. Because when the spirit calls you have to respond – and that can lead you down some strange paths...

"Just another winter morning
Spider web wheels of liquid frost
The stillness of a crow on a frozen birch
And silence in the hedgerows

Then from the misty distance
Faintly at first
A breath
A stirring of muted music
Drums and horns across the lawns

Closer, closer still
And the parade of pandemonium
Bursts into our safe, sheltered suburbs!
With noise and clamour and glamour and noise!
With shivers and tingles and bells and cymbals!
Beautiful women and beautiful men
With antique clothes, outlandish manners
Wreathed in smoke and smiles and oils
And freaks and creatures and dogs and demons
Garish and greedy yet insouciant too
Eyes meet, worlds collide
We step back, we crack, we lower our eyes
We swallow, we stare
We are glued to the moment
Right now, right here

Here comes the parade!
Louder - marching, laughing, crashing
Right up to your front door!
Boom!
A thunderflash
Light and noise
Obscene in the early morning!

And then silence returns to the street
Smoke settles on the lawn
The crow looks down from the frozen birch
And, like the rest of us – he waits

And a scarecrow man in rags and feathers
Tattooed teeth and matted hair and painted hands
Stands smiling, unperturbed, at your front door
Opens his arms, opens his mouth
And yells your name!

He holds candy and skulls!
And snakes and jewels!
And he smiles and he bows
And he offers you through
Through to the carnival
Through to the freak show
Through to the distance behind the houses
Through to the rough blue, tense and luminous
Of a new day somewhere
Somewhere else...”

Or of course you can choose to ignore the summons, turn away from the offer, the risk, you can choose not to evolve. You can choose to live your life at a mundane level.

For some, the spirit will come in the form of Jesus or Mohammed. For some, the peaceful lure of Buddhism will beckon. Something from the Ancients of Europe may speak to you. And also from the East may come for you the Devas, the Shining Ones, exotic deities such as Krishna, Lakshmi or Ganesh. Sometime the exotic element is part of the appeal. Sometimes the element of risk, of becoming an outsider, is attractive. Sometimes it’s the common sense element, or freedom from too much ritual, that’s attractive. Buddhism gets a lot of adherents that way.

I got called. Shiva walked in on my life. I didn’t even notice at first. When I realised what was happening, I chose to join the freak show. It was scary at first. I was a strict Buddhist, hot on morals, ethics, the whole Dhammapada (path of the law) thang. I didn't know where the new trip was going. Still don't. But I don't care any more. I'm actually still pretty keen on making the world a better place, treating all beings with respect, all that karma-dharma-samsara-nirvana palaver. But I feel different. More settled, less frantic about "getting there". I think I'm already there – I think you are too. We've just got to realise it!

All these long centuries of human spiritual endeavour, all that praying, all that striving, all those moments of exultation, all those dark nights of the soul. All that fighting too. All these religions, all these systems, ways of getting ourselves "saved". Religion has a long history, and we can learn a lot by studying its roots and its many and varied cultural flowerings.

And all these religions, or at least all the ones that I can think of, and that includes Tantra, Paganism and Shamanism, as well as all the Hinduisms, Buddhisms and Christianityisms etc, share one thing in common. They all uphold the concept of a layered universe – a worldview that contains the notion of many different levels of reality, states of being. There are underworlds, realms of spirits, some of whom are friendly, some of whom are either neutral or actively antagonistic to mankind. There are heavens, or at least realms where "higher" beings dwell. Many various other worlds, both above us and below us, extend vertically from the central level of mankind.

This idea of a layered universe seems to be universal. Most religions have come up with this concept, independently and organically. The earliest blossomings of Neolithic religious thought, and Shamanistic paradigms from many different cultures, some very isolated, feature just such a notion. It's hardwired into us. Our neural network makes it a given. We are programmed to experience the world that way.

Now, anyone who's ever done regular meditation for more than a year or two will sooner or later come to the strange realisation that, contrary to popular thought, our minds are not in our bodies. In fact, the physical body, with all its sensations and processes, can be experienced as being in the mind. The body is in the mind, not the other way round! Further, we can experience the whole world as being "in the mind". This means that all that stuff "out there" – everything that's material, solid, corporeal, physical, "REAL", is "in the mind". The whole "physical" universe of planets, star systems, vast distances of empty space - all that is IN THE MIND! Our minds hold all that!

If you haven't done a lot of meditation this may sound preposterous to you, but some of you will know exactly what I'm talking about – the whole universe, its people and animals, its energies, all happens within the mind. And it's not even your mind, or my mind, it becomes impersonal, just "the mind".

And our minds hold the multi-tiered universe as well as the “real universe”, with its planets and solar systems and big bangs! How can we reconcile the two models? EASY! Think about it for a moment. The vast and still expanding “real” universe, which we still know next to nothing about, is still only on one level – the human level. From this unimaginable huge and mysterious expanse we call the universe, expand even more unutterably vast worlds, on non-human levels. And it doesn’t end. We can’t really even talk about it much. It’s too, too immense.

Realising that everything, however solid, material and “real”, is in the mind, this makes a mockery of the distinction between “real” and “imagined”. The tiered universe is as real as the physical one. Shamanic experiences, religious states of being, are as real as getting a stomach bug or learning to play the flute.

So in this multi-level universe, which we spiritually explore “in the mind” – which doesn’t make it any less real, we are still spiritual nomads, seeking certainty, seeking understanding, seeking our place, our role in it all. Brok and !skian still gaze out from behind our eyes, still sit with us in meditation. They are still part of our spiritual search and our religious community.

And we - we are still wanderers...

CHAPTER TWENTY - WOMBS AND WILLIES – A CHAPTER ON SYNTHESIS.

Tantra, unlike some other religions, isn't afraid of the cunt. The feminine principle of fertility, the womb of all creation, the source of all matter, symbolised by the yoni, the female organ of generation, is held to be sacred. And of course this harks back to Neolithic times, when we were learning the art of agriculture and domesticating animals. Many primitive sites and dwellings are very vagina-shaped in plan. These ancient sites, the first temples really, are obviously intended to symbolise entry, or rather re-entry, into the womb of the Mother Goddess, and, by extension, entry into eternal life, constant renewal.

These special places are obviously artificially created, "controlled" cave spaces. Their alignment with the Mother Goddess current accentuates their womblike qualities.

These sacred wombs are quite different from the earlier, Palaeolithic sacred caves, which though superficially womb-like, are more to do with entry into an underworld of animal spirits. In those days, the journey itself - entry, penetration into the dark, difficult, remote and sometimes dangerous depths of the earth, a cautious, painstaking crawl into the unknown, was more important than the womb symbolism of the caves. It was more to do with "possessing" those dark places of mystery and perhaps the "crossing-over" places of the spirit animals. It was partly about laying claim to the underworld, partly about participating in the processes that took place on and through those rock walls, the boundaries between the worlds. Though the journey involved an entry into a womb-like space, similar to the later Neolithic "temples", it was the identification with the "penetrating" aspect of the journey that made it more masculine in nature, more aligned with the Horned God, the Protector and Provider of Animals.

Worship of the Horned God, or the God of Animals and Nature, together with the worship of the Divine Mother, the Source of Fertility, the Symbol of Birth, Growth and Death, has survived to this day. Both Tantra and Paganism have kept alive this wholeness of worship. Of course, many Wiccans and many Tantrists choose to worship the feminine principle more than the masculine, and some Pagan groups focus more on the warrior ideal. All this is fine, though actually there's no Shiva without Shakti, no awareness without individual shape, embodiment - and conversely, no creation of the myriad entities without consciousness. Shiva and Shakti, the alpha male and female, define, complement and complete one another. It's in the spark of their coming together that we are born, of flesh and awareness.

Ancient man in his (and her) wisdom, kept this balance quite well. The ancient caves, with their magnificent paintings of oxen, deer, bears and bird-headed Shamans (to symbolise flight of the spirit, transcendence, ascendance), were often also found to contain carvings of (very) generously proportioned female fertility symbols. The later, Neolithic "temples", with their womb interiors, often contained carvings of bulls, the ultimate male image of power and potency. Some ancient sites, Stonehenge included, contain womb shapes, to symbolise the fruitfulness and power over life and death of the Goddess - but they also contain symbolic trees, vertical pillars, that echo the aspirations of the older bird-headed (male) Shamans – ascendance into other worlds, other states of being. Having said that, these pillars also emphasise a "verticality" that can go down, into the underworld, as well as up into the heavens.

In my neck of the woods, that's Norfolk, the discovery of Seahenge was very exciting. By the coast, an ancient circle came to light. It had been created around a huge oak tree, inverted so that its circular trunk and sawn off roots formed a kind of altar. The tree appeared to be growing downwards, into some kind of underworld. Perhaps it was a symbolic ladder between the world of human and spirits. A ladder between the worlds is a common theme in Shamanism.

And speaking of verticals - Shiva's lingam, that's a very vertical pillar! That too, is circled, cradled and contained in every Shiva temple by a symbolic yoni, the sign of Shakti. So the urge to enlightenment, the fire of spiritual endeavour, is circled, cradled and contained by our flesh, by our worldly being and by our affinity with other living beings.

So we can slant our worship and our practice three ways if we wish – towards the male, the female or the balance. And our choice is not necessarily determined by our own gender – any man or woman should be free to worship in the way they consider most beneficial, for themselves and for those who share their lives.

Also in my neck of the woods are "Grimes Graves", a Neolithic network of flint mines, dating from around 3,000BC. Animal and human bones have been found in these shafts, which although were primarily working mines, were probably also symbolic gateways to the underworld of spirits. When you climb down the ladder in your hard hat (Health & Safety!) you find yourself in these claustrophobic little corridors and galleries, and you very quickly become aware of how removed you are from the outside world, with its noise, sunlight and other sensory stimuli. You become intensely aware of your own breathing, your heart beat, the sheer physical presence of those people underground with you. It's very conducive to trance and meditative states of mind. Maybe that was part of these mines' functions, in addition to their harvest of flint.

I recently watched a documentary on TV on the Durga Puja, the creation and worship of a Mother Goddess image. The image was commissioned by the British Museum, who flew to Calcutta to seek out the necessary artisans. These craftsmen of India, who create amazing statues of the Mother Goddess in Her various forms from rough bundles of bound reed, plaster and clay, are carrying on a tradition that has its roots in Neolithic times – many such images have been found in ancient sites in the Middle East, fashioned in exactly the same way. And those Neolithic carvings of the bull –they can be also found in Crete, Greece, Egypt – and of course outside many temples dedicated to Shiva and his number one follower – Nandi the bull. We can trace these ancient principles and practices right up to the present day.

But of course, as I've said before, though we still have Stone Age bodies and Stone Age instincts, and for some of us, a Stone Age religion – we don't live in the Stone Age any more. We live in a global, multicultural, incredibly diverse society. So from the outside it may seem as if there's a dichotomy between our inner and outer orientations. But actually this is true for anyone pursuing a spiritual path, whatever its cultural roots and whatever the cultural roots of the practitioner – there's always going to be an ongoing dialogue, resulting sometimes in widely differing aspirations, between the inner and outer life of a spiritual seeker. The world within and the world outside (actually the same thing, though it seldom feels like it) require different things from us at different times. And though we may have the luxury of religious faith, there's never a spiritual sure thing for the aspirant. One learns to live with uncertainty, ambiguity.

Depressing though it may sound – without this kind of suffering, this spiritual pain, this longing for assurance and certainty – without it there's no growth. Sometimes we only question life when we suffer. Only pain causes us to ask "Why is this happening?" Certainly, the doctrine of the Enlightened One, the Buddha, springs from this very dilemma – what causes suffering? And Buddhism says – because we can't relate to reality skilfully, because we allow ego desires to pollute the clear reality of what's actually happening.

Shiva Shankara reminds us that we suffer because we chase illusions. This may seem timely advice to anyone wishing to align their religious practices with those of our Palaeolithic and Neolithic ancestors. So we mustn't lose sight of the obvious fact that we are, in many respects, unable to see life in the same way as our ancestors. The good news is that it doesn't matter. Religion will always evolve, develop, change. It's the principles that remain fairly constant.

And these principles, that the apparently paradoxical worlds of spirit and matter are in fact constantly interacting, are in fact the same thing, and that we can all achieve intimate, personal contact with divinity, these principles are intact and can be discovered within Tantra, Paganism and Shamanism.

Another coming together, another synthesis, that appeals to me is that of spirit work and soul work. Spirit work may be loosely defined as the urge for transcendence, for personal liberation, the urge to rise above the human condition. Buddhism is a par excellence example of spirit work. Soul work is all about descent, sinking, merging – an immersing in myth, dream, culture, an exploration of inner landscapes. Jungian psychology may legitimately be termed soul work. Here's a poem I wrote quite a few years ago. It was originally written in apology for ripping into a friend, a devout Christian. Then it became a hymn to harmony, unity, synthesis. I was examining the two currents of spirit and soul that, at that time, I hadn't reconciled. It's called The God Tree.

"I have been sharp with you and entertained angles unawares

But now I wish to make amends

Your God's tree does not shelter or comfort me
But I didn't mean to shake its limbs
Or cause them to become knotted and shocked
Contorted in defence's cause

What causes me to shatter into blossom
That is vulva purple or thorn white
(And from both the fragrance of released musk)
Is that two streams feed and colour my roots
And each is seemingly poisonous to the other
And innocently, greedily vie to dominate and drown the tree
It's from this weeping, creaking timber that I speak

One stream is silver clear and nudges brightly as it surges
Tumbling noisily over roots and stones
Happy to arrogantly elbow leaves and drowned butterflies
From its looping cord of light
Ever hungry and renewing
Reaching, needle sharp, through every night

Ah, but the other is old and dark, wormwood bitter to my thoughts
But salt blood of my darker heart
Wherein men of iron have drowned
And stories floated, myth-logged
Seemingly just beyond our fathers' grasp
Here the dead moths find a fertile grave and transcend to pale angels
That shiver between the worlds
Here the heartblood colours the blossom
From easter-milk to a rich and sombre wine
And the flooded roots, already stained black
Still hungrily suckle on each clotted drop

And so, groaning, my God-tree stands at your left hand
And our roots reach into each other's land
And one child-white dawn
From the purple womb of night skies born

The flowering branches may yet knit
To form a shelter for this one man, and for all"

I'm thankful to report that the poem was well received - with grace, dignity and forgiveness. Phew!

I feel that the aim of any authentic spiritual path should be that holistic state which Jungians called individuation – a blend of completeness of soul, having access to the wisdom of the collective unconscious, a harmonious synthesis of all one's energies (soul work) and some kind of awareness of personal responsibility, personal power and transcendence (to a degree) over worldly (human) conditions (spirit work).

It's good to find a path that nourishes both spirit and soul, which is why I advocate Tantra, with its journey into other worlds, other states of being, devotion to divinity, its inner alchemy – all of which may be termed soul work – and with its equal emphasis on improving personal karma and rising above the pashu (animal) level of human existence – which of course is the very definition of spiritual work.

I'm sure there are branches of Paganism and Shamanism (and other paths too) that achieve this level of balance but, as far as I know, only Tantra sets out, as part of the original game plan, the twin aspirations of dissolving into divinity (and the worlds of the divinities) and achieving personal power and emancipation.

One more example of synthesis before we wind this chapter up...

When I was a young boy I used to forcibly hold my eyes tightly closed, relax myself deeper and deeper, and watch the geometric shapes, the stars, lines, streaks and grids, that would swirl and press against the inside of my eyelids. The pressure used to hurt sometimes but thankfully I never really damaged myself. The weird thing was that, the longer I continued the process, the harder it became to breathe. Nothing was blocking my nose or mouth yet it would feel as if I was being suffocated, crushed beneath a heavy weight. I'd persevere though - my aim was always to hold on until "the tunnel" appeared – a swirling snot green vortex, like smoke rings, that would eventually open (and often fail to open) into a circular patch of deep, beautiful blue, like the sky seen from the bottom of a well. Just once or twice in my childhood I managed to "climb up" into that world, "up" to that level. Mostly I didn't. But in my head, if I held on until the tunnel appeared – I won the game.

These kind of "behind the eyes" shapes and visions are called entoptics and are very common in prehistoric cave and rock art. Stars, meshes, diamonds, lightning flashes etc appear everywhere, in both ancient and not-so-ancient tribal art. The ancient shamans would record the shapes they experienced as they fell into trance and journeyed "through the tunnel" into other worlds. I think the spiral motif that occurs everywhere in European Neolithic sites is a rendition of "the tunnel". And remember Shiva's damaru drum – that funnel that opens up into other worlds? Its shape and its sound both point us towards crossing the borders of the material, into the world of spirits.

Many of these entoptic shapes also end up as tribal tattoos. Very nice too. I think it's good that we record significant events on our lives on our very skin. But it should be personal to each individual – not just panthers, bluebirds and Mickey Mouse (for fucks sake!)

Anyway, I used to associate that blue distance with some kind of twilight summer world where all my heroes (like William Tell, Robin Hood and The Lone Ranger), together with half human-half animal beings (like Rupert the Bear!), lived eternally, forever engaged in some kind of happy adventure. I was also vaguely aware that the journey to this world was potentially fraught with dangers. The Bogey Man and other ghostly creatures could be waiting, hoping to divert me "sideways" into the swirling abyss around the tunnel. Yep, I was a strange child. But not too far off the truth!

It's very easy, when dealing with psychic stuff, to get taken off the path, to get swirled sideways, to be seduced by promises of personal power or by fascination with side issues, diversions that suddenly appear central, pivotal, vital. It's like chasing a butterfly when trying to negotiate a maze. If you're not careful, just one wrong step, one unwitting turn of direction, can be disastrous!

When I first read about entoptics I was very pleased. I felt it was another example of synthesis – a childhood practice merging into my adult paradigm.

Sometimes though, it's harder to reconcile disparate images from one's childhood. Read on...

CHAPTER TWENTY ONE - SACRIFICIAL LAMBS.

"Life feeds on life." One of my students said that, and she's absolutely right. All life exists at the expense of other life. Whether you're a vegan, a vegetarian, a carnivore, something has to die so you can live. Life has to be sacrificed to sustain life. That's nature. It took me many years to come to terms with this simple fact.

Growing up as a child, I always thought of myself as shy, even a bit prissy. I didn't like coarseness, such as when other boys my age would hold belching or farting competitions, replaced much later with communal masturbation and cigarette smoking! I always felt that I was letting myself down if I participated, that people shouldn't behave in such ways. And yet I did all the usual boyish things – chased rabbits and lizards, leaped over streams, threw penknives around, jumped out of trees, stole cigarettes from my parents, tried to look up girls' skirts. And the few surviving photos of me as a boy show what looks like a right little bastard! The inner boy I was experiencing doesn't seem to match the external image.

Like many people with a modicum of self awareness, I was able to look at my parental influences, my childhood upbringing, later in life and make conscious decisions about what to keep, what to discard. And of course, sometimes these choices change as you grow older. We grow into being more, or less, sociable, we grow into a settled vocation or a life of moving around the country. We grow into meat or non-meat diets, we grow into different lifestyles. We grow into different relationships. We even grow into different religions!

Some people, of course, lack the ability or the courage to lift their gaze above the emotional horizon, to see where they've come from, where they might go – they get stuck in reaction, and then another reaction – their whole life is spent as a karmic ping pong ball. And of course, it's never their fault when things go wrong!

Personally, I grew into my fierceness, into being a leader. I had to sacrifice my unwillingness to compete with those other boys in their "manly" games. But at first I wasn't a good leader, whether it was being in a band, in an American Football team, in a coven. I was too willing to sacrifice people, especially my family, my wife and kids, close friends, in the pursuit of... whatever it was I was pursuing at the time. I allowed no other voice but my own, felt no one's needs but my own. I was ruthless and callous. I was always successful at what I did but it was always a narrow vision because it was only one man's, not a team effort. It took an awfully long time to move away from that kind of mindset, and I regret it all now – not bitterly though

– I've become a much better person through my regret. I'm grateful for the pain I caused myself through regret – I grew through it, it's my karma. I can still be single-minded, ruthless in pursuit of a goal, but I will not allow myself to be cold to others any more – that's a sin to me now.

And of course I can't go back and undo any injury or insult caused to others through my coldness and selfishness. That's my karma too.

Here's a bizarre and powerful meditation I had recently, which brought all this back to me...

I'm sitting, trying to still the mind, when I find myself in a forest clearing, sitting with Jungle Shiva. He tells me to go hunting every day, to look for something to kill. I know He means things like moral cowardice, hypocrisy, selfishness. He repeatedly stabs His trident into the dust to illustrate His point. The metal tips gleam through the fine film of dust. He moves to squat behind me, holds me, supports me. I always really enjoy that feeling. I find my mind has drifted for a few minutes. I apologise to Him but He laughs. "What does it feel like when I do that?" I ask Him. He tilts His head, considering. "Your body turns to small stars, like dust, but it holds its shape." That's His reply.

And then He's gone for a moment. I can't see Him. But I can understand what He means. I can still feel His arms around me like a presence, though I can't see Him. Then He comes back.

I try again, flying around the clearing. Then suddenly everything changes! It's really bizarre! I'm in a room like a doctor's surgery and a respectable young couple have brought their son in to see me. He's about eight years old, quite pale. I somehow understand that he's autistic in some way, very withdrawn, and that I'm supposed to help him. I tell the parents that I can't guarantee anything but I'll give it my best shot. I tell them to leave the room and under no circumstances to come back in until they're told to – no matter what they might hear. They agree and leave.

All hell breaks loose! There's screaming and banging and furniture overthrown and I'm thinking "Shit! They'll think I'm murdering the kid!" But somehow all this commotion isn't coming from the boy, but from inside him. He's a puppet of these forces.

Suddenly there's an enormous looming presence in the room. Right in front of me. I take a step back! I flash on Shiva's three horizontal stripes on my forehead – it's my instinctive reaction to this kind of danger. (Physically, for those that are interested, I tend to make "leopard" fists, like holding a tennis ball, but with the fingers together and the backs of the hands flat) It's a shaman. He's tall and grizzly and wears a bear's head as a kind of hood. He wears bears' teeth around his neck. He looks very powerful.

It's obvious that he's been "hiding" inside the child. He looks at me with a kind of "What now?" look. He doesn't seem particularly bothered. I make a bright, burning white light, another automatic defence. When I can see again the scene has disappeared and I'm back in Shiva's arms in the clearing. He smiles. Again, in my mind's eye, I see the bright glint of metal in the dust...

Well, that's it. That's all that happened. It was afterwards I did all the introspection. Was I the parents looking for their middle class respectability to be restored by the curing of their son? Nah. Was I the child, unable to contain the shaman's power? Nah - but closer. It was to do with that power, and the responsibility that should come with it. I was the shaman. I'd dominated others, literally not allowing them a voice, not allowing them to interact, to participate in decision making. I'd made them all autistic, unable to communicate. I'd locked them inside their own heads. I'd contained and concealed the extent of my influence over them within their unconscious collaboration. I'd sacrificed them on the altar of my pursuits. I'd turned a blind eye to the consequences, for myself and for them. What a horrible thing to do. I deserved all the pain and regret that was to follow in later years. Every bit of it. No excuses, no appeals. Karma is very precise, very fitting.

I sacrificed the "Well, what a man I am!" feeling for true regret and a desire to make good. I perhaps sacrifice my dignity and your sympathy by telling you all this...

And of course, further analysis reveals further possible interpretations of this meditation experience. Perhaps I was the parents after all – part of me knew it was time to heal the child. Again two alternatives – either because they (I) genuinely cared about the child (within), and were willing to try unorthodox methods to help the boy – or maybe it was them who needed healing – they wanted a "normal" child to preserve their middle class respectability. (I'd like to point out that I'm not middle class!)

Or maybe I was the autistic child, unable to communicate because the shaman within was too strong. I couldn't channel that amount of energy successfully, so it became blocked. There's an element of truth in that – I recall being unable to hold all of Shiva's energy at one point – how could I? How could anyone? But eventually I'm drawn back to the strong intuition that the shaman had been deliberately hiding inside the child, concealing his strength, going to ground where no one (presumably his "enemies") would ever think of looking for him. It's a clever thing to do, if cruel. It's the same as hunters wearing the skins of dead buffalos in order to creep up on a herd. So why was the shaman hiding himself. Who is he wishing to avoid? Or is he "stalking" humans? Are humans his prey? What's going on here? Maybe Shiva is trying to show me how to be a hunter. If so, parts of my pretensions about being such a caring and compassionate person (which I am –honest!) are going to have to be sacrificed. Again. Perhaps my task is to do this without becoming cold to others again. Hmm.

The idea of sacrifice is as old as mankind. Way back when in those Palaeolithic caves, men and women were leaving offerings to the spirit world. Seashells and animal teeth have been found, stuffed into cracks and crevices in the walls. The concept that we have to surrender something to attain or obtain something seems universal throughout history. And this is perhaps the origin of the barter system. Animal sacrifice, and sometimes human sacrifice, was routinely performed throughout the ancient world – in India, China, Greece, Egypt, everywhere. The man that was to become the Buddha in India in the sixth century BC sacrificed His luxurious lifestyle, His entire family, His royalty, in order to pursue the spiritual life. He was among the first to advocate that such sacrifices were far superior to any number of dead animals burning in front of an altar. He told us, "All life runs away from pain, fears pain and suffering. So don't cause pain and suffering." He might have paraphrased that saying for my benefit, "No one likes to feel coerced, cowed, impotent. So don't make people feel that way. Even if they collude and co-operate in that process. Especially when they collude and co-operate" And the sad truth is that we all collude and co-operate in our own suffering. We all invite it in, even if we don't know we're doing it. One thing we really have to sacrifice for spiritual growth is our own wilful blindness, our refusal to see how we cause suffering for ourselves and others. We bleat about our suffering even as we throw ourselves on the sacrificial altar. Again.

In fact, The Buddha (and perhaps Lao Tzu too) was also the first to switch spiritual focus away from sacrifices intended to appease and petition the Gods towards a personal endeavour, individual aspirations towards some kind of transcendence, even divinity. This was a revolutionary switch, real thinking outside the cultural box. And He placed suffering squarely at the centre of His philosophy. And karma - personal responsibility for our suffering - that too became central.

Jung, another giant, and also not afraid to think outside the box, said that neurosis, existential suffering, happens because the soul has not found its meaning. In other words, we suffer when we haven't realised what it is we're here for, what we're supposed to be doing. Until we discover our task in life, we'll feel permanently displaced, unsettled, alienated.

Remember my student's concerns (in the "Divining the Divine" chapter) that a spiritual practice can get narcissistic, self centred, self serving? Well, she's right of course, we all have to guard against the possibility of that happening, but actually the reverse should be true – an authentic spiritual path should take us away from narrow ego concerns, towards a greater empathy with all life. In fact, a spiritual path is nature's way of doing its work through us. And by nature, I don't mean merely the seasons and the weather and the dolphins (who are NOT as nice as you might think!) but the bigger current of evolution, the growth and development of consciousness. A spiritual path is evolution carrying itself along, in us. We are evolution's vehicles.

And to perform that collective task effectively, for the common good, we have to paradoxically become true individuals, responsible for our actions, for cleaning up our self-created mess. Gods and Goddesses won't do the work for you, but They will give you the tools for the job, they will encourage you every step of the way, They may even give you a helping hand occasionally. But the task is yours, the responsibility is yours. The achievement however, the good that ensues - that belongs to all creation!

Suffering is inescapable. It's a central element of human life. And it's how we relate to life's inevitable trials that defines us as a conscious, skilful being – or a sacrificial lamb.

As I write this it's midday on December 31st. It's a mild but wet and breezy day, with a mean vibe, a feeling of worse weather to come. I was in the middle of my training at a friend's house a couple of hours ago. It wasn't going well. I was tired and grumpy, I was forgetting bits of forms that I shouldn't forget. I had a phone call from my son, who was in the grip of a teenage-like angst attack. His puppy had crapped on the floor, made a hell of a mess and he felt responsible. I don't know what he wanted me to do but our conversation left us both feeling worse than when we started! I went outside again, rescued a worm from the pavement, then watched in astonishment as a blackbird immediately swooped down onto the grass and ate it! Ho hum! Then my training was interrupted again, my irate wife on the phone demanding to know what I'd said to upset our son so much. Getting better and better...

I managed to finish training, being interrupted only once more by a neighbour, looking extremely pale and stressed out, presumably by the whole Christmas thing. She said she'd just ordered her husband to go and perform useless errands somewhere, anywhere, just so she could have the house to herself for a couple of hours. Finally, when I sat down to meditate, I was disturbed by the sound of sobbing from the house next door to my friend's. One of the women inside was obviously not having a good day.

Now, I know most of the people in the above scenario, and they're all decent people, trying their best to make their way in the world, helping others as they go. And yet they were all, myself included, in some kind of private hell. There was an enormous gap between the way things were going and the way that we would have preferred them to go. Nothing new of course, but it's more noticeable when it all happens at once.

It's the central task of Buddhism, and of Jungian therapy too, to invest our natural suffering with significance, to give it meaning. We have to ask ourselves, "Why am I suffering?" and further, "What is this suffering asking me to do?" The first answer, to the first question, usually all boils down to letting go, relaxing more into the flow of things, letting the Dao (the way) find its own level, with a minimum of interference from our ego based desires and aversions. The more we can "relax our preferences" as Ajahn Sumedho so sagely puts it, the less we'll suffer in everyday life.

The second answer, to the question "What is this suffering asking me to do?" – well, that's more difficult. Shamanic wisdom, and again, Jungian therapy too, would assert that suffering occurs when we aren't living authentic lives, when our lives are not aligned with the work that our soul wants to undertake. And usually the answer is found in the dragon's den, or in the magical cave guarded by serpents or buratahongs (bogey men, half crocodile, half ape, with a dash of scarecrow and "alien" added for good measure), in other words, in those inner recesses of our psyche where the most resistance is encountered. Usually, the greater the suffering, the greater the possibility that the one thing we really need to do is the very set of actions we most wish to avoid. So we throw up lots of smoke around the cave mouth, assert that we can't find our way in, or we shrug and say, "Let's try another cave!"

And we can play that game all our lives. Let's find another sacrificial altar. You light the fire and I'll bleed a bit.

I know from personal experience that the worst place to be is when you hear yourself say, "I know I've got to do something but I don't know what." Most of the time we suspect that we do know the answer but it would be too painful to examine, let alone implement. Often you can actually feel your mind skidding away from revelation at the last moment, ending up back at square one – "I know I've got to do something but I don't know what." But this kind of mental approach, this evasion, has got to stop.

It takes enormous courage, an immense act of will, to actually enter the cave, the labyrinth, to confront one's own unwillingness to participate in self emancipation, to open one's ears to hear the answer we dread, the actions we must take...

So often we refuse to search in the very places where meaning is hiding, where significance dwells, because that's where our deepest fears also reside. Ask yourself, "What is the one thing I don't want to find out about myself?" Then explore all the stuff that arises from that!

One of the reasons I prefer to teach Taiji and Qigong, rather than be a healer, is a) to empower people, give them the means of their own deliverance from various ailments, and b) to kick them out of the "My world is broken. Can you fix it for me?" mindset. In other words, out of the passive, sacrificial lamb mentality, into a pro-active programme for self development. We all need to assume responsibility for our own suffering. Only then does it become meaningful. Only then does it become the path to liberation. As the slogan asserts that I saw on a wonderful pagan t shirt – "The truth shall set you free – but first it will piss you off!"

And that's so true! I was talking to a friend and confidant about my experience with the bear shaman hiding himself in the autistic child. I actually heard myself say these words...

"So the implication was that he was wearing the body of the child as a hunter wears a buffalo skin to get closer to the herd. But if that's so, why was he doing that? What, or WHO, was he stalking? (pause)..... Oh. It was me, wasn't it? Duh!"

Yep, Dumbo, it was you! Congrats on your incisive mind! The shaman wanted to confront me, wanted me to feel his power, wanted to show me the part of me that I consistently deny, my personal power. And I walked right into his trap like a sacrificial lamb.

The lesson is the same, not becoming cold or unfeeling towards other people, but the other lesson is not to be so naïve, to realise (again) that not everything on the spiritual path is sweetness and light. We (I) need to stay alert, be wary of ambushes and distractions. Time to wake up again!

CHAPTER TWENTY TWO - SHAKIN' ALL OVER.

Tantrists believe that the entire world is shaking, all the time, that everything is created from vibration. They believe that, through the lovemaking of Shiva and Shakti, consciousness and physical form come into being simultaneously, born from Shakti's womb, infused with the awareness of Shiva.

They believe that the entire universe is held together by vibration. They believe that all life vibrates at certain frequencies. Further, they believe that every single entity, every organism, represents a different frequency of vibration. So all life is both held together, united, in vibration and is held apart, differentiated by vibration. Thoughts have vibration. Words have vibration. Light has vibration. Time has vibration.

When you look at Tantric art or Tibetan thangkas (religious scroll paintings) you can see the energy, almost feel the picture, the world in the picture, vibrating with power.

Sometimes, in the world of Tantra, when vibrations are compatible, things can slide through, into, around each other. So thoughts can be transmitted over long distances. Tantric "magicians", adepts can cover long distances very quickly, or even appear in two different places. Time can run backwards, or be frozen. Gods, humans and animals can communicate. The adept can visit different worlds, different planes of existence, different states of being.

Tantrists are consciousness engineers. They seek to alter their ways of perceiving themselves and the world(s) around them in order to achieve darshan with the deities, to dissolve into the divinities. They often employ spirit helpers or beings from other planes, intermediary Gods, dakinis or Bodhisattvas. They use drumming, chanting, hallucinogenic drugs etc to aid their awareness altering.

And of course, most of this is true of Shamans, which is why I've devoted so much time and space to them in this book. Shamans believe that the world, all the worlds, and everything therein, are a vibration. They believe that these vibrations, and therefore all energies, can be influenced or manipulated. Shamans are consciousness engineers too, and employ drumming, chanting, hallucinogenic drugs etc to aid their awareness altering. They employ spirit helpers, intermediaries, in their work.

Both Tantrists and Shamans hold the cosmology, the world structure, together for those around them, and employ that cosmology in their various endeavours.

Both Tantrists and Shamans are involved in a kind of voodoo. They seek to either become possessed, or to channel the Gods and Goddesses, the helpful spirits, which in Shamanism may be animals or even plants. After that, the paths diverge a little, Shamans traditionally undertaking healing, lost object location, initiations, and purification ceremonies. Tantrists have similar, but far less central functions, their main endeavour being "internal" magic, union with the deities.

It could be argued though that both Tantrists and Shamans work with imbalances. Shamans with evil, disease-causing spirits, and Tantrists with ignorance and emotional hindrances. In their active pursuit of such goals, they're both hunters! Both are intensely aware that there is no such animal as objective reality, that what you expect to perceive and feel is exactly what you'll experience. This of course aids both healing and spiritual aspirations.

Both believe that there's no difference between the sacred and the secular, the holy and the everyday. Both therefore keep a close eye on the natural world, looking for clues, anomalies and connections. Both deal in synchronicities, as synchronicities enhance the perception of interaction between various elements of the universe and hence enhance meaning, significance, and therefore religious faith too. Both treat the natural world, all relationships, conversations, bird flight, animal movement, weather patterns etc as an oracle, as an expression of spiritual harmony or "unrest" or as clues as to what work should be undertaken.

Both are familiar with other realms, Shamans traditionally working with the spirits of the dead, the spirits of animals, the spirits of plants, even demons. Tantrists work in the three realms of Nirmanakaya, Sambhogakaya and the Dharmakaya, that is, the natural world (including humans), spirit planes (most of the work is done on this level, which may also be termed mythos, the world of the imagination, though this sounds rather derogatory and patronising), and (rarely) the formless God/dess levels.

So, the wisdom and the practices of Shamanism and Tantra are compatible. Tantrism can be traced back, through Shamanism, to our Palaeolithic and Neolithic ancestors. Both tend to be culture specific, Shamans and Tantrists working within the culture, the symbology and worldview of their ancestors. I believe that this must remain true for authentic Shamanism. There is a wealth of plant and animal lore and a plethora of spirit helpers and hinderers that must be either inherited or passed down through initiation. One can't learn to be a Lakota, Siberian or Inca Shaman over the internet. One can however learn valuable basic Shamanic skills from almost any source. These skills perhaps can then be imbedded into a cultural setting and become part of an authentic Shamanic practice.

For Tantrists it's easier, I believe. Unlike native plants, animals and localised spirits, the Gods and Goddesses are archetypal energies and though They may have bloomed in various cultures, need not necessarily be confined to them. Shiva, for example, is generally regarded as a product of Indian religion, but His prototype is older than India, older than any country. Indian culture, Indian belief nurtured Him, and I'm grateful for that, but India doesn't own Shiva. India doesn't own Kali. India doesn't own the Buddha. Egypt doesn't own Anubis. Greece doesn't own Pan. Northern Europe doesn't own Freya. And Jesus is NOT an American!

So the modern day Tantrist has the luxury of working with any deity, with any practice. Results are all that matter. (That's true of Shamanism too!) Cultivate your own world vision, your own relationship with the deities, your own personal experiences of the invisible world, rather than your book library or your intellectual knowledge.

Boom Shiva Ho! YOU are the experiment here – be a good Tantrist and see what you can make of the material at hand!

We're fortunate, in a bizarre way, to be living at a time when we can watch our culture visibly shrink and contract. We can see the creeping tide of Americanisms in the English language - nothing necessarily wrong with that I hasten to add, but it seems to be accompanied by over-emoting, a lack of public restraint, phoney emotions, a growing "I'm the victim here." mentality, a faintly hysterical form of Christianity and a general dumbing down in the media. TV programmes seem to be adapting the "say something for ten minutes, have an ad break, then repeat the information again, in case the dumb asses in their armchairs have forgotten what they're watching" approach to programming and presentation. And if I hear one more "news" interview begin with the words, "So how did you *feel* about that?" I shall scream!

There are less and less programmes on serious matters, and those that do slip through the net usually consist of a bunch of mindless, gutless "personalities" mouthing their officially sanctioned opinions of the matter at hand. The so-called giant thinkers such as Stephen Hawking seem to have lost the big picture. And you'll never see Terence Mckenna, expert on Shamanism, psychedelic drugs and New Age phenomena, and probably the most articulate man on the planet, deliver a lecture on any BBC programme! (Well, ok, partly because he's dead, bless 'im!)

As Mckenna asserts, though I feel he over-emphasises the message - sometimes "culture is not your friend." This isn't true of course if you live in a Shaman-friendly environment, within a culture that respects and honours the visionaries of other worlds as much as it does visionaries of industry, science, art etc. But most of us live in a culture that not only fails or refuses to honour such visionaries (though the recent outpouring of public affection for the deceased ex-frontman of the Pink Floyd – Syd Barrett – was encouraging), it actively represses and forbids such "seeing" and the means (psychedelic drugs) of such seeing.

But Mckenna makes a pertinent point, and as usual, does it beautifully, in denouncing culture as an enemy of those who wish to "see". Culture hardens off our perceptions, our assumptions, conditions us to think and behave in certain ways. And it's insidious, we don't notice it – we think we're free of conditioning. Far from it. The way we function has been funnelled, narrowed down into little trickles of freedom and autonomy. We are very, very conditioned beings.

But of course, happily, as soon as we even begin to become aware of it, even as we ask the question, "How am I conditioned by society?", the evidence starts to become incontrovertible, we begin to see all too clearly how our thoughts, our attitudes, are shaped by the influence of parents, upbringing, peer pressure, "education", the media, religion, political proclivities etc.

As soon as we become aware, even a little, of our conditioning, its influence on us shrinks.

But if our perceptions are distorted in this way, by all the influences around us, then everything we see, every conclusion we arrive at, is going to be distorted isn't it? Here's an enlightening Buddhist story on just such a way of perceiving...

There was a young monk (a westerner, though it makes no difference to the story) who joined the local Buddhist temple as an apprentice. He was a nice enough lad, but very full of himself, he thought he was special simply because he had opted to follow the Buddhist path. He prided himself on being a very aware person. One morning he was meditating and a very senior monk walked past. He stopped, looked closely at the young monk and said, very kindly, "You look just like the Buddha when you sit."

Well, of course, the young lad was delighted at first. But then the senior monk did something very strange. He leaned over the young monk and whispered. "Do you know what I look like when I sit in meditation?" Of course, the young monk said nothing – he wasn't that stupid! The senior monk continued, "I look like I'm going to fall asleep." Then his voice rose to a roar! "BUT I NEVER DO!"

This shook the young monk; he was actually physically quaking as the venerable walked away. What on earth was all that about? Then it him like a hammer. The old monk was trying to help him. He could see the Buddha-nature, the potential for enlightenment within the youngster. He saw the Buddha in everyone. He saw the Buddha wherever he looked! And the old monk was warning the youngster – I may look dopey when I sit but I guard constantly against falling asleep, in other words, falling into delusion.

The lad dropped his (natural) youthful folly right there and then, and vowed to emulate the old monk, to always guard against the delusions of pride, ignorance, envy, ill will and greed. Later, when he was renowned for his wisdom, he would recount the above story as the seed of his enlightenment.

So, if we're full of the world, wherever we look, that's what we'll see. If we revere Buddha, or God/dess, then that's what we'll find, wherever we look. But we have to be careful. We may be fooling ourselves even here.

Everyone is familiar with the term "fetish". A fetish is an object that we allow to assume, or we invest it with, an importance way beyond its everyday function. So called "primitive" tribes had objects, such as totem poles, or sacred trees that were described by short sighted anthropologists as "fetishes". It's within the field of human sexuality that most people learn about fetishes. Some people can only achieve orgasm or full sexual functioning by focusing on rubber wear, women's knickers, whips, uniforms etc. Here, the "sacred objects" are infused with power, they carry the full sexual charge that we would expect to find in the whole process of wooing, seducing, petting, screwing and sharing a cigarette or cup of coffee afterwards. The fetish carries all the sexual electricity, all the satisfaction. In fact, the electricity and fulfilment depend on the fetish being present, exerting its power.

And people can do that with religion. We read of a man who achieved enlightenment and liberation twenty five centuries ago in India. We call Him the Buddha. He told us to test His teachings for ourselves, even to discard any parts of it that seemed either ineffective in our lives or ran against what we regard as common sense. He empowered to think for ourselves, to try and emulate Him, find our own way to liberation. He gave us teachings and guidelines, and more importantly, practices – actual things to do. He told us to rely on ourselves.

All well and good. So usually the first thing Buddhists do is buy a statue of the guy and turn it into a fetish! We put Him "out there". We hope that if we lead good enough lives, somehow we'll be rewarded with enlightenment. We indulge in bizarre practices, like sitting still, doing nothing for thirty minutes at a time. We even go off on "retreats" (what are we really retreating from?) to sit and do nothing with others.

Nothing of this is actually harmful but it reeks a bit of a kind of displacement. The Buddha is here and now, not in a monastery, not at the end of a "virtuous" life. The Buddha's wisdom and compassion pulses most strongly, most potently, most provocatively, in the very parts of us we most wish to conceal – especially from ourselves.

Meditation quickly reveals to our conscious mind the horrors that lurk within us. Sometimes it seems as if our entire head is full irrepressible chattering lunatics. Once we learn to disengage (not suppress) from this bedlam, we start to not believe them any more, not to buy into what they're saying. Then we have a bit more space and energy at our disposal to investigate what the Buddha called the three characteristics of existence. First is anicca – impermanence. Nothing lasts forever, especially our insights, thoughts and opinions. They're always changing. Second is anatta – emptiness. Everything is essentially hollow. It's an illusion. Everything we think will bring us fulfilment turns out to be two-dimensional. Nothing comes on its own. It's always part of something else, something we may not want. Third, and especially powerful because of anicca and anatta, is dukkha – dissatisfaction. Nothing, and that means nothing, is going to bring us lasting happiness. No relationship, no job, no possession, nothing is going to give us eternal happiness. It's an impermanent, hollow, dissatisfactory illusion. So there!

But that's what meditation is for. To bring this home to us. So we can wake up, change our orientation, change our practice, become saturated with the divinities, stop looking for personal satisfaction, power, prestige, enlightenment, all that stuff. Just to be with the divinities is enough. Then you no longer care whether you become enlightened or not, whether you're going to reincarnate or not, even whether you're happy or not. Sounds crazy doesn't it? But the one thing that becoming saturated with the deities brings – is meaning. And meaning is a really powerful drug. I confess I'm hooked on it!

That's the genius of Tantra. We don't have to go looking for Buddha in a temple, or in the latest Dalai Lama book. We can go looking for Buddha (or God/dess) right here, in the untidy, stinking but fertile, darkness covered garden of our own minds, even in our shameful paucity of humanity, in our poverty of empathy, in our shrivelled little egos, in our optimistically-giving-to-charity-regularly lifestyles, in the bits of us that are not nice, not acceptable, not condoned or praised by our society, our culture. Whatever energy rises to the surface – anger, resentment, lust – all these energies are just the divinities in disguise. If we learn to see the face of God/dess or Buddha behind the dark mask, we may just be able to see each and every energy for what it is – the universe working its karma out through us.

And when we understand that, then perhaps we don't have to express that energy through anger, resentment or lust any more. And it'll be a genuine evolution, from something base, destructive, to something positive and potentially elevating, beneficial. It won't be an act of will, ie- ego.

I used the term "saturated with the sacred" a few times in this book. You have to become saturated in this way to function with full spiritual efficacy. By all means pay your taxes, visit the dentist, earn a living, give society its dues, but unless your inner orientation is fully towards the divinities, then your experiences, perceptions, insights and achievements are going to be limited, to a greater or lesser degree, depending upon the amount of gravitational pull our society exerts on you.

And this orientation is not necessarily towards being "good" or trying to please everyone. You can't. It's impossible I know. I've tried. It's about trying to see the divinities in everything that happens, and asking, "What's the lesson here?" What energy is trying to evolve – and into what?

Life is messy. No one is in total control of themselves or their day. Those that think they are, are under a delusion. Those that think other people are, are also under a delusion. But our perceptions, our experiences, our whole day, can be transformed, so there is a degree of autonomy.

For example. Today, I trained in my hard qigong, threw up a bit (I always do, it's not a spectator sport!), went into the city with an elderly friend, and helped her carry two lampshades home. Then I began this section of writing. That's it, that's all that happened. Externally.

Internally, it was a very different day. I meditated after training and who should turn up but Skanda, one of the sons of Shiva, the other being Ganesh. Skanda is an enigmatic deity, supposedly an accomplished yogi, also associated with war and the planet Mars. Like Krishna (there appear to be overlaps in Their symbology), He's sometimes depicted as blue and He wears a peacock father (the peacock is His vahana, His vehicle animal). Known as Karthikeya in North India and Muruga/n in the South, He doesn't get mentioned much in books on Shiva-related matters and He's not as high profile as His older brother, Ganesh. He is, however, very popular in some places, especially Sri Lanka.

I know very little about Him, have no connection with Him, so it was quite a surprise when He stood there in front of me, very real, very vivid. He was very handsome, with high cheekbones and an aquiline nose. He was dark blue in colour and wore a peacock feather in His long black hair, on the left side. To be honest, at first I had no idea who He was. I thought it might even be Krishna but some inner voice corrected me. He waved a peacock feather in front of my right eye, so I was looking through the "eye" at the end of the feather. The world turned a little darker, and I could see light particles like sperm swimming through the air, except that these "sperm" were the size of pigeons! I could also see demons, shaped like long legged crabs, and squids, dark brown and black in colour. They were squirmy and horrible! I felt an instinctive revulsion and wanted to kill them. I was surprised at how easy it would have been for me to feel totally comfortable with blasting them to pieces. They felt predatory, ancient and hostile. Now I think about it, they were similar to the kind of sea monster one encounters when clearing the sex chakra (Look it up! Or read The Real Rasa – it's cool!). Maybe I was being shown the true nature of my sexual consciousness! I'm joking – I hope!

After my mental battle with these creatures, Skanda leaned over me, then He tapped me three times on the top of the head with the peacock feather, but whether that was in blessing or admonishment I have no idea. He said not a word, just disappeared. So what the fuck was all that about? I opened my eyes. The sun was illuminating the bare branches of a chestnut tree. They were glowing green with moss and lichen, extraordinarily beautiful. And in the lower branches was a sparrow hawk, regal and totally motionless, only a few feet away. When I moved, the hawk swooped away in a flash.

Recovering, and still puzzling over my experience over a cup of tea in my friend's kitchen, the radio played the full version of "Like a hurricane" by Neil Young. His guitar solos seemed breathtakingly haunting, deep and majestic beyond belief. In my heightened state of awareness, every note was perfect, achingly so. I felt alternately racked and elevated by the bloody thing! What a trip!

Waiting for the bus into the city, my friend and I were entertained by a flock of about twenty starlings playing in a huge puddle in the road. At any given time there would be ten birds in the water, five hovering and a further five either coming into land or taking off. It was like a precise, three dimensional ballet, quite something to watch. Every bird seemed to know exactly what to do, and when, to maintain the illusion of a never ending stream of birds.

And the strangest thing is that several people walked past, never even noticing this fantastic display. How can people not see this?

So, as can you see, my inner life is very different from its outside appearance, and different from anything an observer would surmise from just stalking me throughout the day! Where I, or you, put our perception is where we'll get fed. What our perceptual orientation is will obviously influence what we get from each day.

Don't get me wrong. I have crap days too. But usually my life is suffused with meaning, with significance, lessons to learn, blessings to enjoy, tasks to undertake. In fact, I think my bad days aren't those when I get a cold, pull a muscle, fail to inspire my students, have a row with a friend, receive this month's bank statement. No, the bad days are those when meaning retreats, when significance is hard to find, when purpose is hiding away somewhere. We can usually endure anything if there's a good enough reason. But to live without meaning would be a form of hell for me. I quake, shake all over, at the very thought!

CHAPTER TWENTY THREE - DUSTY TRAILS AND FROGGY KISSES.

I'd had a bad morning. I woke up with a painfully stiff neck because I'd slept on my stomach with my head almost twisted face upwards. (I'm a pro-active sleeper. I go looking for it in the far flung corners of the bed.) I somehow, somehow managed to drop my mobile phone into my cup of coffee. Oh yeah, ha ha! I can't believe I did that either. It fizzled, chirruped a little, then died on me. The hard drive on the one pc in the house that holds all the important stuff (not the manuscript for this book thankfully) decided to quit this earthly existence, our new puppy Oni (part boxer dog, part Bulgarian shit demon) had left a series of fragrant souvenirs on the living room carpet and I managed to pull my groin in training for one of the more energetic broadsword forms.

So I sat down gingerly to meditate and decided to try to just let go of the whole day. I sat there feeling virtuous. I let go of my expectations of the day ahead, I mentally let go of all my preferences, likes and dislikes, I even lined up all the people in my life that I care about, told them I loved them and said goodbye. I really tried to just let go of everything. It was like falling into the sky. The bittersweet poignancy was almost unbearable. Then Shiva turned up...

He asked what the hell I thought I was doing (I paraphrase here of course) and I replied that I was trying to let go. "Why?" "Er... because I'll have to let go of everyone eventually, say goodbye, so I'm practicing now." There was a pregnant pause. Then He spoke.

"But in every life you've been surrounded by people that love you. You spend every life surrounded by people that love you. Some people come into your incarnations again and again and love you. It's the fact that you can't recognise them you should be mourning." Then He was gone.

Oh.

I felt, rather than saw, the glinting grind of the trident penetrating the ground.

I suppose He's right. Duh! We all suffer from a form of spiritual Alzheimer's. We don't recognise that we've been here before, have met some of these people before, have made some of these mistakes before. The trauma of the death and rebirth process wipes out all our conscious stuff. All that's left is our shadow, our unexpressed, unincarnated unconscious urges. That's what we become.

And He's right again in saying that it's our lack of power, our lack of training, that we should be mourning. But it's not too late to do something about it. We have to be skilful though. If we spend our lives just trying to be "good", we'll create, by our repression, yet more shadow material to be incarnated next time around.

Jung said that the task of man(kind) was to bring the unconscious into the light, in other words, to own our shadow material. This doesn't mean we have to become more selfish, greedy, vicious, lazy, negative etc – that's not what the world needs. But we have to acknowledge and transform those aspects of our psyche, rather than repress them. We have to work with them, take them in another direction. Take punk rock as an example – it was an outpouring of anger, disillusionment and alienation. Music had grown bloated and pretentious, irrelevant. And although there was inevitably some violence on and off stage, most of the energy of the punk bands went into creating a valid, powerful and timely artistic expression. It was "real" again. It was within the reach, the ability and the understanding of those grown distorted on a diet of synthesizer-fuelled symphonies about elves and wizards. People wanted to sing about poverty, politics and inequality again. And how I loved The Clash! They were like a firework going off! Of course, punk, like all fashions, had its day, came and went. But it came at the right time, for the right reasons. It was healthy, necessary and very exciting and enjoyable. The shadow material of that musical period, the middle-to-late 1970's, roared into broad daylight looking for a fight - and I for one welcomed it.

Our darker qualities can be brought up into the conscious mind. If we're brave enough. There, they become the material we work with. If we're brave enough. With practice, our base qualities can be transformed into spiritual gold. Once we acknowledge, own and honour these energies they transform automatically. To use a metaphor we're all familiar with – if we kiss our frogs, they become princes. Or princesses. Or whatever.

I had an unsettling dream last night. I was atop a huge, flat topped mountain, gazing out over an endless vista of hills, canyons and plains. I knew I was on a vision quest, hoping to find the meaning of my life, some clue as to my future direction. Somehow a canyon nearby, dark and steep sided, seemed important. It seemed to symbolise the plunge into the darkness of our unconscious mind, the descent of the aware mind into the abyss of personal myth and history. I felt I had to investigate it.

I turned myself into an eagle (as you do!) and plummeted into the canyon. As I descended, it turned out not to be so dark after all. Duh. Caves, labyrinths and canyons always look darker from the outside don't they? It opened up into what was quite a wide valley, carpeted in prairie grasses and scrub trees. A small group of Native American Indians were riding slowly through the landscape, on a dusty trail, narrow enough to force them to ride in twos and threes. I landed in front of them, turning back into human form (as you do!) and addressed their leader. He seemed very dignified, wasn't fazed at all by my sudden appearance. I asked what they were doing and he told me they were on a quest. The Great Spirit had told them to go out searching. "For what?" I asked. "We don't know," was the reply, and he seemed quite patient, quite resigned.

"So how will you know when you've found it?" I asked. Again he replied quite calmly. "We don't know." I didn't know what else to say, and the dream ended.

As unsettling as this dream was in its implications, I admired tremendously their patience and their faith in their vision quest. The spirit had called and they had answered. They had no idea where they were going or why. But it didn't matter. They had obeyed the call and believed that all would, presumably, be made clear at some point.

The implication for me personally was that I wasn't meant to get clear answers about my own future at the moment, the hint being that if I were to know where to look, I wouldn't look in all the other places that would not only lead inevitably to the correct site of revelation, but would also contribute to my knowledge and understanding, ripening me by stages, so to speak, ready for the conclusion of my personal quest.

There are no short cuts to enlightenment.

Fuck, fuck and double fuck with a side order of fuckety fucks! So no nice, clean cut, concise and elegant conclusion for me then! Patience is not one of my strong points. Neither is subtlety. Neither is speaking in riddles. But I guess I needed to be told this. I trust the information and it rings true. Shiva's trident glints and grates into the dust again. The point is made. As much as I'd like to be told "Go there. Do that," it doesn't happen very often.

Ambiguity, living with the authentic mess, is all part of learning to be a responsible, adult and spiritual being. But one thing is stripped of ambiguity, thankfully. When the spirit calls, you know. And you usually know what you have to do. And you have a clear choice – to follow the summons or not.

So I choose to follow. Every time. At the moment I don't know what the next step is. I'm trying not to care too much about that! This just going forward, one foot in front of the other, trying to stay open for clues along the trail, not knowing what the hell it is I'm looking for, is presumably the latest frog I have to pucker up for!

And actually, sometimes just heeding the call is enough. That acceptance is all that's needed to help everything click into place, and before we know it, we're bowling along quite happily again. Remember I told you about Halloween Shiva and how scary it was to meet Him? And how chilling I found the challenge that I had to formalise my psychic world a little, including visiting parts of those spiritual realms that I find very easy to avoid (including anything to do with the dead, as many of those "spirits" are overloaded with yin qi, negative energy)? Well, as soon as I accepted that I had to do as I was told, and started to hone my (limited) psychic abilities (including dusting off my deck of tarot cards), acknowledging rather than trying to avoid certain shadowy levels of the invisible world (mythos, sambhogakaya, the spirit world, call it what you like), then it got easier. It all went quiet. I haven't seen Halloween Shiva since. I guess it was just another test to see if I was willing to open myself up to things I'd been ignoring. Pucker up time again!

This feels like a healing time for me. A time to rest and recuperate. Jungle Shiva has a long house (an ancestral hut, an extended family glorified log cabin like those used in the rain forests of Amazonia and Borneo) which He sometimes leaves me in for "three moons", in other words three symbolic days. What this means is that on three consecutive occasions when I see Him I have to go into the hut and stay there. It's like being grounded! But it's intended to cleanse me and recharge my batteries. I don't mind because I meet other people, other beings in the long house and it's quite interesting. A few years ago a very eminent Shaivite scholar died. I met him in the hut last year. I'm ashamed to say we didn't think much of each other! He was a very pure man, very knowledgeable, very erudite. I come from the "dirty" end of Shaivism, the path which is much more shamanic, chaotic, visceral. I thought He was a wanker, he thought I was a savage. Shankara forgive us both (especially me!)

Shiva (or any of the deities for that matter) doesn't need more High Priests. The deities need people to speak for Them, give Them Their voice back. We've sidelined Them, reduced Them to psychobabble, to history books, to irrelevance. They need a rabble, a horde of individual voices, rather than a tamed congregation! We've forgotten Them. That's why, despite our laudable (if flawed) levels of health care, morality and our ecological and spiritual aspirations, we're a sick species. The gap between physical reality and spirituality is too wide and needs to be reconnected by a bridge constructed of willing souls.

Less organised religion. More religious thought. Less state, less church, more Godliness. And I don't, repeat DON'T, mean fundamentalist, anti-women, anti-gay, anti-Christian, anti-Muslim, anti-Pagan, anti-druggies, anti-anyone garbage! It's time to face up to our collective humanity, time to create a world where people don't need crime, crack, warfare in order to live with a "buzz". And I don't mean a liberal, green, wishy-washy Utopia either, though that would be an improvement on what we've got.

As in the days of old, nature, ecology, the health of the planet, has become bound up with spirituality again. And that's good. We all want to recycle more, create less pollution etc. It's hard though because half the stuff that I throw out every week I never asked for in the first place. Free newspapers, endless leaflets, three layers of plastic on everything I buy. And I'm the one being told to get my act together! I'm the one who may have to pay extra taxes for not being green enough! I didn't want this crap in the first place! However hard I try, I'm not going to save the planet by myself. And neither are you. We just have to keep lobbying for sane, reasonable laws, laws that will help the planet without crippling us. We keep forgetting that we're part of nature, not separate from it. We seem to be labouring under the delusion that if we put enough concrete between us and the surface of the planet we'll somehow become exempt from the laws of nature! If, on the other hand, we make a concerted effort to heal ourselves we'll automatically cut back on the neurotic, sick and destructive behaviour that pollutes our inner and outer environments.

We managed to eradicate slavery from most parts of Mother Earth, but most of us are now shackled to a treadmill created by a need for material possessions such as a home and car, the need to pay taxes (on everything!) and the need to pay to get away from it all occasionally. We're materially, though not necessarily financially, better off than ever before, yet we're still not happy. We're getting overweight, lazy, physically and mentally soft, intellectually atrophied, artistically sloppy, more aggressive, more dependant, more self pitying, etc.

I'm not a politician. I'm not a world leader in art, religion, politics or culture. I'm an isolated little man in late middle age, in the rural backwaters of England. But like many others, I'm recognising that I feel less and less part of this world of ours. Further, I feel less and less like I want to be part of it! I can't afford to run off to the forest to play at being a shaman. That would be childish anyway. I can't afford to start a new chain of temples dedicated to all the old deities from all over the world, from all historical, or prehistorical, periods. That would be crass and pathetic. I can't afford to write endless books haranguing our spiritual poverty. That would be tedious.

So it's the same problem for all of us. What to do? How do we start to work for evolution? How do we become part of a current that addresses the need to reclaim our spiritual roots, our shared humanity, our individual and collective way forward?

How do we plasticize, concretise, make tangible, make real and material, our yearning and our determination?

Well, the answer is to keep doing what you do. But involve the divinities in it. Then what you do will change. And so will you. And then what you do will change again. And so it goes... Simple as it sounds, it's not, obviously. It requires a commitment and a willingness from us to undertake the necessary inner alchemy that informs and transforms our outer efforts.

As ye olde worlde cook books of England used to say, "First find your frog..."

We have to become saturated with the sacred again, in order to "see", to heal, to create, to destroy if need be. To evolve.

CHAPTER TWENTY FOUR - NEUROSES, NEIGHBOURS AND NEEDS MET.

If we manage, even to a small degree, to reinvent ourselves, to begin to heal our self inflicted sicknesses, to own and acknowledge our shadow material and the recurring patterns it has been generating for most of our lives, and for most of our parents' and their parents' lives, then we can not only influence the future, what gets handed down to the next generations, but we can also cleanse our own DNA, we can affect ourselves at a cellular level – and we can heal our ancestors. Our self healing travels out, like ripples in a pool, towards the future and the past.

This also implies that if we can inspire future generations to heal themselves, and the various cultures of this planet, and the planet itself, then we can reap the benefit too, right now. Perhaps that's what's happening to some of us, we're feeling the psychic ripples of our distant, inspired, descendants.

I need hardly add that the whole process of self healing is a sadhana par excellence, and a legitimate way to honour the divinities.

It's always a tempting conceit to judge and interpret ancient cultures in the light of our own. Most archaeologists and palaeontologists guard themselves against this tendency quite rigorously. But the unspoken assumption is that we're the chronological centre of the universe. Everything that's ever happened has been leading up to this moment – to us. If we can rise above that conceit however, it throws the whole of our belief system into disarray. Perhaps the apex of human civilisation, the chronological centre of humanity is or was the Victorians, or the Aztecs, or the Neolithic farmers! Perhaps everything from, say, 500BC has been in decay! We don't know. Perhaps the centre shifts constantly as we evolve (and as our ancestors and our descendants continue to evolve), perhaps it's one civilisation, one isolated incident, one individual, that stands as the summit of mankind's journey one day, and it's something entirely different the next day, and the day after that.

Maybe it's nothing to do with humans. Maybe the whole history of this planet is leading up to something wonderful that's nothing to do with us as a species. Or maybe it's already happened...

And, ultimately important in this planet's history or not, humanity has certainly made an impact. For the relatively short time we've been around, our activities have impinged heavily upon our environment. And nowadays, with the global village we all share, that means the impact that any of our neighbours has upon the village will inevitably affect us all. No country lives in isolation any more. Our financial security, our power sources, our raw materials, our cheap labour – all are intimately bound up with the politics, the climate, the fortunes and misfortunes of our neighbours.

It would seem to be a mark of sanity to live in harmony with one's environment, to protect resources, to glorify diversity of wildlife, to find methods of harvesting crops and animals that minimise damage to the environment and to the future environment. It would seem to be a form of neurosis to pay lip service to this subject while actually still damaging the planet – our home. Hmm. Guess what?

We shit on our own door step. We shit on our neighbours' door step. We say in public how fragile, how beautiful the balance of nature is, how important it is to preserve and protect the planet. But actually, we just go on shitting! We actually don't want the hassle of changing the way we function.

I'm no more green than anyone else. I merely want to illustrate our modern mindset, which is quite schizophrenic. We operate on two levels, one of them being total fantasy. We pray, but keep on shitting. We sermonise, but keep on shitting. We regret, but keep on shitting...

Ok, enough sermonising, let's bring the whole energy of this book back to Tantra, and to a personal level. But we're still on the subject of shitting!

A student of mine was close to tears a few nights ago. She's recovering from a long and unhappy marriage. Her husband wasn't a bad man, but he had some problems, was a bit obsessive in nature, used to eat the same meal every day, from exactly the same brand names etc. That sort of thing. He was, is, a decent enough bloke, but my student had endured his obsessions and his emotional distance for decades. One day she just had enough and announced she was leaving. That was a year ago. She now has her own place, she's doing ok. But the guilt hit her a few nights ago – and it hit her hard. She's always tried to be a good Buddhist, to minimise the damage she does to others. She takes the principle of ahimsa, harmlessness, very seriously. So the realisation that, in her words, "I've broken his heart." was very painful for her. She felt she'd shit on him, on his dreams.

My first instinct was to comfort her, to reassure her that she was right to have wanted to move on or she would have drowned, become numb, betrayed her own evolution. And all this is true and I said it. But more seriously, from a Tantric viewpoint, and I guess from a psychological viewpoint, to remain in guilt, though a healthy first reaction, is actually to remain in denial, in distance.

Guilt is a barrier to keep understanding out. To divide oneself. To keep the divinities away.

By all means feel the guilt. The soul knows damage has been done, to self and other. But to remain in that space is counter-productive. What my student must do now is to turn lead into gold. She has to own that pain, she has to know, feel, how fragile the human psyche can be, and how much impact our actions have on each other.

We have to feel how the web of karma shivers and shakes with every deed, word and thought. Then we can learn to become more skilful in our dealings with others.

But she also has to become aware that, just as life feeds on life, so emotions feed on emotions. One person's triumph is another's humiliation. One person's liberty may be the result of another's bondage. One person's happiness may result in another's misery. It's impossible, impossible, to go through life without hurting someone. We shouldn't actively seek that out, but we can't avoid it coming to us. Even the Buddha no doubt royally pissed his family off when He abandoned them for the holy life. They must have felt that keenly.

My student needs to be aware of how her husband fed upon her loyalty for years, how he repaid her with distance and inconvenience. Without resentment though – after all, she bought into it. So it's ok, they've both had their payback now. No doubt they're both still smarting. But they both need to know how they damaged each other. Then they can avoid the same pattern in the future.

She needs to use this. She has to lay down all this guilt, this confusion, this regret, at the feet of the divinities. It has to become an offering, an untidy, chaotic emotional bundle maybe, but still an offering. The God/dess will accept it, help her transform it into something more positive. It's astonishing. We don't have to be very clever, very sophisticated to do this, but the potential for healing, for learning and for self knowledge and self transformation is vast. In addressing the Gods and Goddesses we address the deepest part of ourselves. By offering our pain, we offer it up to the deepest part of ourselves, for healing, for reconciliation, for the restoration of harmony and balance.

Jung said that every neurosis (every pain) is an offended deity. So my student has to offer her pain as a placatory rebuilding of a connection that got broken somewhere. The bridge between her and the offended deity has to be repaired. And that connection may well be to do with listening to her heart, her soul - the God/dess within. The lesson may be - when to nurture, when to release.

Kali, Shiva, Pan, Hevajra, Vajrayogini – these, and all, deities have nurturing and "destructive" qualities. They know when to bind and when to dissolve. My student has to relearn this. And I know she will. She's smart, honest and determined. She listens too.

Maybe, today, this incident is the chronological centre of the universe. Maybe everything hinges on this. Maybe this one striving is the lynchpin of evolution. No pressure then!

When I sit in Shiva's long house, when I'm reluctantly healing myself (it always feels like I should be doing something else) or allowing myself to be healed, I'm aware that it's not just for me. That's why I can sit still long enough! I'm aware that future generations and past descendants (not that there's a difference) are depending on me. And not just on me – the world is waiting for you to get your act together too.

Brok and !skian have an investment in my efforts. I have an enormous investment in their efforts too. Shiva needs me – no devotee, no deity. I certainly need Him. We're all bound together in the shining, immaculate karmic web of endless becoming. We're shipmates!

So self healing is important. It adds to the general levels of sanity and self knowledge in the world, as opposed to neurosis, self harm and ignore-ance. When I'm sitting in the long house, in psychological terms I'm abiding in that part of me that's still in the jungle, untouched by civilisation, uncontaminated by society's demands. I'll return to this theme soon.

I think I need to reiterate why I've devoted so much space in this book to Shamanism and "primitive" religious practices. A trip into the city this morning left me feeling justified. I visited a relatively new book store and jolly good it was too. There were lots of books on various religions, including Buddhism, Tantra and Hinduism, psychology books, earth mysteries, ufos, Shamanism, Paganism, Wicca, prehistoric art and language. Lots of Batman books too (we all have our weaknesses!). I could have spent a fortune in there. But even after leafing through all these wonderful books, I was left with that hollow feeling. I think it was that, with the exception of some of the books on Shamanism and Wicca, most of these books were still "selling the dream". I could sit in the in-store coffee shop, sheltering from the atrocious weather, leafing through my new purchases, listening to Bjork (followed by Coldplay – from one extreme to the other!) and just generally feeling good about myself. Drinking my organically grown Bolivian coffee and gazing at pictures of Aboriginal rock art, I could convince myself I was having a wonderful, spiritually relevant, multicultural experience. All well and good if it inspires me to actually go and do something, but the nice experience, pleasant though it may be, doesn't carry any practical value.

Different store from last visit, more books, same problem. Well, for me anyway. I admit, only slightly grudgingly, that we need books on Buddhism, Tantra and Hinduism for beginners, with background information, user-friendly topics, nice pictures etc. The difference between these and the books on Shamanism and Wicca is that the latter are usually more practice-orientated than the former, containing more practical exercises, techniques, things to actually do.

I'd like to drag Tantra, Shiva, Kali, the whole kit and caboodle, kicking and screaming if needs be, away from India and the mystic East and into a new current, one that's less culturally orientated, less culturally coloured. In other words into a current that carries less cultural baggage, a current that allows you to evolve your own paradigms, your own set of efficacious practices.

I guess what I'm trying to say is that if we can journey back far enough into ourselves, into those parts of ourselves that exist below culture's radar, those parts of us that still live in the forest, in the caves even, we may be able to encounter the deities in a much more archetypal form, in the bodies they wore before culture coloured them with its own values. It's as if we still allow the Gods and Goddesses a place in our lives, entombed in clinical jargon, in the days of the week etc, but don't allow any interaction, which is harmful for both parties. Why brick these archetypes up? We need them. They're the deepest part of ourselves after all, the archetypal energies that bind, drive and define our world.

And from a Buddhistic perspective, the naked, pre-civilisation self we may encounter in these forests and caves of the psyche may be easier to work with, towards enlightenment and transcendence. From a Tantric perspective, the naked, pre-civilisation self and the naked, pre-civilisation deity may have an awful lot in common, may in fact be the naked ground of being itself.

I sat in meditation this morning and I was surrounded by glowing blue forms. Very ethereal, very beautiful. They were androgynous, sexless, like neon outlines of seated terracotta warriors, like electric sketches in the air. There was no movement, no hint of individuality, no personality. They were alive but not living, if that makes sense. It was a forest of awareness – naked, beautiful but almost sterile. And striding through this ethereal host came Shiva, mud and ash daubed, filthy, laughing...

I was being shown that physical form is vital for consciousness to evolve (at least for most of the "levels"), that there's nothing unholy, profane, ungodly about our bodies. The angelic beings I saw in meditation may have occupied some ground of being but it wasn't useful. It was like an unplugged stereo – everything was there in potential but lacking the vital connection, in this case to physical form. Maybe they were consciousnesses waiting for rebirth or something, I have no idea.

Imagined heavenly realms, where we can shuffle off this tiresome, trouble-burdened physical body and exist as beings of pure light, aren't to be scoffed at, but we have to realise that even these states are temporary and are karmically conditioned. These blue beings weren't evolving because there was no possibility of interaction, of growth. Freedom from form, it seems, can be as sterile as mud, as much an evolutionary dead end as unknowing, inert matter.

So my wishing to journey “back” into the caves and forests of myself, to encounter and interact with my naked self and with the naked divinities, isn’t just some religious escapism, a back to the womb regression, a naive wish to return to the state of the “noble savage”. It’s an authentic Shaman’s journey, through my inner terrains, to some kind of pre-civilisation ancestral cave, where, together with Brok and !skian, I can come face to face with the prototype God of my choice.

And in that cave, that part of myself, my unconditioned, unpolluted Julian Wilde can worship, and receive instruction, teaching, from a culturally unconditioned God.

This isn’t barbaric. This isn’t anti-humanity, anti-ethics, anti-electric cookers and i-pods. This, dear reader, is pure Tantra – me and the deity, naked, naked to ourselves, naked to each other, face to face. Darshan.

CHAPTER TWENTY FIVE - SACRED SPACES AND THE DIVINITY LINK.

But of course, it's not necessary to dance around the handbag at all. You can meet the deities, just as you are, cultural and emotional baggage intact. They don't care. You can't hide anything from Them anyway. So let's play a little "how to" shall we? Let's work through a couple of exercises to get your Tantric juices flowing.

We'll start with the creation of a sacred space, then move on to calling for a divinity.

So, Health & Safety first! (Groan!) Let's protect ourselves. There are several ways to do this, and in fact one of the worse and most cumbersome is the physical drawing of a protective mandala or the traditional sacred circle, using chalk, salt, green boughs and virgin's blood (kidding!). Both the mandala and the magicians' or witches' circle are unnecessarily complicated. They also dictate to you where you can perform your personal rituals. You don't want to be forever vacuuming salt (or virgin's blood) from your living room carpet, do you? It's a lot easier, and ultimately better practice, to create your sacred space around you, using your mind, the powers of visualisation. As I prefer "primitive" methods to classical Indian procedure (who'd a thunk it?) we'll use, by way of example, the natural elements and protective animals.

For all these exercises, I don't really care if you stand up, lie down, squat, sit cross legged or do handstands. The main thing is that you're relaxed. Lock your doors, and yes, turn off your mobile phone. You can have background music if you like, but nothing too loud or intrusive. No heavy dub! Dim lighting or candles contribute to the atmosphere.

For protection by the elements, imagine yourself in a space you find appealing. It can be in a forest clearing, in a hut, by a seashore, in a cave, on a boat, anywhere. Then visualise yourself surrounded by fire, water, air and earth. These can be in any order – if you picture yourself on a boat for instance, then imagine yourself surrounded by miles of open water. Then imagine that water surrounded on all sides by swirling, thick fogbanks (air), way off in the distance. Then imagine sheer cliffs (earth) and rocky crags looming out of the fog. Imagine rivers of molten lava intersecting these mountains and cliffs. Nothing is going to get through that! So you can relax safely on your boat.

Or you could imagine an enormous ring of fire, say a hundred metres across, banked up on either side with great earthworks, surrounded yet again with dense smoke (air) or deep canals (water). Or see yourself high upon a mountain top (earth) in the clouds (air) – you don't have to use all the elements. As long as you feel safe, you're free to make your own inner landscapes.

You can (but don't have to) augment these inner landscapes by adding guardian angels, spirits of people you've known and loved, even of those you've always admired but never met, great warriors or pioneers etc. Or you can use animals...

There must be an animal you feel an affinity with. I love wolves. But anything is usable. Eagles. Bears. Bulls. Hunting dogs. Leopards. All good traditional guardian spirits. Experiment. See what you feel most comfortable with. Imagine these animals coming from the four directions, one direction at a time (use as many animals as you like), surrounding you, protecting you. If you like, pick a different colour for each direction, for example, following the colour of the sun and sky – white or grey for the east, yellow for the south, red or grey for the west and black for the north. These represent dawn, midday, evening and midnight. Use anything that makes the picture in your head more vivid.

Say a prayer for protection to these animals, and to any other spirit beings you summon. Be polite, but you don't have to be long-winded. Just ask them to look after you until you've finished the exercise. It's also polite, actually quite important, to thank them when you've finished.

Or you could combine all of the above and have different animals for each element. Dragons for fire, eagles for air, dolphins for water and cave bears for earth. They could surround you from the four quarters, each bearing a symbol of their element, for example a burning torch, a feather, a cup or chalice and a rock respectively. There are no rules here. Make this whole thing personal to you.

You could just visualise a stone circle. Or a temple. Or a cave. Anything. It's results only that count in this endeavour. The reason I prefer these simple methods is that firstly they're effective and secondly, the deities don't need all the fancy ceremonies and ritual regalia in order to visit you. If They want to come, They'll come!

I don't want to itemise these procedures, over-describe them, as I'd like you to have to discover what most resonates with you. Find your own way.

Once you get used to creating your sacred space in this way, or any other way, and you find what works for you, it'll get easier and easier to put yourself in that space – a matter of seconds. And eventually you won't even have to make a sacred or safe place consciously – it'll just happen automatically. Eventually you'll dwell permanently in a safe space.

And once you're familiar with this procedure of creating a sacred space, the centre of your own mandala, you can invite the divinities in.

Of course, if you're hoping to call upon a deity with an associated mantra, as in the case of our four "high voltage" deities from earlier in the book, it helps to use their sacred syllables. Otherwise, just sit in your sacred space and imagine the chosen deity in your head, hold their image in your mind's eye. Pray to the deity. Again, you don't have to be long-winded, flowery, obsequious. Just tell the truth. Say that you're embarking on a spiritual quest and you'd be grateful for Their company, guidance and protection along the way. Ask Them for clues as to which direction to take, which practices to adopt.

Don't expect too much at first. It takes practice to create a divinity link. It'll get easier in time to create the safe place and to have darshan with the deity. Use pictures, mandalas, yantras, music, anything that attunes your mind to the required "vibe". Eventually the divinity will make an entrance.

Don't have fixed ideas about what will happen, what should happen. This is your path, so your experiences may be very different from (or very similar to) those that I've received. And this is ego – to assume that you know what should happen. And it's ego too (though quite natural) to be disappointed with your experiences, to compare your experiences with those of other seekers. All ego – things will unfold as they should, so be humble, patient and grateful.

In fact, my only real dictate is to please be respectful. Depending on your personal worldview, you're either interacting here with supernatural beings, or with tremendous energies from deep, deep within your psyche. Either way, these forces are beyond your control, potentially volatile and very, very powerful. Treat them with due reverence.

One more thing. Don't assume, if you manage to embark upon a relationship with a divinity, that your life will instantly become easier, problem free. It won't. It may even become more difficult, as you're forced to deal with personal issues that you've ignored, neglected, avoided until now. You may feel the tug of the world even more keenly, as it attempts to pull you away from your spiritual practice. Or it may be the other way round – suddenly your friends, your relationships, your work, your pastimes, all seem shallow and unsatisfying. It's hard to keep a balance.

Sometimes I get transfixed between two levels of being, between two ways of experiencing the world. Shamans call this the first attention or the first seeing (the worldly) and the second attention, the second seeing (in the west we used to use the term "second sight"), which is the interaction with the "invisible", the world of spirits, the sambhogakaya. It's horrible when I feel pulled in two. I just have to make more of an effort to give each world, each attention, its due.

And it's important to retain self awareness. A fall into grandeur or delusion is just as unhealthy as being over sceptical, cynical about the spiritual path and the experiences it bestows.

So why bother with any of this? Well, I'm assuming that, because you're reading this book, you have more than a passing interest in knowing what lies beyond this world, what the meaning of life is, how you can become more than you are...

And your answers are here, locked in your own unconscious, held by the Gods and Goddess, by the animal spirits, by the spirit of the land itself. And here is where you start to figure it all out. Here is where your journey begins. In this sacred, safe place you've created for yourself, you initiate the process...

Let's just remind ourselves of our basic Tantric principles, shall we? Firstly, the entire universe, the multiverse, is made up of vibration. Different rates of vibration create different materials, different substances and energies, including consciousness. We, as humans, are born of two vibrations, one material body, courtesy of Shakti or the Mother Goddess if you prefer, and one consciousness vibration, courtesy of Shiva. You can substitute the name Shiva for any name of your choice.

This is a simplistic way of explaining things, as each level of consciousness has a different vibration, and our physical bodies are a chord of vibrations, more a symphony than a monotone.
Our multiverse has way, way more than three dimensions of space, and time is cyclical not linear. We exist as a shining net of energy, all inter-connected. Everything has an effect. Everything has an effect on everything else.

There are many levels of reality. The overwhelming majority of these are NOT socially or culturally sanctioned. States such as ecstasy and trance are often derided as hysterical, not grounded in "reality". This is shameful, and ultimately detrimental to humanity's evolution. Tantrists recognise three main sectors of reality. These are all multi-layered too.

The three main categories of reality are: the nirmanakaya (illusion body), the material, concrete, physical world, the sambhogakaya (body of shared bliss), which is dreamtime, imagination, out-of- body experiences etc, and the dharmakaya (law or truth body), a formless, indescribable, incomprehensible realm.

We could also categorise these realms as the conscious mind, the personal and collective unconscious and the transcendent, the truly "out there".

Tantrists seek experience and learning from the sambhogakaya in order to eventually attain the dharmakaya, which in personal terms means liberation, transcendence, enlightenment, conscious integration with the rest of the multiverse.

As well as performing regular puja (worship) and meditation, Tantrists seek to utilise all experiences, all energies, "good" or "bad", in the spiritual quest. All so-called negative or shadow material (that which some Shamans call the dark ally or dark twin) can be honoured, owned and processed, transformed, pressed into service. This is the equivalent of turning lead into gold.

To achieve this, one must be vigilant, a hunter, ever watchful for opportunity. The dark ally is always around, always causing dissonance, Freudian slips, and synchronicities. The Tantrist must be awake for these moments and seize upon them, utilise them. As Jung said, the task of humanity is to make the unconscious conscious. Terence McKenna uses the phrase "exteriorise the soul". Shamans would say, be the hunter, or you will become the hunted. Buddhists call this faculty mindfulness.

The ultimate aim of Tantra is total union with the divinity. To channel the deity so profoundly that all sense of separateness disappears. We can practice this at all times if we wish. We can even prepare for our inevitable dissolution (our physical death) by practicing our relationship with the deity, our divinity link, during dreams, orgasm and other levels of non-rational consciousness. This is why so many Tantric books swerve off into sexual matters – and stay there! If we prepare ourselves now, our connection may not be lost during the death trauma, giving us an enormous advantage in our continuing evolution.

I mentioned in "The Real Rasa" book (buy it, it's way cool!) that sexual practices such as Tantric union and Tantric masturbation are useful for training the divinity link in "extreme" states. It's also useful to practice chanting a mantra, or visualising a yantra, or a deity, as you fall asleep. If you wake up during the night repeat the process immediately. This, at the very least, trains the "border" awareness, the mindspace you inhabit when neither completely asleep or wide awake. It can also improve your meditational abilities. In a busy lifestyle this is an invaluable sadhana. We all have moments during the day when we can practice flipping our consciousness into "deity mode", visualising a chosen symbol of the God or Goddess of our choice.

I hope you can gather from the above few paragraphs that this work isn't easy, isn't convenient, isn't a pastime, isn't a pleasant, blissful, angelic journey. On the contrary, it's a slog - it's a long, dark, disturbing odyssey. It'll probably threaten your ego security, your sense of self, how you function with other people. Your values will change, your priorities will change. You'll encounter monsters, demons and aliens, as well as bodhisattvas, spiritual guides and divinities on the journey. Most of these will spring from your own psyche. Exploration of your inner terrains will reveal bleak deserts, treacherous swamps, mystical lakes and awe-inspiring mountains. You'll have to overcome all these in order to keep moving towards your goal. Your goal may even change somewhere on the journey! It certainly happened to me (several times!).

I had an unusual experience the other morning (Yes! Another one!). It was early, quite cold and very overcast. The sun was low in the sky, shining almost horizontally under the dark clouds. I was walking almost due east, towards the city.

It was quite a beautiful sight. The road stretched out ahead of me, climbing almost imperceptibly, wide and shining, silvery gold in the sunlight. Lots of cars and people on bikes were moving toward the sun, the edges of their silhouettes shimmering as if they were about to merge with the light. Like a Turner painting, it gleamed as if painted with gold leaf and quicksilver. Every mote, every shift of light seemed charged with significance. It was like a mass ascension into some heavenly realm. The people, the city buildings, the wide and shining boulevard, all like some utopian vision, like matter turning into spirit.

So I stopped and looked the other way. I'm funny like that. As you'd expect, the road stretched back, sloping downward slightly, dark grey and almost deserted. And yet it had its own beauty. The gunmetal sky pressed heavily down to the horizon, pregnant with rain, pregnant with meaning, with something about to happen. The naked trees shone in the horizontal light, gleaming palely with an other-worldly aura. They seemed very alive, almost moving, against the forbidding dark clouds. The scene was like something from the Lord of the Rings movie, a dark avenue to an underworld realm peopled with elves or orcs.

So there I stood, surrounded by beauty. One road beckoned upward, as if towards pure spirit, transcendence. One road led gently down, into the world of the soul, where myths meet dreams, where imagination becomes reality. One avenue of light, one avenue of darkness and mystery. One yang, one yin!

But of course we all know that we have to have balance, we have to give both our aspirations (spirit) and our cultural roots and buried wisdom (soul) their due. We need to balance our roots and our blossoms. We can't go in two directions at once. The road I was standing on was actually the inner ring road of the city, so either direction would lead me back to the place of origin, where I stood. But how long would the journey take? And what might I miss on the way?

Or I could adapt the archetypal Buddhist perspective and stand still long enough for the world to turn around me! Or I could shrug the dilemma away and go and find some breakfast.

At any given moment on our spiritual trek through the inner terrains, the pull of soul and spirit will exert different gravitational pulls. It's a wise man or woman who can keep this balance.

Remember we discussed the term "vajra"? It translates from Sanskrit as diamond or thunderbolt. I prefer to regard it as liquid diamond or free flowing crystal. Vajra is hard, clear, indestructible. And yet it's fluid, endlessly so, rolling like a river around and through all obstacles. In our forming powers (siddha) we should try and emulate vajra. In training the mind as we fall asleep or at the point of orgasm, even when we sneeze, we should be stern and disciplined. Careful though, or sex can become joyless. Give yourself a day off (a free orgasm!) once in a while! Keep on track, even on holiday, at work – every peak moment of consciousness, if you sneeze, cough, if something makes you jump, then train yourself to immediately turn the mind to the deity, or His/Her mantra, yantra etc. The body and mind learn things by repetition, so sometimes habit can be your friend. Habitually turn the mind to your goal.

But be prepared to flow with it all, to change methods if something ceases to be effective. Be prepared to follow the dictates of the deity or your own instincts. Remain awake, monitor yourself. Be careful especially of complacency and hubris. As soon as you think you're the bee's knees (what the hell does that mean, exactly?) or that everyone should be pursuing the same path as you, then you're unwittingly setting in motion the juggernaut of your own downfall. It's like a hunter walking through the forest, full of fantasies about catching a wild pig or shooting a deer, not realising that there's a predatory, silent and fanged presence breathing down his neck!

And apathy is a pitfall too. As I asked above, why bother with all this, especially if it's going to lead you into dark, difficult and disturbing places? Life can be hard enough at the best of times. None of us are totally impervious to illness, injury, loss, heartbreak or boy bands. These sorrows are always around somewhere. But that's the point. If we're going to suffer anyway, if it's a given that we're going to get old and die, probably encountering numerous problems and disappointments on the way, then at least make those sorrows work for you, let them impart meaning and significance into your life. It's no good trying to keep them at arm's length, hoping that your money, your relationships, your job, will provide enough of a barrier to keep these sorrows from overwhelming you.

Let's be honest for a second. Really honest. We all have regrets. We all feel bad about someone we neglected or hurt. We can all wish we'd taken that art course instead of going into insurance, or that we'd travelled more when we had the chance. No one spends their last minutes of life wishing they'd spent more time at the office, avoided that heady, if foolish, one night stand with Bob/Betty at the motel, or had watched more crap on TV, do they? Life is for living, and enjoying and for learning. To heed the call of spirit is a grand endeavour. It won't protect you from sorrow any more than a mortgage, a toy boy or a new car will. But it will grant this incarnation a meaning and a strong potential for the next time round.

To chase and then have to defend and preserve a life dedicated to material and emotional comfort is to bind yourself more securely to the wheel of birth, death and rebirth, centuries of further suffering and bondage. Despite the world's opinion, it's not smart or cool. It's not the most skilful way to live.

In my life now, the divinity link is the only game in town.

CHAPTER TWENTY SIX - A CRACKING OF BONES!

So why do all this stuff? Why bother? Well, first let's sum up so far... What I call the divinity link is a training of the mind, to cultivate not only an open two-way dialogue with a deity, but also to retain this connection, this spiritual/psychic umbilical cord intact throughout all extreme states of consciousness, such as dreamsleep, pain, orgasm, panic, shock - and dying.

The divinity may be regarded an external entity, a member of another species if you like, a consciousness-construct accreted around spiritual aspirations, a discarnate spirit, a real concrete being, or a part, an expression of a part, of our deep psyche. The divinity may be all, some or none of these things!

After a while, the distinction between "me inside" and "deity out there" becomes meaningless.

We can train this link with the/our divinity by habitually flooding our conscious mind with images, mantras, symbolic diagrams such as yantras and mandalas. Or we may discover for ourselves, through practice or inspiration, a word, a picture, a sensation, that creates the path of accessibility. We can practice turning our minds to these passwords or pictorial entry points whenever we're falling asleep or in some state of emotional arousal, even when we sneeze or stub our toe - especially at these times, try to make it a reflex action, an automatic response.

This kind of practice is probably the easiest, most accessible sadhana there is.

So why do all this? Is there any personal advantage? Any evolutionary advantage? Does anyone draw any benefit from all this?

Firstly, on a personal level, I would claim to have benefited from this kind of practice. I have received information that has proved useful, guidance as to future direction, inspiration and reassurance and admonishment when needed. I have had my ethical frame work dissolved and redrawn. I have been able to view myself, relationships and situations from various perspectives and I have gained relevant insights. I have been able, to a certain degree, to de-condition myself. By far the most important thing that has arisen from all this is that my life has a meaning. I have a reason, beyond the material, to get out of bed in the morning. I have a goal and good reasons for pursuing that goal.

I'm not a Shaman. I don't heal the sick and I have no idea where you left your car keys. But then again I am a Shaman if that is defined as helping people to heal themselves through the principles and practices taught to me by my Qigong master. And through other methods such as "shamanistic counselling", talking to people about their problems from a shamanistic perspective. And I'm a Shaman also if you define Shamanism as consciousness engineering. I don't have access to ayahuasca and other hallucinogenic drugs so I have to use my latent abilities, which can be trained and honed. I believe that psychedelic plants and fungi that occur naturally in the living world are there for a purpose so I don't condemn their use. I don't trust "lab rat" drugs though. I have no quarrel with any of the information brought into print by ayahuasca and peyote pioneers so I assume we're both on the same page.

Like the peyote, mescaline and ayahuasca riders, I believe we have the potential to speed up our spiritual evolution. The mushrooms and vines are one way to do it – and seemingly a very effective way. I can understand that many yogis and meditators would be quick to defend their chosen path and claim that it too will lead to insight and liberation. However I doubt that more than one in a hundred of these practitioners will achieve the same depth of insight as the average stoner puking his or her guts up in the middle of the Amazon rainforest! To be fair, a lot of stoners claim that only the drugs work – anything else is a waste of time. They're wrong too!

Everyone becomes a missionary for their chosen path. It's healthier to assume we've all got just part of the truth. "Even" Wiccans and Pagans, if they work hard, can achieve a better symbiosis with nature, with the spiritual mysteries of nature and "supernature", a lot quicker than someone sitting cross-legged and chanting Aum for a decade. Classical Buddhism and Hinduism are very hot on ethics. The systems make a lot of sense. And meditation is important. But these are the foundation of your practice. You'll keep revisiting the teachings but your understanding of them should grow and develop. If you do the same thing for a decade you'll get very good at it – but that's about all.

In Taiji we're quite happy to work on a form for years. Then the teacher brings a new weapon along or pushes the self defence to a new level. We quickly realise that everything we've been working on is very useful, but we still have to adapt those skills, apply them differently.

Results are what count. Noble aspirations are necessary and laudable, but these aspirations aren't necessarily enough of a catalyst to transform one's perceptions and habits. Hence the efficacy of plant gurus. But the plants have their own agenda, which you'll have to follow, and dancing and chanting and drumming and all that stuff can get you there too. But if you're not careful with any of these methods, they can become an end in themselves, rather than a vehicle. Always keep the big picture in mind.

"What do I want?" "Is this getting me there?"

So – anyway! I'm a Shaman if you define my work as healing and my practice as not so much finding lost car keys as finding those parts of ourselves that we've lost, those realms deep inside us that we used to be so at home in and now have lost the code to tap ourselves back in.

And that's the evolutionary benefit, the wider picture. We've locked ourselves out of the cave in our heads. We've been wandering the backyard for millennia, gazing up at the stars, wondering if our destiny is "out there". We've made a fetish, a juju, out of Buddha and Jesus and Krishna and Apollo. We don't actually talk to Them, or want Them to talk to us any more. Among many others, I'm here to remind you how to get back into the cave, that dark, deep, sacred place where you used to meet the ancestors and the animal spirits. You can find a place where your personal demons and divinities, your personal archetypes, and your cultural archetypes, meet and meld. From that place, that spiritual bedrock, you can put down roots and grow again. Your practice can become personally relevant to your life, in a very real way.

I can't give eyesight to the blind but I can help with spiritual myopia! First lesson – you've been conditioned to see reality in a certain way. When you question this reality – and most people never do – you'll question it in a conditioned way. But it's a start. Question everything – especially your own conclusions. We all want clarity and certainty and it takes enormous courage to dwell within the question as it were, to deliberately remain open to ambiguity, and to the stress and anxiety that can arise from this internal balancing and juggling. Spiritual gold is often found in this pulling apart, this uneasy tug of war.

I would call myself a Tantrist but that carries an awful lot of baggage too these days. People assume I'm fascinated by sex (instead of er... moderately interested?) and that I spend all day on the brink of orgasm (only when there's a "y" in the day!). Every system you can name immediately conjures up mental connections, connotations, labels. To call myself a Tantric Shaman or a Shamanic Tantrist just sounds... wanky!

I once asked Shiva what I was. He laughed uproariously and said "A devotee!"

I was meditating this morning and suddenly there I was in Jungle Shiva's forest clearing – one of my favourite sacred, safe places. He sat there, caked in mud and holding a bone between His nose and upper lip. He caught my eye, sniffed the bone, cracked it between His teeth, sucked on small pieces. He bared his teeth at me. "Everything you sniff should nourish you."

In my usual subtle way I replied, "What does that mean?" He grinned.

"Everything you perceive can feed you spiritually." Again I subtly interrogated Him. "How does that work then?" He looked at me hard, but still grinning. "See the world, everything that happens, as the miraculous, significant event that it is. If you want to be a hunter then keep your eyes open in the forest! Learn to read your world."

I intuitively understood this lesson, as I'd had similar before. The danger of course is reading so much meaning into everything that you end up paralysed or unable to comprehend the simplest event – "Why did the postman wear a hat today? It's doin' my head in!" Or your friends can accuse you of paranoia or reading too much into life – "Things just happen sometimes!" Well, yes they do, but karma exists, it's real. And life consists of connections and patterns. The fact that your mother used to lock you in a closet and the fact that you have relationship problems may not be isolated incidents! And people that don't see their own patterns are doomed to repeat them – perhaps for life after life...

So we have a choice. If we wish, we can train ourselves to read the world around us as if it was one of those crazy ayahuasca or peyote trips that feature so heavily in some books on Shamanism. For this reality, this dimension, is just as weird, just as crazy, just as self-transforming, just as pliable, just as misleading, just as obscure, just as meaningful and educational, just as "out there" as anything a plant spirit can show you. If you don't believe me, try going through a day as if you were on acid, seeing this world for the first time. Watch the craziness unfold before your very eyes. Honestly, you couldn't make this "ordinary life" up. In contrast, Shiva's jungle clearing is an oasis of relevance and sanity!

So let's go back. I'd just been told to perceive the world as if I was on an intense hunting trip, looking for signs that other creatures had passed this way...

I looked at Shiva and the small pieces of bone scattered around Him. "How does this help others?" I asked. Big mistake! He spoke sharply. "You're not here to help others!" Then He softened again. "I know you want to help others, and you will, you do. But right now to think of others is either a distraction or your ego."

This is one of my weaknesses. As a teacher, I instinctively think of others, and how I can relate my experiences to helping others. All very laudable, but it can develop into a kind of vanity if I'm not careful. The teachings I receive are for me – for me to internalise, to work through, to make my own. To simply repeat stuff, parrot-like, is dangerous. To hand on unprocessed material is careless, possibly dangerous. A teacher can only teach what he or she truly knows. Book learning doesn't count. The experiences of others don't count.

And of course, while I'm thinking of others, I'm watering down my own experience. I'm not paying attention.

Shamans often divide their orientation towards healing or becoming a warrior. To be a warrior is to use gained knowledge for self development, to use gained wisdom and experience for spiritual power. That's also more aligned with Tantra. And it seems to be my path. So I'm afraid you'll have to find your own car keys!

Anyway... returning to Shiva's back yard... I was being admonished, if you recall...

Suddenly there was a loud roaring sound from off to my right and standing there was Ganesh! He was huge and fierce, wearing shiny dark armour and I could see trees bursting into flame around Him. Black smoke was billowing up into the sky and there were all kinds of explosions and metallic clashes. Jungle Shiva just smiled and said "Ah. Ganesh." And He bowed. I was very surprised. Why was He bowing to His own son? Then the faintest whisper of the word "ego" brushed against my inner ear so I bowed too. Ganesh did look awesome! I'd never seen Him in that mode/mood before.

Ganesh is traditionally worshipped at the start of any venture or project. He's believed to get rid of obstructions. This fierce Ganesh I was now looking at and thinking "Way cool!" was presumably a reminder of how hard it can be to get rid of ego and habitual tendencies on the spiritual path. These crusty old routines and hardened chunks of hubris won't be brushed off with the tap of an elephant's trunk! They need explosions and fire!

Shiva seemed quite calm and happy. I think He was teaching me to be humble (of course) but also (I think) He was bowing to the Shiva in Ganesh. He was paying tribute to Shiva Tattva, to Shiva consciousness, which I assume Ganesh has buckets of!

Shiva picked up a small stick and drew a diagram in the dust. It consisted of a central square, with a square growing out of each corner, making five in all. He made it with one line, so it looked a bit like a Celtic decoration, or the Tibetan palbu, a sacred knot. He pointed to the central square and said "Ordinary consciousness." Top left was "Dreams and unconscious." Bottom left was "Meditation." Top right was "Death." Bottom right was "Shiva Consciousness." And as soon as He'd pointed to the Shiva Consciousness square, the whole knot diagram redrew itself around that square! The lines moved like wriggling snakes. Shiva Consciousness became the centre.

A fairly clear teaching then. We can make any state of consciousness our central square, our chosen field of operations. But Shiva Tattva, or rather the training of Shiva Tattva, will redraw the topography of our consciousness. It will certainly change the inner terrain, or at least we can see the terrain from a better vantage point. We can see more clearly the places we'd like to visit and how to get there from where we are now.

For me, at the moment, my goal and my practice are the same – attaining constant Shiva Tattva, or what I call the divinity link.

I used to crave enlightenment, liberation, all that cosmic stuff. But actually, Shiva Tattva, which I'll define as a conscious integration into all life forms, an aware unfolding through all that tsunami of physical and non-physical evolution we call life, is easier to develop and maintain. It's also far trippier! To do anything other than working on my divinity link – and that includes Shadow work and Shamanic consciousness engineering – would feel so... pallid.

CHAPTER TWENTY SEVEN - THE LETHARGY OF LULLS, LIONESSES & MORE BLOODY SNAKES!

I was meditating the other morning, when whooah! here comes Halloween Shiva, rising over the crest of a hill like a bad moon risin'. Oh joy. He always looms slowly up into vision like some beast from the deep, all pale and luminous, His hair floating around His head like a drowned sailor and the serpent ornaments all wriggly and 'orrible. I hadn't seen Him for a while.

He sat there all aloof and remote, cold and yet burning with a dark radiance, like a black sun. Everything around Him seems to float in zero gravity. I had some sort of half formed question in my head about autonomy and choice in one's life, and it was still only half formed when His very presence, austere, untouchable, dreadful, seemed to answer it for me...

We're largely driven by our conditioning, much of it unconscious, yet we still have choices at any given moment. We're always at a crossroads. It's the Tantrist's task to make these unconscious conditioning forces conscious, to bring every energy within us up to the surface for examination, so that we're aligned to the deities with all our being, not just the ego mind. Some of these uncovered energies aren't pleasant.

Halloween Shiva feels almost evil – and yet I know He's not. He contains, holds, many dark energies. And these energies are turned to spiritual ends, to liberation and transcendence. Lead into gold again. With Him these dark energies, murder, cruelty, emotional coldness, deceit etc, aren't hidden deep down – oh no, they're boiling within Him like lava. But these energies are never used for such base purposes as oppression and violence. They're just the fuel that gets burned off.

It's like having a car and driving someone to hospital, yet refusing to give a friend a lift to meet their drug dealer. The petrol in your car is neutral – the purpose of the trip may not be. Halloween Shiva boils chillingly with awful, awful forces, yet with Him they're directed to positive ends.

Doesn't make Him any less scary! And I don't get turned on much by His world, the world of dead spirits, elementals and hostile psychic predators. It's a world with an overload of yin energy. It's a world I need to be more comfortable in though, obviously.

Vasuki ("divine being"), King of the Nagas (serpent beings), coils from around Shiva's neck and spits at me. I become aware of my guts inside me, rolling around my abdomen like snakes, my nervous system spitting sparks around the pathways of the body, like snakes. I can even feel these thoughts writhing around in my head, like snakes. I really like snakes. Not.

And Vasuki is telling me, "I'm in you. Your whole body/mind complex is snake-like. You're a pit of vipers! So lighten up around serpents, ok?" And of course, serpents and dragons are traditionally guardians of great treasure, in this case self knowledge and power. We have to get round the snakes, round the dragons, to get to the loot. We have to look deep into the eyes of those very parts of ourselves that we find most loathsome.

We need to be challenged sometimes or our spiritual path will be one of opting for that which makes us feel good. And actually – that's not a spiritual path, is it?

Jungle Shiva had another, unique, way of illustrating this lesson. I was sitting with Him once and He grew tusks out of the corners of His mouth like a wild boar. He made grunting noises. I always feel very close to Jungle Shiva so I came straight out with it – "What's all that about then?" He grinned (no mean feat when you're sporting eight inch tusks from your mouth!) and said, "It's the Year of the Pig. Be a pig." Okay, I'll bite. What do you mean? Another tusky grin. "Root around in the shit until you find something to feed you."

Of course. Root around in the pigsty of my own unconscious until I find something to work with, something that will eventually nourish me. Good one.

I really feel that discovering the whole concept of Shadow, our repressed selves, our lives unlived, and addressing the issues that inevitably arise through this discovery, was one of the most important things I ever did in my life. It feeds my practice. In fact, Shadow and Tantra are very parallel paths. Add Shamanism, with its "dark ally", to that list.

Through flooding our conscious minds with an image or sound of a deity, we start to attune the unconscious to that vibe too. Eventually even your dreams will be full of Tantric stuff.

Actually they already are. The deities, archetypes, unknown parts of you, romp through your dreams, wearing masks. Try to remember the dreams. Look for the message, the teaching.

Eventually your daydreams, your meditations will channel stuff up for you. And it all starts with turning the mind towards the deities, or deity of your choice. Or power animal, or your shadow. Or a spirit. Or your chakras. As I recommended in the previous chapters, why not practice visualising your Yantra or God/dess image, or saying your Mantra, in those moments when your mind empties, such as when you sneeze, have an orgasm, or when something startles you. Practice as you're falling asleep and as you wake up. It has to become a very intimate, very constant presence in your life. You have to become saturated with the sacred.

Someone asked me a very reasonable question. How can I avoid getting carried away with all this? How do I know if I'm losing touch with reality?

Actually I don't care much about the concept of reality any more! I pay enough attention to the world and the inner world so that I can maintain my practice without forgetting to put my trousers on, pay my bills and keep in mind that sometimes a cup of coffee is much better than meditation, that sometimes you need to just go out with your friends and dance and flirt. Most people are ok. If you're the addictive type, than you'll get addicted to the practice. I have. And I don't care. It's my path, I'm walking it. Others can do what they like. As long as we don't hurt each other, what's the problem?

And actually, it isn't about losing touch with reality. It's about expanding your ideas of what reality is, pushing back the boundaries of your personal reality.

And as you can probably see, all this practice – what's it got to do with India or with a Hindu or Buddhist path? Nothing really. The deity you feel drawn to may be an extract of Indian, Nepalese or Chinese culture, but that's about it. Tantra is a Sanskrit term but that's about it. The word Shaman is a Siberian term, not applicable to the Amazonian Rainforest or the Dakota Plains, but that doesn't stop people using it to describe the practices carried out in these locales. Tantra is a way of looking at the world, a set of techniques and practices. Tantra is as relevant, as applicable, in London as in Lahore, in Manchester as in Madras, in Kentucky as in Kathmandu. Tantra's net is worldwide.

Ok, time for a question. Suzie asks, what can she do on those occasions when it seems nothing is happening, when things have gone a bit flat? This is from a woman who converses with Kali on a daily basis! Well, firstly, there'll always be peaks and troughs in our spiritual practice, there'll be times when nothing much seems to be happening. If it was bang, bang, bang all the time, we'd never properly assimilate and process the material that comes up in meditation or in dreams. There's also a risk of just becoming addicted to the process of receiving revelation. One can become a Shiva junkie! Or Pan or Kali or whatever. Then you just get off on the fact that you're able to acquire knowledge, you feed the ego, you never actually get to act upon the wisdom. What's the point of that? So it's healthy to have gaps, to have lulls.

If the lull goes on for too long, and I'm talking weeks here, there are a couple of things you can try. Firstly, just go back to basics. Meditate and sweep the body for sensations or just watch what's going on in the mind. Go back to mantra or yantra work. Or you could try switching your attention. Instead of waiting for the deity to come to you in meditation, look for Him or Her in the daily hustle and bustle of "ordinary" life. Try and find where They're hiding themselves in other people or in situations. I guarantee you'll find something!

In fact, this is a perfectly good sadhana in its own right. If flooding the conscious mind with images and mantras doesn't seem to be working, then reverse the process, just stop trying, behave as if you're already in a world of spirits, of power animals and deities sending you clues, revelations, knowledge. In other words, just open up your intuition to the world around you. Let the dreamtime seep up into your consciousness. It's sometimes astonishing what can happen.

So anyway, don't panic. A lull is ok!

What can definitely be scary though is when you find yourself seemingly afloat, lost at sea without the structure you once depended upon. Whether it's Hinduism, Buddhism, Christianity, Paganism that you're leaving behind, when, at some point, you realise that you're forging your own way, following your own path, with only synchronicities, dreams, intuition and received revelation as your signposts, *then* panic can set in! You wonder how you'll cope, what your moral compass will be, how you'll avoid self delusion, inflation etc.

But this is how it should be. Any genuine spiritual path will have its unsettling, challenging periods. No one can promise you enlightenment by numbers. There ain't no such animal. Finding your own way is difficult, yes, but rewarding too. Don't be afraid. But stay humble, be patient. You're probably a decent enough person, sensible enough to realise when you're using people, talking bollocks or living in a "I'm the only one who understands the universe" fantasy. You have to trust yourself to some extent. Stay awake and it'll be ok.

Another question on this reality theme. "What if you become irrational, divorced from reality?" Hmm. What reality? No such animal. Reality is just another name for mass consensus. A lot of what I do, experience and talk about is irrational in the sense that it belongs to the world of dream, myth and the unconscious. It doesn't stop me functioning in the "real" world, which to me is a world of Maya (illusion). I soon know when I'm saying things that people find uncomfortable or "ridiculous", so I just shut up. No problem!

When you've left a religious structure behind, when you're following the body sensations, dreams and intuitions that become your new teacher, of course you'll wonder if you're just slipping into a fantasy. That's natural. You have to test your path sometimes, make sure it's not making you lose all your friends, or damaging your health. But – if it's working, then commit yourself to it, don't be half hearted. As you progress, for better or for worse, you'll care less and less about the opinions of others.

Sometimes we receive encouragement, validation. Here's a recap of a dream that cheered me up...

I need to get somewhere. A guy pulls up in a car, he's obviously part of my golden shadow since I don't recognise him and couldn't even describe him, apart from a "successful, prosperous" vibe (says a lot about me, doesn't it? The car is an open top sports model, very racy. He offers me a lift, which I gladly accept. The really bizarre thing is that he has three golden lionesses riding in the car with him! One is in the front, next to the driver, and keeps lolling her tongue out into the airstream. I ride in back with two others, thinking to myself how very, very cool all this is.

Now, these aren't his "bitches", though they seem devoted to him. They obviously represent powerful, regal female energies. In retrospect I wonder if they weren't the triple Goddess, maiden, mother and wise hag, though to be honest they all seemed the same age as each other.

We pull up outside an official looking building and as I thank him for the ride he gives me as a gift a huge golden dog, like an Alsatian or a wolf. He rides off and I enter the building. Once I'm in the building I realise that I've had to leave the dog outside. I hadn't even noticed but presumably someone is taking care of him. I sit down at a desk. A stereotypical, overweight, shirt-sleeved police chief is chewing a cigar and barking into a phone. He shouts at me that's he's not impressed, my intuition won't make the arrest, he needs hard evidence. As he's ranting at me, another officer comes in, walking the golden dog. It won't stay outside. It feels like a triumph to be reunited...

I know now that the golden dog is the gift of a power animal, a guide and guardian. But at the time of the dream I had to do all the necessary analysis. I didn't know whether the dog was a power animal or another part of my shadow, or even my soul. I felt it was possible that the lionesses represented the collective unconscious and the dog, more domesticated, civilised, represented my personal unconscious.

Hopefully, more revelations will follow. I'm just happy that, despite the rules of the official building, which presumably is my social "self", the dog refused to be parted from me. It's determined to be with me. Which makes it almost inevitable that this is what will happen.

It's this kind of dream that keeps you going sometimes...

According to the fictional/actual (and who cares?) teacher of Carlos Castaneda, Don Juan Matus, there are four traditional enemies of the Shaman, and by extension, anyone who's into engineering their own consciousness and their own cognisance, their ways of perceiving. These four foes are fear, clarity, power and old age. In modern parlance we could render these into anxiety, absorption, functionalism and depression or apathy.

If we live constantly in fear we'll never try anything, never move outside our comfort zones, never take a risk. Therefore the chances are that we'll never accomplish anything. A healthy respect or sense of mystery, even awe, is entirely appropriate in matters of the spirit, but we shouldn't let our fear of the unknown stop us from exploring different, even repressed, parts of ourselves, or moving into disciplines, practices that we find faintly unsettling. With Jungle Shiva I'm very comfortable, with Halloween Shiva I'm very nervous, all as it should be. But it doesn't stop me from moving forward, or from questioning any information I receive.

If we allow clarity of seeing with the second attention to become too one-sided, in other words, if we start to lose interest in the outside world, get obsessed with our psychic abilities, we can drift off into self absorbed trance states, not paying due attention to all the clues and information unfolding all around us in this realm. I have to watch myself on this one. I can get a bit remote and distant at times.

If we start to treat other people in a functional, instead of relational, manner, in other words, if we allow others to become extensions of our own ego, instead of the mysterious beings that they are, then that emotional coldness can freeze our perceptive abilities. Any information can be contaminated by our increasingly narrowing field of vision. The true warrior should have emotional detachment when necessary, but it shouldn't be a 24/7 state. That's asking for trouble – and a karmic kickback.

Lastly, if we allow depression or spiritual apathy to become an option, we set ourselves up for more suffering. Allow me to expand on this a little. I was talking to Elaine the other day, and she was uncharacteristically quiet. She explained that she was a little blue as "yet another cycle" had become clear. It's inevitable in the process of exploring one's psyche that one's own recurring patterns of behaviour become horribly clear. The patterns of others as well. Some we inherit from our parents, or their parents. We all tend to react in certain ways to certain situations, handle our relationships, our careers, our problems and challenges in certain, predictable ways. We repeat patterns again and again during our lives. It takes a lot of guts to find these patterns (some of which may actually be appropriate) and to challenge our karma. Elaine was naturally enough feeling a little down after finding another pattern. But to give way to depression, to a feeling of "what's the point?" is to probably allow the pattern to harden even further. Depression robs us of the energy and motivation to challenge our cycles. We need scolding, cajoling and encouraging out of our apathy or melancholy. If I know Elaine, she'll rise to this challenge with relish!

"Your turn today, my turn tomorrow". As I mentioned in my last book (sorry for all the plugs!), that's one of my favourite quotes and it's from the post-apocalyptic novel "Riddley Walker" by Russell Hoban. And sure enough, it's my turn to feel blue today. I woke up in a hollow mood on an empty grey

Sunday morning and was walking to a friend's house to do some heavy duty training in the hope of burning off the lethargy when I saw my mother (who died 45 years go when I was 11) standing over the other side of the road. A heavy grey fog seemed to envelop both of us and she was visibly upset, cradling what looked like a handbag full of (identity) papers to her chest. She kept saying "look at me, look at me!" in a very sad way. She died of a brain tumour and at one point had to have all her long dark hair shaved off for an operation. In those days it would have been really an outlandish way to look. I think she felt that her illness and her appearance had robbed her of her identity, her motherhood, her sex appeal, her self esteem, everything. I did my best to tell her that I remembered her as a vivacious, funny person, who had encouraged me to love books and learning, and the art of comedy too, for which I was very grateful. But I was overwhelmed with sadness too, coming face to face with her in this way. What on earth had brought all this on?

I didn't really want to stand in the middle of the road crying, but I knew I had to pursue this, plunge into Halloween Shiva's world, to try to hunt down the meaning and value of this experience.

After training, which didn't go well, as you can imagine, I sat down to meditate and tried to get back to see her. It was hard because the emotions were so raw on both sides. Eventually my father turned up (he died some ten years ago) looking quite cool, calm and together, and between us we managed to create a better atmosphere. My mother told me that the brain tumour came about because there were thoughts in her head which she was unable to articulate or even own. Back in the late '50's, early 60's, there wasn't such a liberal culture as there is today. Today she would have been able to say or do whatever she liked, something at least which would have relieved the terrible pressure in her head. I think she also feared hurting others with her revelations, so decided to let the tumour kill her instead. Though unnecessarily self destructive and naive, that's a very heroic thing to do. I have an inkling what those "unbearable" thoughts were, but it would serve no useful purpose to elaborate further.

The spiritual warrior/hunter's path, the Tantric journey, is never short on material to work with. After I'd done my best to break through my mother's self-flagellation and tell her how much she was loved, I sat down and talked with Jungle Shiva. He asked me how all this had helped me. In other words, what meat was there on these bones?

And I guess the answer is that lack of self forgiveness and an almost wilful emotional self harming is as much an indulgence as depression and apathy. They all prevent action, they all prevent progress, they all serve as a distraction. To fail to assume responsibility for one's actions can take many guises!

And I was very depressed, all day and half the next. A psychologist would probably describe me as being in the grip of an anima mood, in other words, a girly sulk! But there was also a black, raging maelstrom inside me, locked in and draining me of the ability to formulate thoughts and words clearly. I felt simultaneously drugged and electrified. It was horrible.

Sometimes of course, a depression has to be listened to. It's a sure sign that something's wrong, that something in the current set-up – relationships, work, lifestyle, ways of doing things – something isn't working. So we have to have the wisdom to decide – is this a depression that wants me/you to stop and pay attention, or is it a cry for action, to start to stir ourselves out of our mood indulgence?

At this point, I should perhaps quickly remind you, dear reader, why self healing is part of the Tantric/Shamanic path. Basically, it's good to know oneself and to rid oneself of emotional flaws, potential handicaps and distortions of perception. It's hard to do a crossword puzzle if you have a headache, it's hard to listen to music if you're in a filthy mood, it's hard to pursue and receive information through meditation or dreams if you're carrying excess emotional baggage. And if you don't do shadow work there's a danger of projecting all your unprocessed, unconscious material onto your spiritual search. So self healing is a legitimate element in the whole divinity link process.

When we bring into consciousness the cyclical patterns of our ancestors, when we realise how we're carrying on their habitual life rituals, then not only do we break ourselves free of that genetic and karmic inheritance, we also free our ancestors. The blessing flows to them too. And of course, to the future. Everyone benefits. So healing yourself is not an act of selfishness, it's a soul retrieval for everyone connected to you, past, present and future.

I talked to my mother again later and everything was a lot calmer. She told me more about her life. The saddest thing was that I felt she was simply born too soon. Her personality and her aspirations, her lifestyle, would have been far more suited to the 1980's, 1990's and the 21st century. Post-war Britain was no place for her. And probably the brain tumour wouldn't necessarily have been fatal today, I don't know. But that was her karma and she lived it. Apparently her latest incarnation is called Penny, is fifteen years old and lives in Gloucestershire! And this girl sings all the time, something my mother apparently wanted to do. Oh well.

Problems, recurring problems, are part of life. Let's just give this subject just one more poke with a stick, shall we? Read on...

CHAPTER TWENTY EIGHT - THE EAGLE AT THE END OF THE UNIVERSE.

Tantra arose from Buddhism, then found itself even more fertile ground in Hinduism. Both these great systems have a lot to say about suffering and its inevitable, unavoidable involvement in human life. To be human is to suffer. We suffer the natural shocks of the flesh, we suffer from old age, decay and eventually death. We suffer when we want something we can't get. We suffer when we've got something we can't get rid of. We suffer when things change against our will. We suffer when we long for change and it doesn't happen.

The human body/mind complex has a thousand holes through which suffering can enter. And it always does! At some point we will suffer. It's guaranteed. Buddhism calls this suffering "dukkha", which actually means "that is which unsatisfactory", so it covers not only normal human disappointments and catastrophes but also the more subtle sufferings of merely existing as a human being, the all-pervading feeling of loss, the question "is this all there is?" In other words the spiritual hollowness of much of modern life.

Millions of authors more erudite than I have written on this subject, so I won't dwell for too long on the orthodox Buddhist view that dukkha has to be recognised as an integral element of human life, that it has to be engaged, accepted and transcended. I'd like to look more closely at one of the most common, and most invisible causes of dukkha, namely ignorance.

Again, ignorance is one of those subjects covered *ad infinitum* by Buddhist scholars so I'll home in on one small part of our ignorance, a topic that touches the edges of Tantra, Shamanism and Shadow Work. That particular form of ignorance is the ignoring of our totality and the immensity of our world. Let me explain.

We are not a flesh and blood machine with a small spark of consciousness adrift in a vast and implacable universe. Rather, we are a knot of consciousness in a huge, linked network of consciousness/es. Or like clots in cream. Most of the time we're unaware of this. We can feel our own thoughts scurrying around in our head, we can sometimes feel this in others. What we can't do, and it's a good job too as the pain would be intolerable for most people, is feel the thoughts, the lives and the continual evolving of every single life form on the planet. And by life form I mean not only non-human forms such as moths, lizards, sparrows and gazelles, but also plants and rocks. I guess one way to look at it is to see ourselves and all life forms as pond weed in a large pond. We float in seeming isolation but touch each other, brush up against each other, occasionally crowd out each other as we grow and multiply. However, from the viewpoint of someone in a hot air balloon a hundred feet up, we're one green blanket, a single organism. If we could see ourselves from the viewpoint of the actual pond water, it would be very different. We'd feel ourselves being sucked up into the floating roots of the weed, in a hundred thousand simultaneous slurpings. We'd undergo a hundred thousand processes but they'd feel like just one process happening in a hundred thousand different parts of our being.

To be in dreamtime, or in shamanic "seeing", or in Shiva Tattva if you prefer, we experience the whole working of the world as a vast network of simultaneous activities and events and processes. This also has the effect of increasing our sense of self, away from the flesh and blood machine, away from a single clot of consciousness, towards the entire network of moving energy. We realise that we ARE the network, and that the sense of isolation and hollowness was a figment of our ignorance. Because we tell ourselves, and are told, over and over again, that this is the way the world is, this is what reality is, this is how things work, we buy into our own ill-informed machinations. We buy the lie.

And we pay a terrible price.

Dukkha grips us. We feel lonely, powerless, afraid. And why? Because we ignore our dreams, the promptings from our unconscious mind and other internal evidence to the contrary, evidence that there is something more "out there", something meaningful and relevant. Where do you think mythology comes from? And why do you think it exists? Because it uses the language of dream and poetry to explain the processes of the multiverse. The problem is often that this body of evidence may prove too unsettling, too threatening to everything we've *invested* in. We focus on various parts of the universe-machine, not on the processes, or the very point of the machine. We seek to bury our angst, our sense of futility, in careers, lovers, weddings, a home, children, holidays, grandchildren, retirement, and a peaceful death.

"Not a bad life" you can murmur to yourself as you prepare to be ground into karmic mincemeat again, or to use Castaneda's graphic image, as the Eagle At The End Of The Universe dries your little scrap of human awareness out in the sun for its supper.

The point, the goal of consciousness engineering, is to retain some awareness, some personal power that will survive the death trauma, enabling you to move on and evolve without the tedious process of having to re-learn the world all over again, and then having to un-learn it all over again later! If you do the work now, and do it well, that indestructible awareness, the vajra crystal, will grow inside your body/mind complex and survive the Eagle's onslaught, survive the awful slaughter of Shiva's sacrificial animals. Nothing will be forgotten, nothing wasted.

And it all starts with that simple turning of the mind towards some kind of sadhana, some kind of yogic work. That's the simple, first step, "Yeah! I'd like to try something like that!" It's not beyond the bounds of possibility to transform the whole way you perceive the world, the whole way you interact with the world, within a few short months – if you find a method and apply yourself to it.

Imagine a bare tree in winter. Let's start at the edges. See how its branches start with thin, pliable twigs, which become gradually thicker. Each twig leads on to a branch, then a thicker branch, then the trunk of the tree. And look at a photo of a great river, seen from the air, how the main body of the river splits up into tributaries and streams. It looks just like our tree! And take a look at a photo of a lightning strike. Very often, it looks like our tree again, or the great river. And some of the veins and arteries in our body look like that too. It's a repeating motif in nature. And it shows us that if we just hold on and apply ourselves to one twig, ie- one yoga, one technique, then very often that practice will open out into lots of other techniques, sources of information etc. It's like the underground tube train network. By changing branches at various points, we can get to anywhere we choose.

A few things to bear in mind though. Firstly, we have to be humble in the face of powerful energies, some of which may spring directly from our unconscious mind and some of which will emanate from various deities or spiritual beings. If we ever get too big for our boots and start promoting ourselves, even privately, within our own mind, as some kind of Tantric or Shamanic expert, then we're heading for a fall. Humans are wonderful beings, far more powerful than they can imagine, but unfortunately prone to falling under the spell of their own ego. So be careful. Being a hunter doesn't exclude you from becoming the prey too! You could easily, easily spend the rest of your life defending your ego and attacking and deriding others. What a waste of energy!

Secondly, we have to assume responsibility for what we do. Don't use the divinities as an excuse to behave badly, thoughtlessly, inconsiderately. Again, this is setting yourself up for a fall. Hubris is the one failing the Gods won't tolerate.

Thirdly, there will be good times and bad times, times of great revelation and insight, feelings of personal power, and times of spiritual drought and depression. These states are meaningful and should be treated as clues, as prey. Don't fall into these moods and indulge in them. By all means listen to what they have to tell you, but a warrior can't afford to wallow in his own crap. That way, you become prey again!

Fourthly (no more numbers!), again and again on the path you'll come up against your own limitations. Frustration is natural, but try and see the positive side of this – further advancement must be possible. If there's a limit, a boundary, a comfort zone, there's also such a thought as "one more step beyond!" It's really hard to retain one's awareness, one's full attention, in times of hardship, but that's the practice. The clue is in the word "practice"!

To become a Tantrist, a Shaman, a hunter, is to enter a far more interesting world (sometimes too interesting – don't get swallowed up!) but it also means that the shallowness and folly of the so-called real world gets highlighted. I can hardly bear to read newspapers any more. By page two, I'm spluttering and shouting, "But that's insanity!" A sense of humour becomes vital.

Everything is energy. Everything. Sometimes, seemingly bad things happen for a reason. Your very notion of good and bad may suffer an overhaul. Don't be alarmed. The absolute golden rule can be summed up in the Buddhist term ahimsa – harmlessness. In other words, don't hurt others. That's a simple rule. A six year old could understand it. But even the most mature of adults can't always practice it.

The path of Tantra, like Shamanism, is a results-count path. All that matters is that your path works for you. If something stops working, change it, or come back to it later. Stay fluid and alert. All these wonderful techniques, yogas, sadhanas are just means to an end. What works for one won't work for another, so find your own way. And you can borrow from any tradition or worldview. Even traditional Shamans from Mexico, Siberia and Australia do that. If you discover power in a rabbit's foot or an icon of Christ – fine! Use it.

And the information you receive. It may be outrageous, grandiose, mundane, it doesn't matter. It's what you do with the knowledge that's important. Again, the information is the means to the end, not the end in itself.

The end, the goal, call it liberation, wholeness, enlightenment, Barry, Griselda – it doesn't matter – is your orientation. The goal colours everything you do. The spiritual hunter no longer acts for profit or esteem but to take one step nearer the goal. I've shared some of my experiences with you. Many, if not all, of these experiences would have been unthinkable to my younger self. I'd always been a mystical lad in my youth but I lacked clear methods and good, realistic advice and encouragement. I've had to do most things the hard way but that means that maybe you don't have to. I've given you enough clues and hints, enough ways of approaching the work of your own personal unfolding. I don't think I can offer much more at this point. So – good luck with it all. I admire your aspiration. Go with my love.

Your life is your dream, it's a story you tell yourself. So, sweet dreams!

My thanks to Elaine and Suzie for their support and their contributions. You can read more of their experiences in next year's book, which I'd like to be more of a collaboration. I'm looking to reading it myself!

Shanti, Shanti, Shanti – Peace to all beings. If you have any questions please e mail me at julian.wilde@ntlworld.com.

I'll be thinking of you...

BONUS CHAPTER!

From the third book in the series "The Lightning Stone – Personal Power in Shamanism and Tantra", to be published in 2008, a preview of the first chapter. Hope you enjoy it.

Julian Wilde – Chapter One - DREAMWALKERS.

Where to begin? There's never really a beginning is there? Just fresh awakenings.

So - the dreamer awakes. Blinking off spiritual sleep, the dreamer emerges, astonished and delighted, not into a non-dream, a cold "reality", but into a greater dream, more mysterious than the last. Vistas, events and processes shimmer, all charged with meaning and content, more than the dreamer ever thought possible.

In a sacred place somewhere the Tantrist pauses halfway through darshan with the divinity. Something has happened, changed, shifted. His or her heart leaps. Somewhere deep inside, a door opens. There is a humming sound, a hint of fragrance. The divinity smiles, "Ah child! Now you sense it!" There's a glimpse of the possibilities of the Deva world, the reality of the Gods and Goddesses, the dream of the divinities. Two pairs of eyes lock and the smile spreads.

The Shaman awakes. From the jungles and wild places of our collective psyche, a forgotten voice begins to make itself heard. Like exotic birdsong or a far off drum, the sound patters in our inner ear. Faint but insistent, the message repeats. From a disconnection with nature a yearning arises, and from that yearning and that whispering voice a new contract can be forged.

That far off drum begins to sound like hooves on the forest floor. As sunlight floods and illumines our inner landscapes, Horned Gods stretch and crack their muscles in the dappled shade of ancient trees. The sweep of light across the twisted network of aged roots is like the hair of the Mother Goddess flitting across the fertile earth. Prehistoric deities are called back into the world.

Shiva plays with snakes in His jungle clearing. Each is more beautiful than the last. All the colours of the rainbow are represented in these iridescent, sparkling, patterned scales. He laughs with delight, ignoring my presence. I try to be serious, trying to hold onto my dull self importance. Even I can't sulk forever and have to join in. The snakes are indeed beautiful.

The dreamtime is back, back from wherever I misplaced it last time. We can connect to that source, to the pregnant void, to the womb of thoughts, dreams and myths, both personal and cultural. We can reclaim our divinity, and the resulting humility and integrity that accompany it.

The archetypes within us, and within the stories we tell ourselves, hold great power. They hold our power too and we can have it handed back to us as soon as we learn how to hold it. The Gods and Goddesses, the spirits, all are waiting. Dreamtime is just under your eyelids, the wisdom like warm air blown into the back of your throat. So sing that wisdom!

Follow the footprints of your dreams and your spiritual calling. The trail may lead through forests, deserts, ancient cities, to futuristic planets or burned-out warehouses. No one knows – not even you until you start the journey.

The dreaming awaits. The constant, unending flow of energy, mutating, moving - creating patterns, forms, sensations, electricity, multiplicity, physical shapes, organisms. The energetic, synergetic, karmically interlocked web of life. The process behind all processes. The pregnant, humming womb of the multiverse. Shakti's creation, pouring forth, blazing with the fire of Shiva consciousness, each life form holding a precious spark of awareness. Each creature karmically linked to every other creature. Stars, planets, spiders, humming birds, lizards, wolves, mackerel and men and women, all burning, luminous with communal dreaming.

Actually, you know, it's not a dream, it's a very real, wonderfully connected web of energies, processes and events. But as it's usually way, way below our sensory radar, it feels like a dream to us most of the time. It sounds like fantasy, like a child's fairy tale. But it's real. The most real thing. Our ordinary, discriminative minds recoil from it.

What we call "our mind" is the tip of the iceberg. Our personal unconscious is infinitely greater. It's where myths live, legends and dreams, drowned pirates, heroes, dragons, witches, spirits, talking animals. And this personal unconscious mind connects to the even greater universal unconscious. We connect directly to the dreaming. We're like froth at the edge of a great tsunami. And we fear the dark rush behind us, not knowing that it's our own long hair, our cloak, our shadow on the water that flaps at the back of our eyelids.

So we get drawn to religious systems that encourage us to discipline ourselves, that teach us our smallness, that lead us to explore our relationship with the divine or the supernatural, and our relationships with others. All as it should be. And these systems can take us all the way – all the way to heaven, to enlightenment, to one-ness, but never, never, never in the way that we expect.

The teachings of the Buddha twenty five centuries ago did much to dismantle the clutch of the ego and demonstrate the personal responsibility of each individual. The Awakened One also left a clear ethical structure to act as our guide, our framework, our moral compass. But to some westerners, with low self esteem or imperfect understanding, that message of detachment can lead to a mechanistic worldview, lacking in laughter and the sharp sting of salty language, the meaningful encounters of everyday reality. It can lead to an unconscious spiritual fascism, based on the cold machinations of will.

The teachings of the Shamans beckon us into an exciting world of spirits and power animals, but here too danger awaits. Fantasy and inflation can engulf the unwary, we may lose our smallness, our humility, and then the enjoyment of the journey becomes more important than the import of the messages, the reclamation of the soul. Spiritual emptiness can masquerade as progress, like a wonderful carnival that entices and enchants, takes our money, then reveals itself as cheap, shabby and tawdry in the cold light of morning.

Tantra and some branches of Wicca encourage the expression and transmutation of sexual energy. A fantastic, potent source of power. But not many people are as sexually mature as they think, as free from possessiveness as they think, as free from the temptation to use others as they think. So – an obvious danger lurks! Anyone that seeks to use such groups for sexual exploitation harms themselves as much as others. But the damage may take longer to reveal itself!

Monotheistic religion is tempting in its moral certainty, in its patent on the truth. But again, the more certain we become about anything, the easier it is to crucify its central mysteries. Certainty can become a cul-de-sac.

The most important questions we can keep asking ourselves are 1) where is this path taking me? & 2) is change actually happening? If we're happy with the answers, then fine, we can carry on. If not, then something has to change. Go back to basics, try another method or technique, shut down for a couple of weeks, meditate on the breath, pray for the wellbeing of all creatures, don't go looking for anything else. Something will shift, sooner or later.

For every path has its dangers. If a path is enlightenment by numbers, no risk, no dark nights of the soul, bliss or money back guaranteed, then the truth is that it's not a spiritual path at all. It's a fantasy. The dreaming is not a fantasy.

From the dark and mysterious, stag and bison haunted caves of the Late Palaeolithic era, through the great Neolithic stone circles, through the dim green cathedrals of the Amazonian rain forests, through the glaring snow deserts and frozen peaks of Asia and Siberia, to the suburban living rooms of Minnesota and Little Hadley-on-the-Marsh, the dream has murmured in our sleep, behind our stories and creations, under our designs and discoveries, our technologies, our treasuring and our treacheries. It's flitted across our unseeing vision as myth and dream and revelation. Sometimes we almost catch it, mostly we don't. Occasionally we remember something, nearly always we don't.

So what does the dream mean? What's its relevance to us?

The dream, or more accurately, the dreaming or dreamtime, is known by many names – heaven, the void, nirvana, samadhi, Shiva Tattva, Krishna consciousness, to creep under Astarte's skirts, to see the face of God, to walk the Summerland, to enter the Heroes' Hall, to rise with Quetzalcoatl to the stars, the list of names is as long as human history.

The dreaming is both the origin of the religious impulse and the goal of the religious path. The dreaming inspires us to embark upon a long, bewitching and dangerous journey, from the dreaming and back to it. From unconsciousness to knowing. From dreamed to dreamer. From vacuum head to vajra heart, from sacrificial lamb to self powered lion/ess. From sham to Shaman.

The dream is evolution in action. Both forwards, backwards and even sideways through time, the various energies we know as life, intelligence and awareness are evolving. Time, karma and meaning bleed in all directions. There are no straight lines in nature! The multiverse seeks its own meaning. God/dess looks for the divine reflection of His or Her countenance in every life form. We are immersed in the dream whether we like it or not, whether we believe it or not. We have the choice to bring the dream up into wakefulness, to consciously live the dreaming, to choose to dream part of the dreaming – or to turn from it. It's up to us what flavour, what rasa we inject into our part of the dreaming. It's up to us how we live, how we express the dreaming.

Some parts of the dreamtime, of the void, of the humming womb, of the web, are bewitching. Some episodes are educational. Some days we feel like a fly in amber, petrified and immobile forever. But all of these are value judgements of the ego mind. From the perspective of the dreamtime, or of a consciousness aligned with the dreaming, everything is ticking along perfectly, just as it should be.

The dreaming never stops. After we die, the dream continues. We move on, get reborn. But part of us stays in the deep dream. I asked my father, who died some ten years ago, what it was like to die. He replied, "It was like being crushed. Then I just faded quickly. I don't remember anything else." So where was he now? I get a glimpse of beautiful, rolling parkland and a huge sweet chestnut tree. What does he do there? "I just walk around and enjoy myself. It's my dream." I misunderstand him, thinking he means that's what he's always wanted. Your dream? Well, do you think you'll stay here, or will you move on? "I've already moved. I think." He indicates the landscape. "This is my dream." *This is my dream.*

Oh, I get it. Part of you is living this as a dream, even now, while you've moved on. "Yep."

Cool.

My mother, who died when I was eleven, can be found at a damp, cathedral-like station of sorrow, comforting those who die ill at ease with their faith. Yet her latest incarnation is now a teenager in Gloucestershire! Part of my mother stays in the deep dream, makes herself useful.

God only knows what parts of me are doing right now!

My God, I should add, is a Stone Age divinity, the Lord of Animals, the Lord of Souls, the super-shaman most commonly known as Shiva, the Auspicious One. I'm not a Hindu. He's not Indian either, though it's the Indian subcontinent that took Him to heart. He appears in many shapes and guises, all with a different personality. There's Dragonfly Shiva, glowing blue, bejewelled, flirtatious, charming, very God-like. There's Jungle Shiva, usually naked, covered in ash and mud, very direct and tactile. There's Halloween Shiva, cold and remote, dangerous, damp and glistening, covered in snakes, accompanied by scary Hammer Horror monsters. There's Pan Shiva, a kind of Horned God hybrid figure, wordless and abrupt. They all take turns to teach, inspire, bully, cajole and nurture me.

And yes, I know how all this sounds. If you're still with me after these statements about Shiva, the spirits of the dead, spacetime etc, then thank you. This book's definitely for you!

I'm not professing to be a visionary or a great medium. I'm none of those things. Though I've discovered most of my worldview and practices for myself, there are many books written by individuals more erudite and more experienced than me that promote similar paradigms and techniques. My psychic ability is very variable. If you held out your hands and asked which one is the peanut in, I'd need a drawn diagram to get the answer right. If you put me in the middle of a strange city, I'd get lost as quickly as an infant. If you asked what's the ancient Greek word for hamburger, I'd have to look it up on the internet. If you ask me to bend a spoon with the power of my mind, be prepared to wait until the sun goes supernova. My intuition however is sharp, sharp, sharp!

So what am I claiming? Well, I'm not claiming anything. I'm just reporting.

And I'm reporting my truth. I'm reporting what's happened to me over the past three or four years. My religious endeavours have led me, over the years, through many fascinating fields to a new, strange and wonderful neo-shamanic spiritual practice. I didn't plan any of it. I regret none of it. I'm happier spiritually than I've ever been in my life. I don't care any more what people think. I know some of my statements are going to sound far fetched, but at least I'm not trying to tie aliens, crop circles, the Bermuda triangle and the yeti in with my worldview. Not yet anyway.

I don't even know what to call myself anymore. The terms Tantrist, Shaman, Shaivite – none of these work very well. And yet my practice seems to combine many elements from these paths. Oh well. Maybe a label will appear later. It doesn't seem to matter right now.

I'm writing this book for one reason only – to be of service. To have found a book like this a few years ago would have been really helpful for me. It would have taken away a lot of self doubt and hesitation. It would have been reassuring to read the experiences of others.

So – thanks for sticking with me. I'll try and define what it is I believe and what it is I do. Where I'm going, we'll discover together in the writing/reading of subsequent chapters. And how I got to this point can be discovered in my two previous books, The Real Rasa and The Divinity Link. No more commercial plugs, I promise. The message of the first book was that anyone can embark upon a meaningful relationship with a God or Goddess. The theme of the Divinity Link was to draw parallels between Tantra, Shamanism and self healing. This book is just a diary, a record of what I've learned and what I recommend to others. No apologies, no long explanations. Just a report on how my worldview and practice is evolving. I hope it's interesting and/or inspiring for you.

Here goes...

I've come to believe that everything is energy. That matter, thought, spirit – all is energy. That we inhabit a huge net of inter-connecting energies. That we and these energies interact, affecting one another constantly. That every action has an effect, a result, which leads to further interactions. This never ends. And it's been going on forever. That time, beginnings, ends are all illusions. Time and space are infinite. They run off in all directions – up, down, forward, backward, into and through many other dimensions of time and space. Infinite worlds and realities collide, knit together, separate. The multiverse is beyond description.

I believe that everything is "alive". That animals can talk. That objects can teach. That spirits are all around us. There are predators out there, protectors too. Archetypes are real. Gods and Goddesses are real. All these realities are part of the dream of the multiverse. And the multiverse is God's/Goddesses dream. That God/dess and the multiverse are *each other's totality*.

What else? Oh yes.

I believe that if we pay close attention, if we employ what Buddhism calls "mindfulness", to everything around us, the dream, the deep, the Dao, the void, the dream of Shiva, will reveal itself. Actually it's revealing itself to us all the time – everything that happens is dreamtime, it's just that we don't notice any revelation, or only notice it when it's so manifest that it's too late to act upon it. We perceive isolated events, emotions and physical sensations, but by the time they've manifested grossly enough to attract our blunt awareness, it's often too late, then we feel like a victim or a passive recipient of the world's currents.

We need a more finely tuned, 360 degree, inner and outer attention. Then we'll be aware of things before they manifest, events before they occur, answer questions before they're asked. Our attention and our ability to respond to and act upon what we intuit gives us "power". Not power over others, though that can be a double-edged by product, but more power over our own processes, over the stories we tell ourselves (our conditioning) and our destiny.

The cultivation of this kind of attention, sometimes know as hunting or stalking, has three effects. Firstly we accumulate vajra – the lightning stone, that diamond-bright, diamond-hard yet infinitely responsive, flexible awareness. We can flow in, through and around the dreamweb with clarity and skill. We can be infinitely responsive, yet adamantine, unshakeable. We become Shamans, sorcerers, people of power, spiritual warriors, hunters, self healers.

Secondly, we are much more autonomous, consciously immersed more fully in the dream, freer from ego anxiety, depression and resentment than before. This gives us the opportunity to cultivate the humility and empathy that prevents us from becoming inflated, delusional, selfish and exploitive.

Thirdly, being more immersed in the collective flow of the multiverse, our consciousness stands a better chance of retaining enough "solidity" to survive the trauma of death and ego dissolution more or less intact. This unique opportunity is a huge advantage, enabling us to further our spiritual evolution without hindrance or hold up. We don't have to waste time relearning the world, then unlearning it again.

So far, so cool! But how we do it. How do we train our awareness, cultivate mindfulness?

The first step is to become fascinated with your own processes. In daily life, employ your hunter's awareness within a conversation with a friend or colleague. Pay close attention. Their words may say one thing, their tone of voice, their facial expressions, their bodily gestures another. This applies to you too, so watch for any mixed messages you may be sending!

When you're alone, or actually, even in company, listen to your own thoughts. Listen to the way you talk to yourself. Does it sound reasonable, or cruel, whining? Does it sound like your voice? Or your parents, your peers or even someone from a film?

Listen to your body. How does it react to different people? Does your heart sink? Does your stomach flutter? Do you pluck at your clothes? Do you make involuntary kicking movements? How do you react to your alarm clock? With fear, anger, eagerness? What bodily sensations, what emotions lurk under your radar when you converse with your partner, your boss?

What themes occur in your dreams? And if you can't remember your dreams, ask yourself honestly, why is that? What are you blocking? What is it you don't want to know? What "bad thing" would a totally neutral observer be able to say to you? What's the one thing about yourself you don't want to hear?

What cultures or religious movements are you drawn to? What qualities do they hold for you? Are they colourful, loyal, at one with the earth, tough survivors? And how about those cultures or religious movements that make your skin crawl? What qualities are they showing you that you don't want to own? Are they treacherous, violent, oppressive, irrational?

How do you habitually react when you're bored, upset or depressed? Do you eat too much, masturbate, lose yourself in a book, get self destructive, phone a friend? In other words what are you trying to make yourself feel? Relaxed, worthy, popular, independent? What are you trying to give yourself with your habitual reactions. Does it work?

Just those last few paragraphs represent quite a few years' worth of work. Read on, enjoy the book, but return to these paragraphs at some point and seriously consider starting the work. Take those first steps through the jungle of your psyche, keeping a hunter's sharp eye on everything around you.

With this kind of hunter's sight, the whole world around you, and within you, becomes your dreamtime rainforest, your hunting ground, your spiritual battleground. You have to travel this world accumulating wisdom, knowledge and experience, cultivating personal power, the lightning stone inside. From now until the moment you die, your task is simply to pay attention and act upon what you learn. Each time you accomplish this (and you know there'll be many failures too!) you'll acquire more confidence in your ability and more faith that the deep, the dreamtime knows what it's doing. Learn to move with this Dao, to dance with the deep.

Learn from animals. Watch how they move, stretch, hunt, relax. Watch how they interact with other life forms and the environment around them. What makes you "superior" to them? Your clothes? Your TV programmes? Your mind? How do you think they think? What do they think? How do they communicate? Come an earthquake or a tsunami, who's more likely to survive?

Watch everything. Even inanimate objects have a presence, can attract your attention, can teach you something. Develop a hunter's eye. Watch everything!

The world, the people around you, daily events, all become much more fascinating, much more significant. You'll learn things about yourself and about others that seem unbelievable right now. But don't expect life to become a toffee-flavoured, rose-scented carousel ride. It's entirely possible that you've coped with life reasonably well so far by blocking out a lot of stuff, by avoiding having to deal with a lot of crap. That's entirely reasonable, but if you want to become something other, something greater than you are now, then you have to pluck up the courage to start addressing the unaddressable, to own the unownable, to assume responsibility for things you didn't even know you'd done! And this can be a real drag. Read on...

Printed in the United States
109706LV00003B/203/P

9 781847 780027